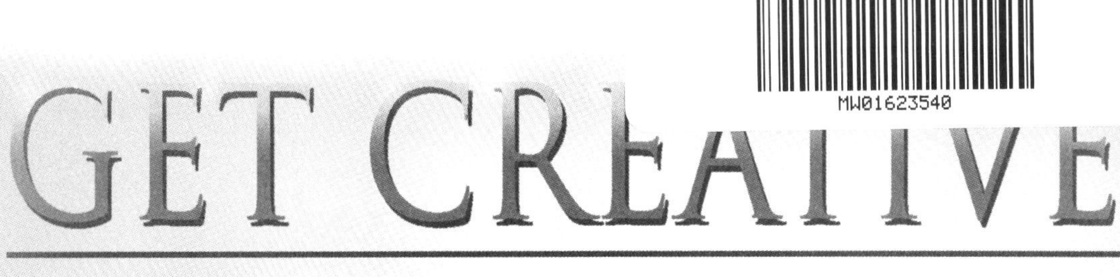

GET CREATIVE

TURN *ON* THE **BRIGHT** SIDE OF YOUR BRAIN

by cartoonist

Doug MacGregor

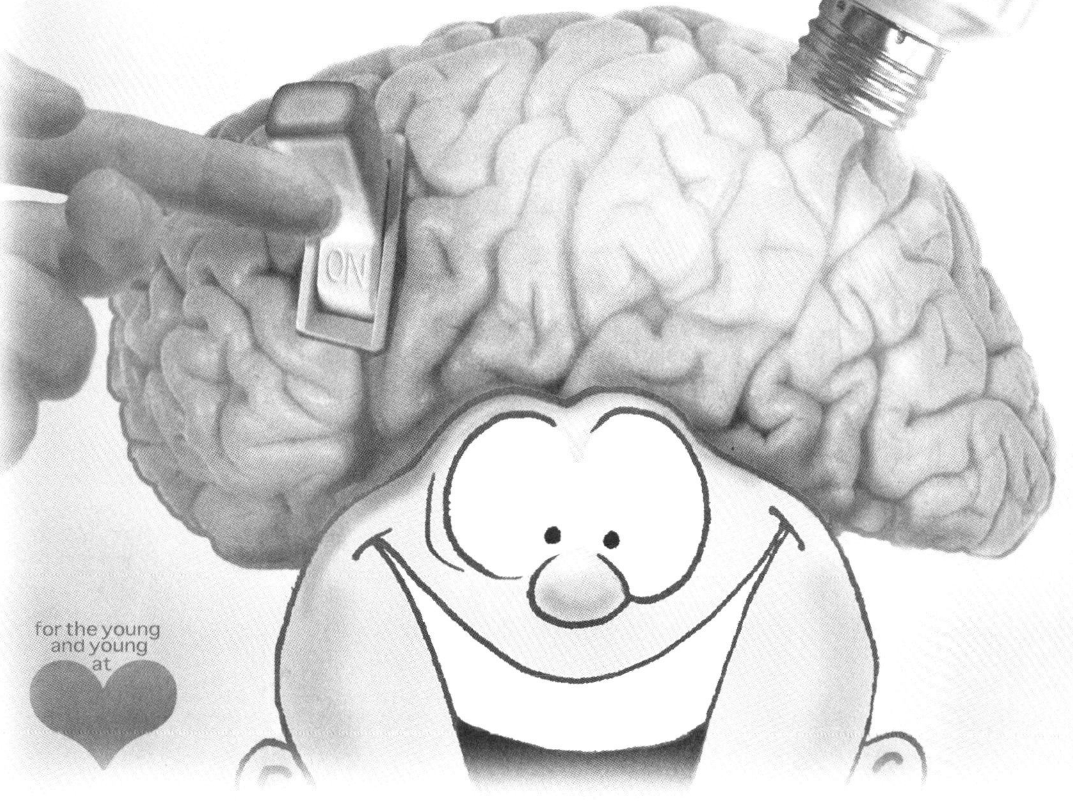

All rights reserved. No portion of this book may be used or reproduced without the permission in writing from the author/illustrator.

Copyright ©2014 Doug MacGregor
Second Printing

Published by Doug MacGregor

ISBN: 978-0-9654843-6-7

Library of Congress
Control Number:
2009909645

For more information
contact the author at:
dougcreates.com

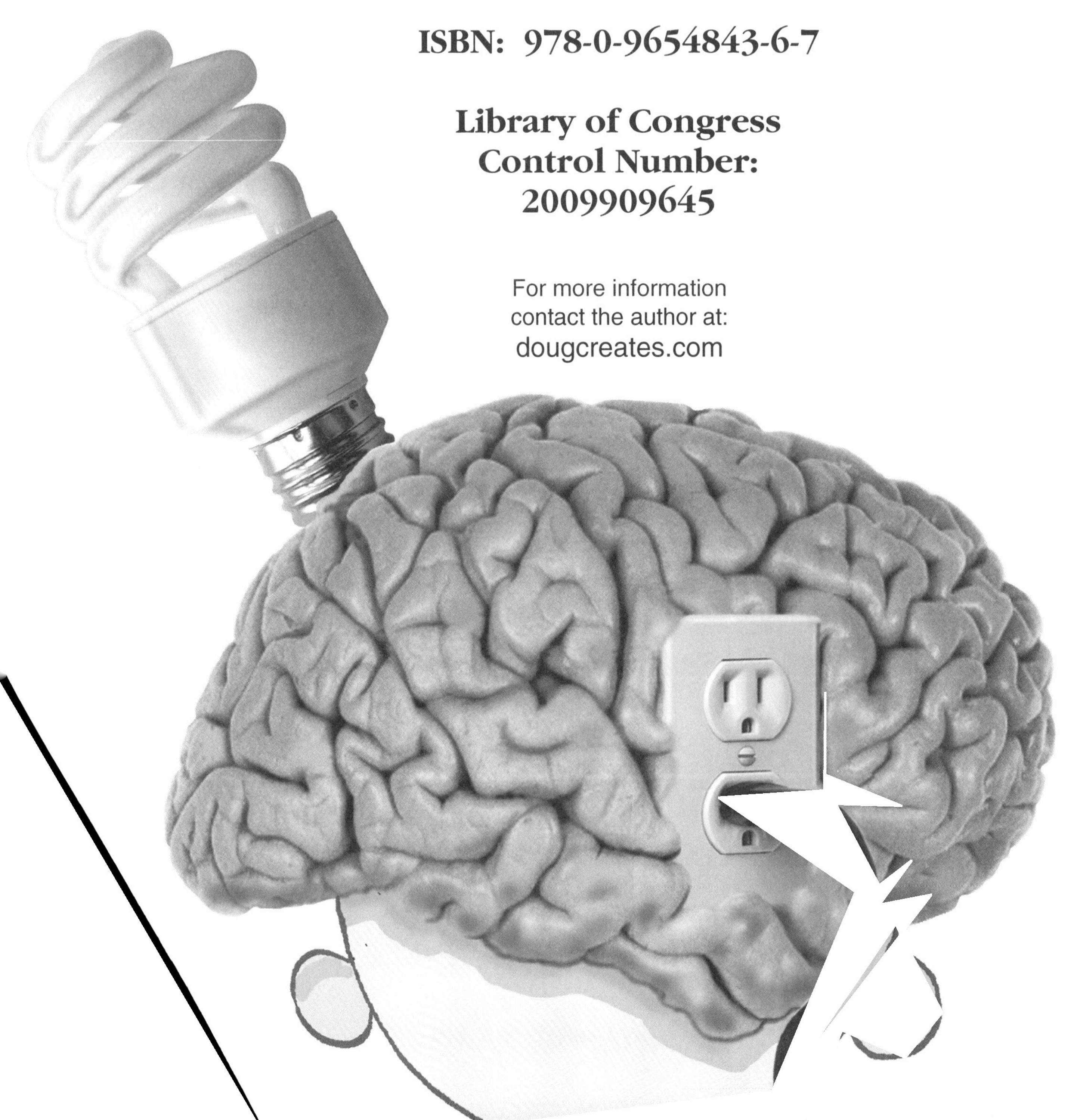

Dedication

For Mom and Dad...

Thanks for showing me how to stay young at heart
by keeping the inner child alive.

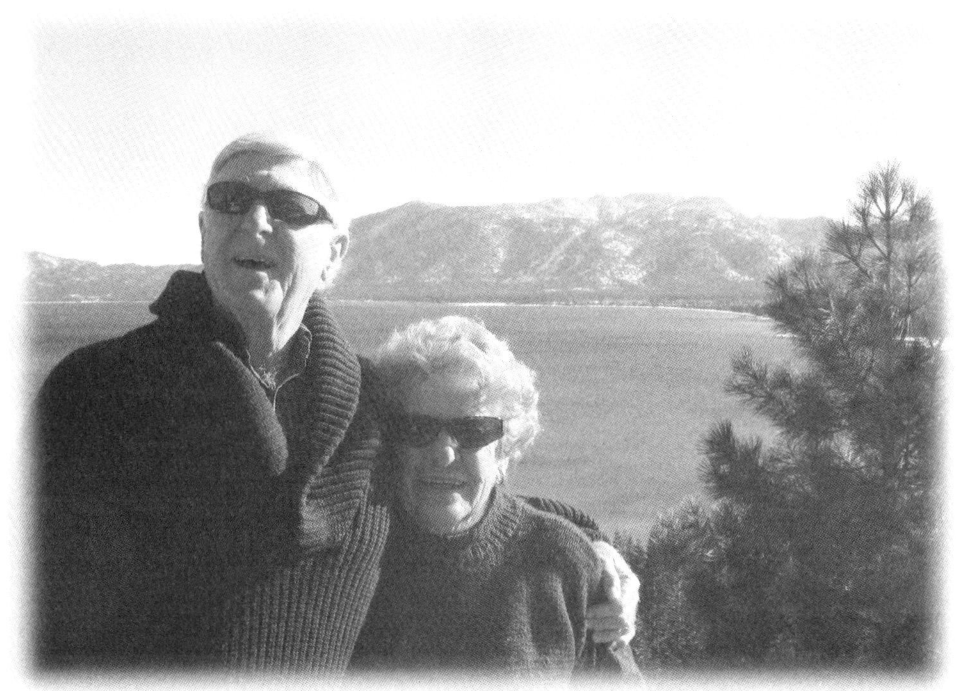

Special thanks to...

Debi Almeida, for all her hard work, dedication,
editing and perseverance in helping me
bring the book to life.

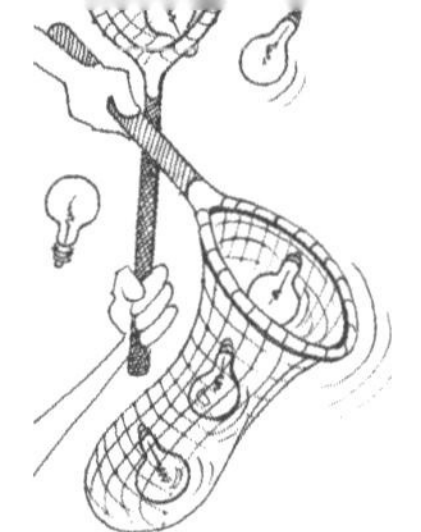

Table of Contents

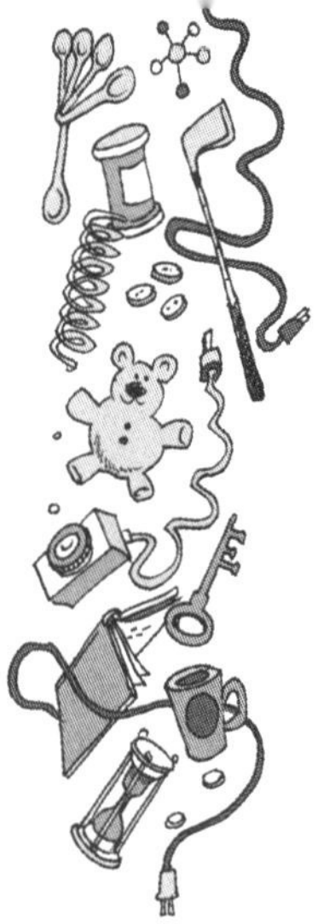

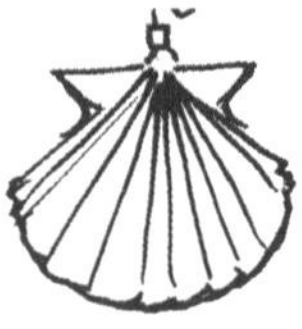

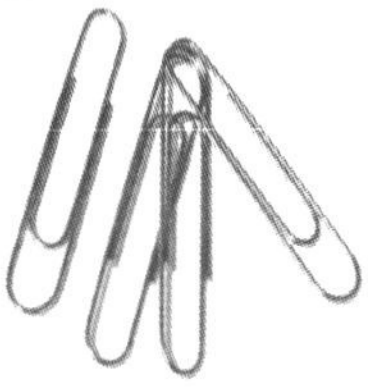

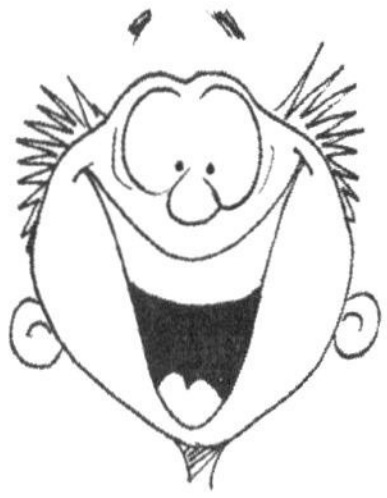

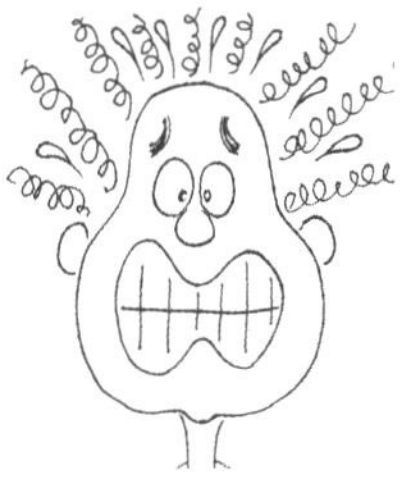

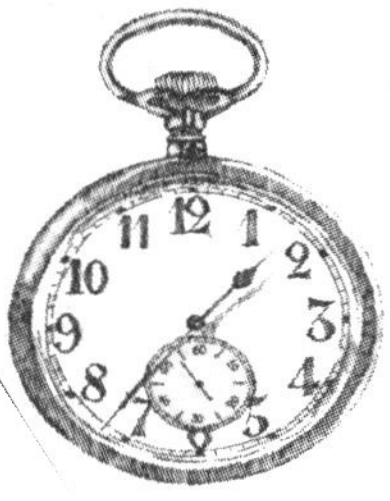

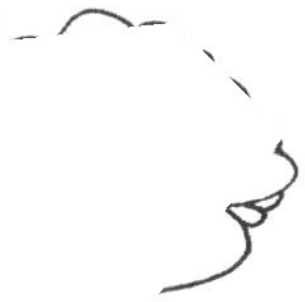

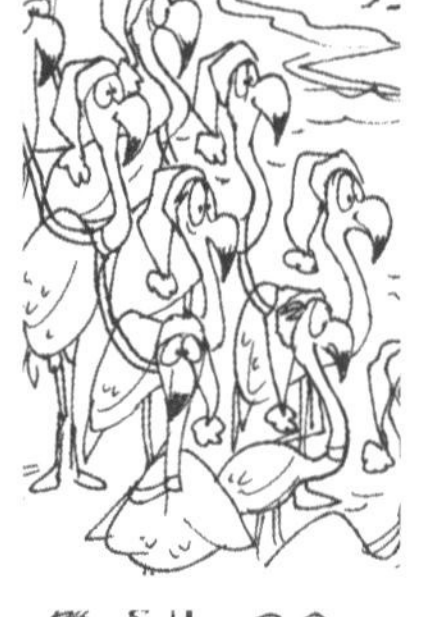

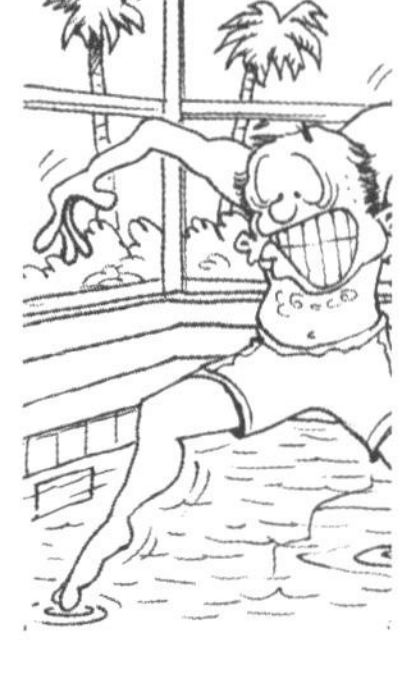

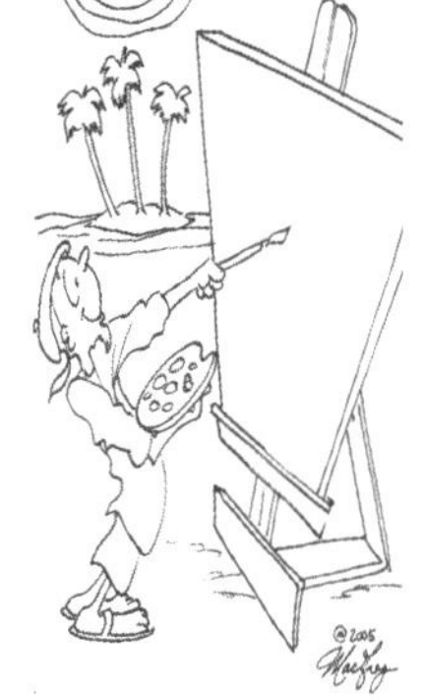

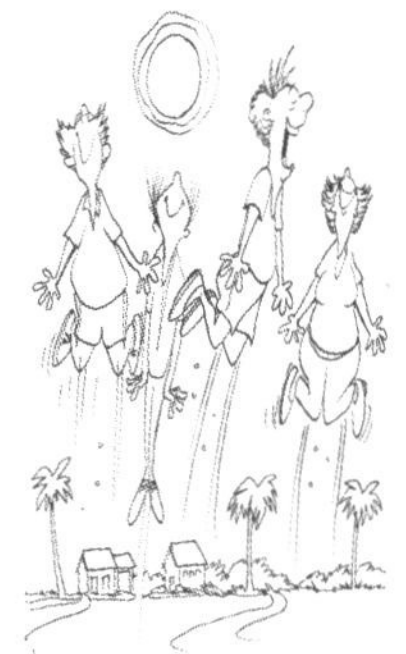

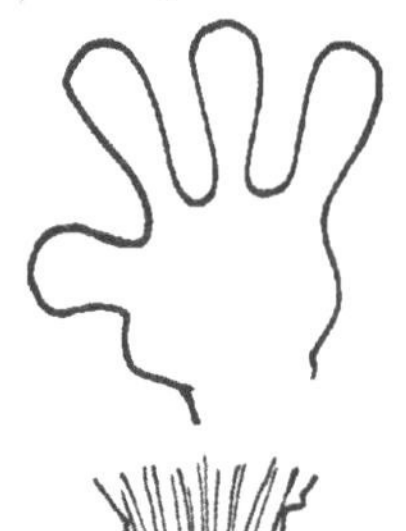

F+ th+ A +

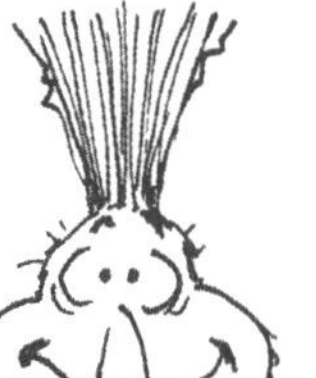

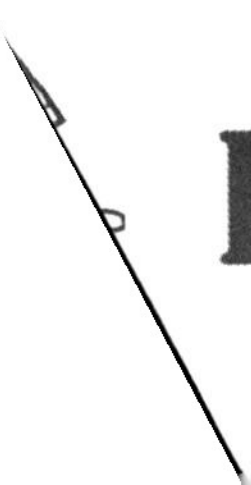

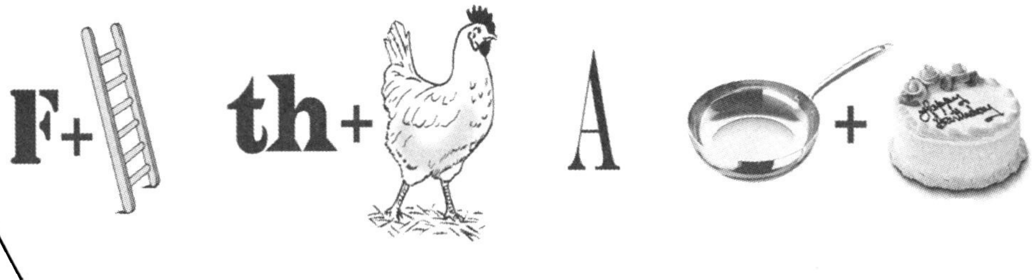

Preface

Let's Get Creative!

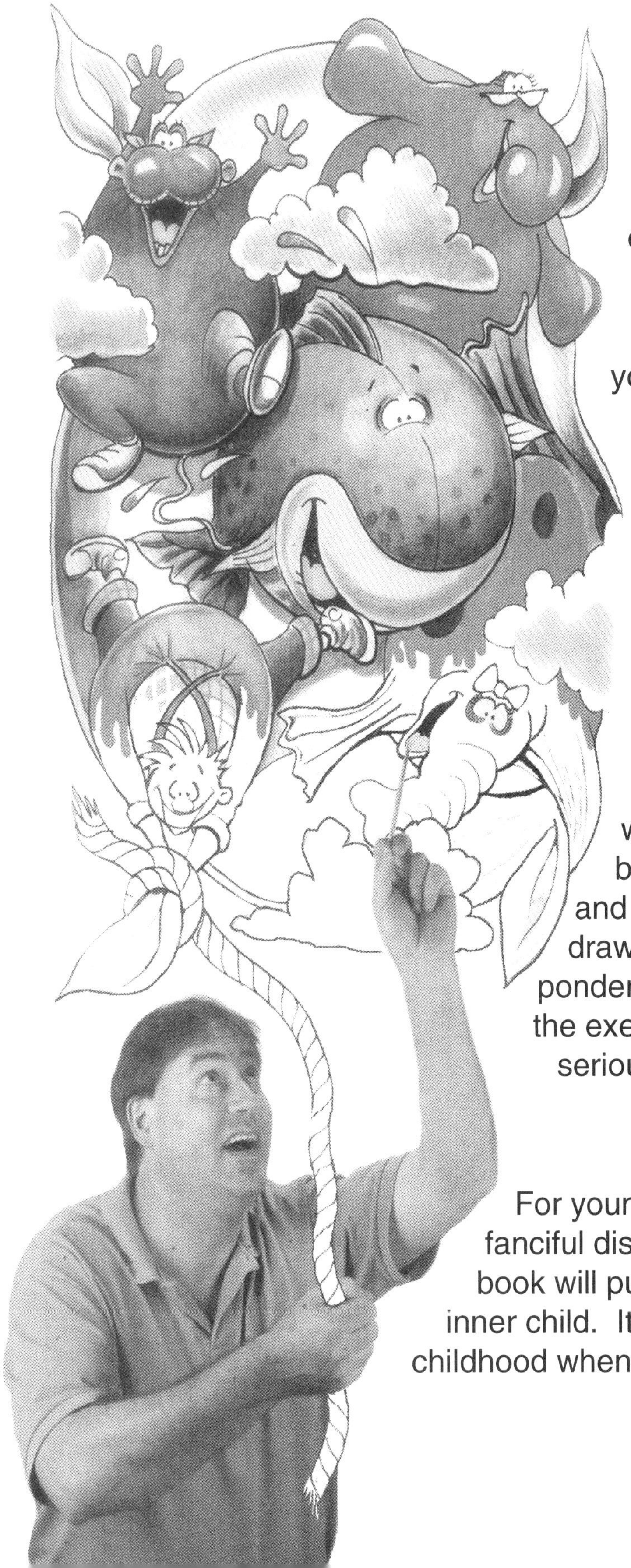

Whether you are an established artist, an aspiring artist, just a person who likes to doodle and draw or someone who just wants to be more creative in everyday life - ***this book is for you.***

It is a book of creative exercises for the young; and young at heart. Being more creative in everyday life is not an easy process. In order for the process to work the brain needs to be ready to create. Just as athletes need to stretch their muscles before working out, creative folks need to prepare the right side (or bright side) of their brain to get started.

To *turn on the bright side of the brain* we'll learn how to help maintain flow for better creativity. There are many verbal and visual exercises to work on. We'll write, draw, doodle, sketch, assemble, puzzle and ponder our way through the process. Some of the exercises are plain silly, some are more serious, others are head scratchers, and some are elementary.

For young folks, this book will be full of fun and fanciful discoveries. For the young at heart, this book will pull and tug at the heart strings of your inner child. It will take you back to a time in your childhood when being creative was much more natural.

- Doug MacGregor

Let's Get Started!

"The future belongs to a very different kind of person with a very different kind of mind...creators and empathizers, pattern recognizers and meaning makers. These people will now reap society's richest rewards and share its greatest joys."

- Daniel H. Pink, from his book *A Whole New Mind*

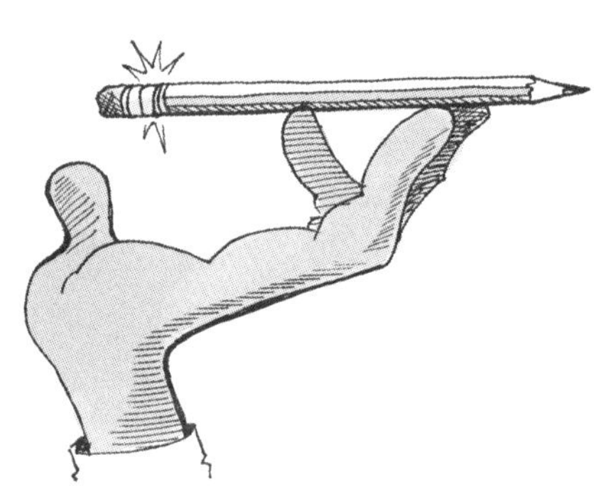

You'll need a few *supplies* to accompany the book.

You'll need a **magic #2 pencil**, **colored pencils** and **crayons**. You'll also need a **blank journal**, a **digital recorder**, **video** and **digital camera**.

Locate a thinking cap and a favorite place to ponder.

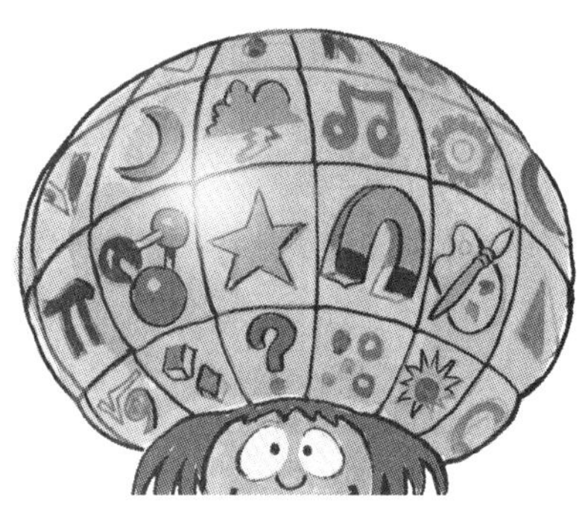

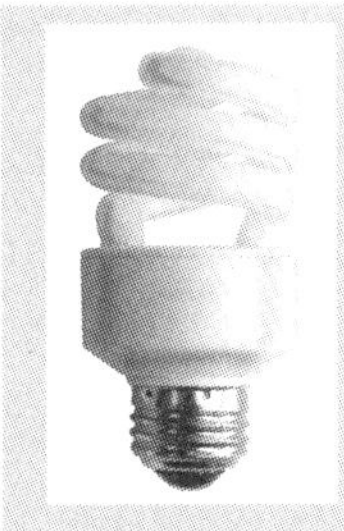

Idea Exercises

When you see the icon, **"Idea Exercise"**, you'll be asked to do a creative task.

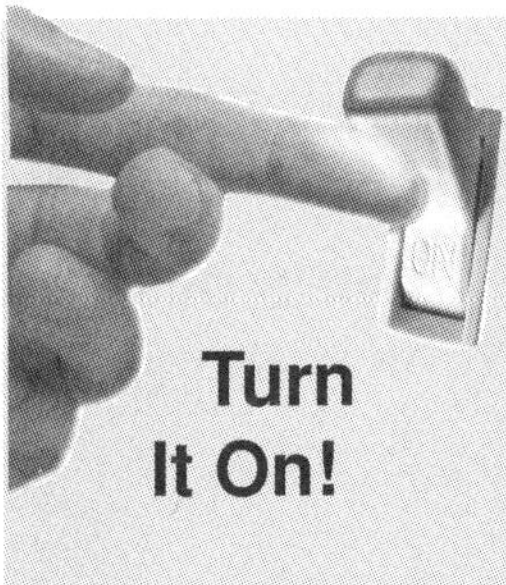

Turn It On!

When you see the icon, **"Turn It On"**, you'll be asked to turn on the bright side of your brain with an additional exercise.

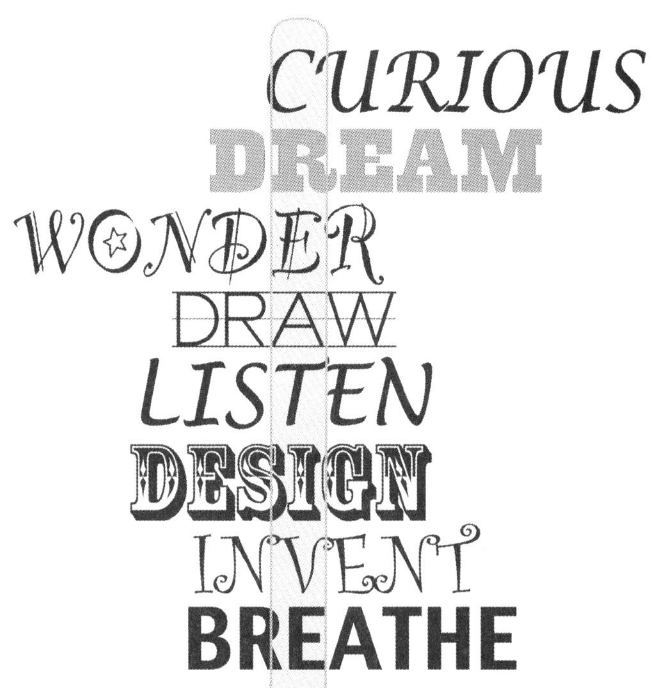

Brain Callisthenics

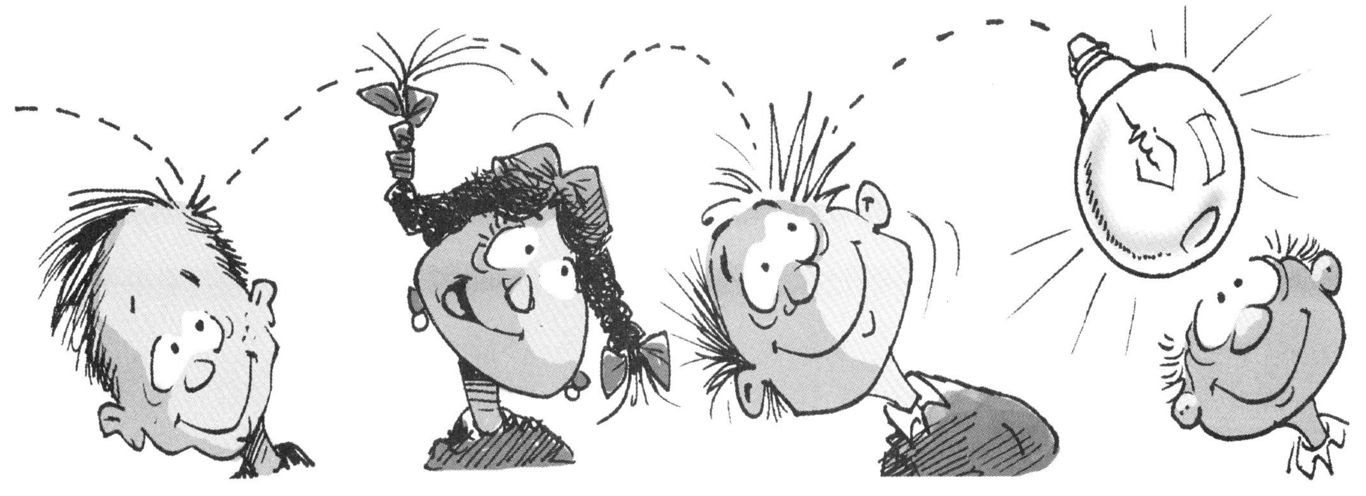

"The brain is like a muscle.
When it is in use we feel very good.
Understanding is joyous."

- Carl Sagan

Know Your Left From Your Right

The brain has two hemispheres. The **left and right** sides. The right hemisphere of the brain controls the left side of the body. The left side of the brain controls the right side of the body. Each hemisphere has different characteristics or specialties that work together or seperately. The left brain is the logical and analytical side. It also handles more sequential and mathematical problems. The right side is the conceptual, intuitive and artistic side. It concentrates more on many of the components of creativity. Here are some of the characteristics or specialties of each side of the brain.

LEFT HEMISPHERE

- Looks for meaning of a word
- Looks for close detail
- Remembers verbal material
- Can follow instructions without pictures
- Good at algebra
- Logical
- Enjoy reading realistic stories
- Tend to be very logical and organized
- All business
- Not easily hypnotized
- Remembers specifics
- Likes realistic stories
- Likes to write non-fiction
- Prefer individual counseling
- Enjoys copying or tracing pictures and filling in details
- Likes planning and order
- Need total quiet to read or study
- Almost never absent-minded
- Read for specific details and facts
- Skilled at sequencing ideas
- Takes longer doing visual puzzles
- Like to tell stories but not act them out
- Goal setting to keep on track
- Watches the time regularly

RIGHT HEMISPHERE

- Visually oriented
- Can match objects by appearance.
- Attentive to speech intonation and inflections.
- Likes to write fiction
- Can memorize music
- Global big picture thinker
- Like to act out stories
- Read for main details
- Good at geometry
- Like to read fantasy and mystery stories
- Likely to be hypnotized
- Looks for the context of a word
- Fun to dream about things that will probably never happen
- Artistic, conceptual thinking
- Like organizing things to show relationships
- Takes shorter time solving visual puzzles
- Prefer visual instructions with examples
- Occasionally absentminded
- Listen to sounds while studying
- Enjoy creative storytelling
- Prefer to learn through free exploration
- Good at recalling spatial imagery
- Very Spontaneous and unpredictable

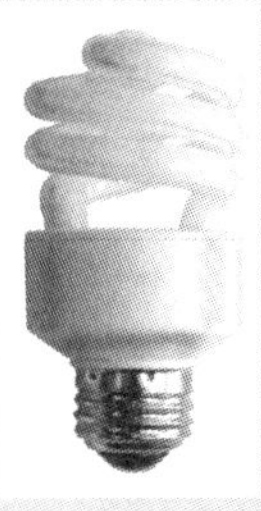

Idea Exercise: Rule of thumb

Join your hands together naturally without thinking. Which thumb is on top? Remember, the left side hemisphere controls the right side of the body. The right side of the brain controls the left side of the body. If your right thumb is on top, it may mean that you are left-brain dominant. It your left thumb is on top it may mean that you are right-brained. This is not scientific, but it will begin to give you an idea of which hemisphere you favor. To learn more, try the left-right brain quiz on the next page.

The Left and Right Brain Quiz

Try this quiz to see if you are more left or right brain dominant. It's easy and fun!

Directions: Read each question carefully. Every time you read a description or characteristic that applies to you, put a check mark at the *end of the sentence*. There is no certain number of characteristics you must choose. In the answer column *circle the numbers* you have check-marks for. Count up the number of L's and R's. Whichever number is higher represents your dominance. If the numbers are close, that means you use both sides of your brain equally.

1. I constantly look at a clock or wear a watch	1.	L
2. I keep a journal or diary of my thoughts	2.	L
3. I believe there is either a right or wrong way to do everything	3.	L
4. I find it hard to follow directions precisely	4.	R
5. The expression "Life is just a bowl of cherries" makes no sense to me	5.	L
6. I frequently change my plans and find that sticking to a schedule is boring	6.	R
7. I think it's easier to draw a map, than tell someone how to get somewhere	7.	R
8. To find a lost item, I try to picture it in my head where I last saw it	8.	R
9, I frequently let my emotions guide me	9.	R
10. I learn math with ease	10.	L
11. I read the directions before assembling something	11.	L
12. People tell me I am always late getting places	12.	R
13. People have told me that I'm psychic	13.	R
14. I need to set goals for myself to keep me on track	14.	L
15. When somebody asks me a question, I turn my head to the left	15.	R
16. If I have a tough decision to make, I write down the pros and the cons	16.	L
17. I'd probably make a good detective	17.	L
18. I learn music with ease	18.	R
19. To solve a problem, I think of similar problems I have solved in the past	19.	R
20. I use a lot of gestures	20.	R
21. If someone asks me a question, I turn my head to the right	21.	L
22. I believe there are two ways to look at almost everything	22.	R
23. I have the ability to tell if people are lying, just by looking at them	23.	R
24. I keep a "to do" list	24.	L
25. I am able to thoroughly explain my opinions in words	25.	L
26. In a debate, I am objective and look at the facts before forming an opinion	26.	L
27. I've considered becoming a poet, a politician, an architect, or a dancer	27.	R
28. I am not easily hypnotized	28.	L
29. When trying to remember a name I forgot, I'd recite the alphabet until I remembered it	29.	L
30. I like to draw	30.	R
31. When I'm confused, I usually go with my gut instinct	31.	R
32. I have considered becoming a lawyer, journalist, or doctor	32.	L

# of L _____

# of R _____

Righting a Blank Check

A blank piece of paper is where we begin. A blank stare into space is our necessary starting point. It's time to wipe the slate clean and empty out your case of mental clutter. Forget the chore list of must dos. Let go of all the stress and duress in your life.

This is *your* time. This is *your moment to create.*

Since your earliest childhood experiences you have left more than a million ideas deposited in the *First Bank of Blank*. It's time to get out the checkbook and withdraw some creative cache. In the world of computing the *cache* in your computer is an accumulation of copied data, a temporary storage area of information the computer has processed. If we visit the *First Bank of Blank* we can pull out as much of our creative cache as we want. It is all there. Deposited thoughts and ideas locked in our unconscious vault are waiting to be retrieved. All it really takes is your account number and your signature.

Can you account for all the ideas you have had in your past? Unless you have consciously written down or recorded every thought you have had since you were a child, the task is virtually impossible. Fortunately, your memory bank, or *The First Bank of Blank*, is not completely empty. The keys to unlocking that memory bank begin on the next page. It's time to try your first "Idea Exercise".

We'll explore how to keep your creative cache accountable by balancing the bright side of the brain. We will also explore how to make lots of deposits so we can *right* more blank checks.

Launch Your Creativity

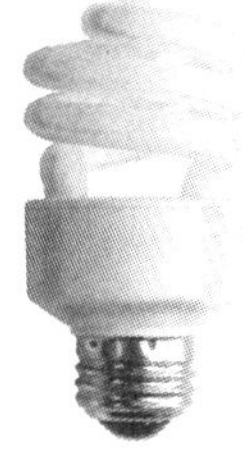

Idea Exercise: Set Your Worries Free

Get out a blank sheet of paper. A regular 8.5" x 11" will do. Grab a pen or pencil. Write down all your current worries. They can be in list form, short phrases or written randomly. Scatter them all over the page. Fill up the paper if you can. If you are worry-free, God bless you, go to the head of the class and put down your pen or pencil. Be honest with yourself.
Concentrate more on your worries than your wants. Think of what is making you anxious, frustrated, annoyed, irritated and tired. Keep writing. You are really doing two things at once. You are physically writing, but you are also mentally *righting your first blank check*. Once you have exhausted your analysis of angst, put it down and take a deep breath. You are almost there. Now go take a five minute break. Get a cup of coffee or a soda. Leave the room you were in, and change your environment for a moment.

Now, pick up your list of worries. Re-read them slowly. After you read each concern or worried thought, say, *"not here, not right now"*. Say it out loud. Don't let yourself feel ridiculous. Take charge. Speak with a declarative tone. Read them all.

Now, using the key to your memory bank, open your vault on making paper airplanes. Laying your paper flat, fold it into the airplane. Once you have finished your magnificent folded flying machine, go outside in the yard and toss it airborne. Send your worries to the wind and say, *"bon voyage."*

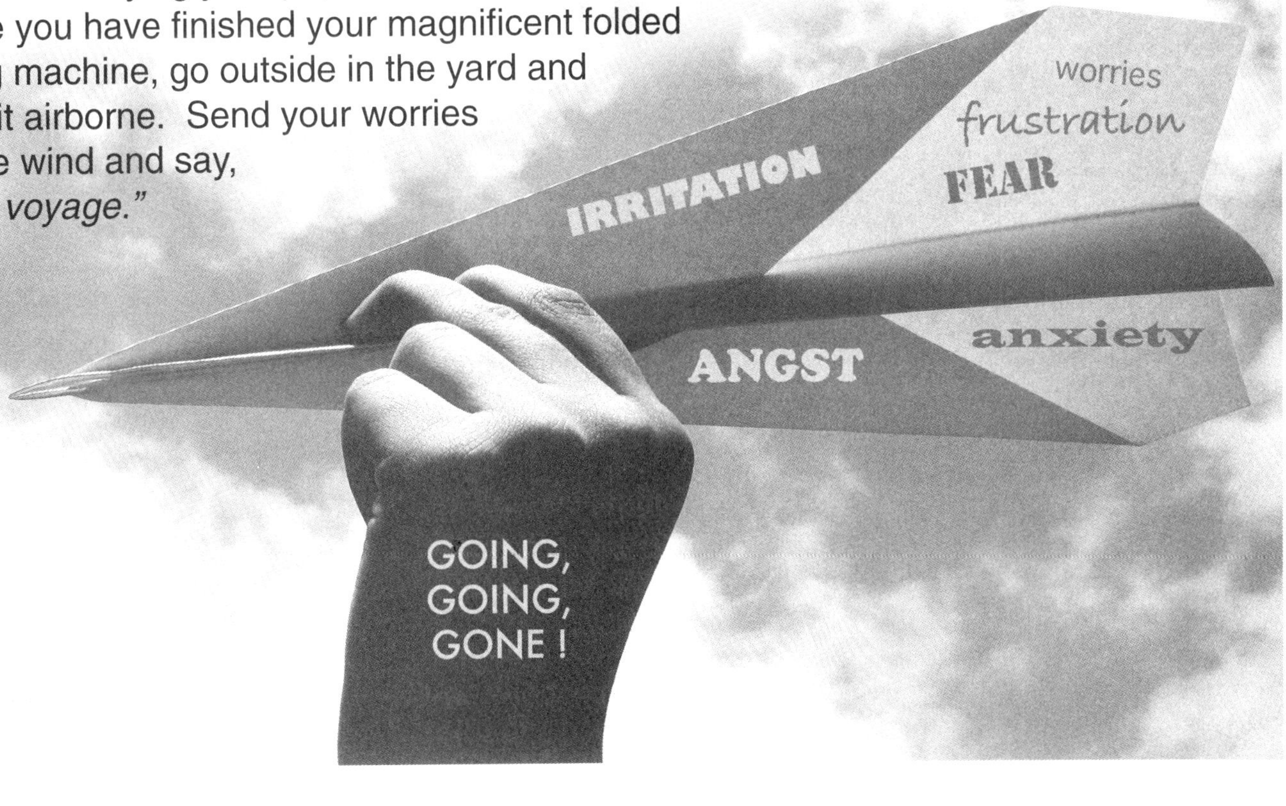

Righting Another Blank Check

The paper airplane is nothing more than a metaphor. By launching your worries in the wind, you jettison some old creative jinxes. You also nix the unnecessary obstacles to fluid thought. Let's try another exercise so we can right another blank check.

Idea Exercise: Painting with a pleasure palette

Find the quietest room in the house. It could be in the basement, the study, a computer room, or maybe even the attic. Go in there and shut the door. Use what you can to create total silence. Put on some of those clunky headphones if you have them, just don't play any music through them. Find a comfortable chair, a sofa or couch in the room. Move one in there if you have to.

Once you feel comfortable, cozy and content, concentrate on the silence. Silence is so rare and because it is, this sensation will feel strange at first. Finally, there are no ringing phones, no TV, no beeping, no talking or yelling Your sense of time should begin to dissolve. Focus on the silence. Close your eyes.

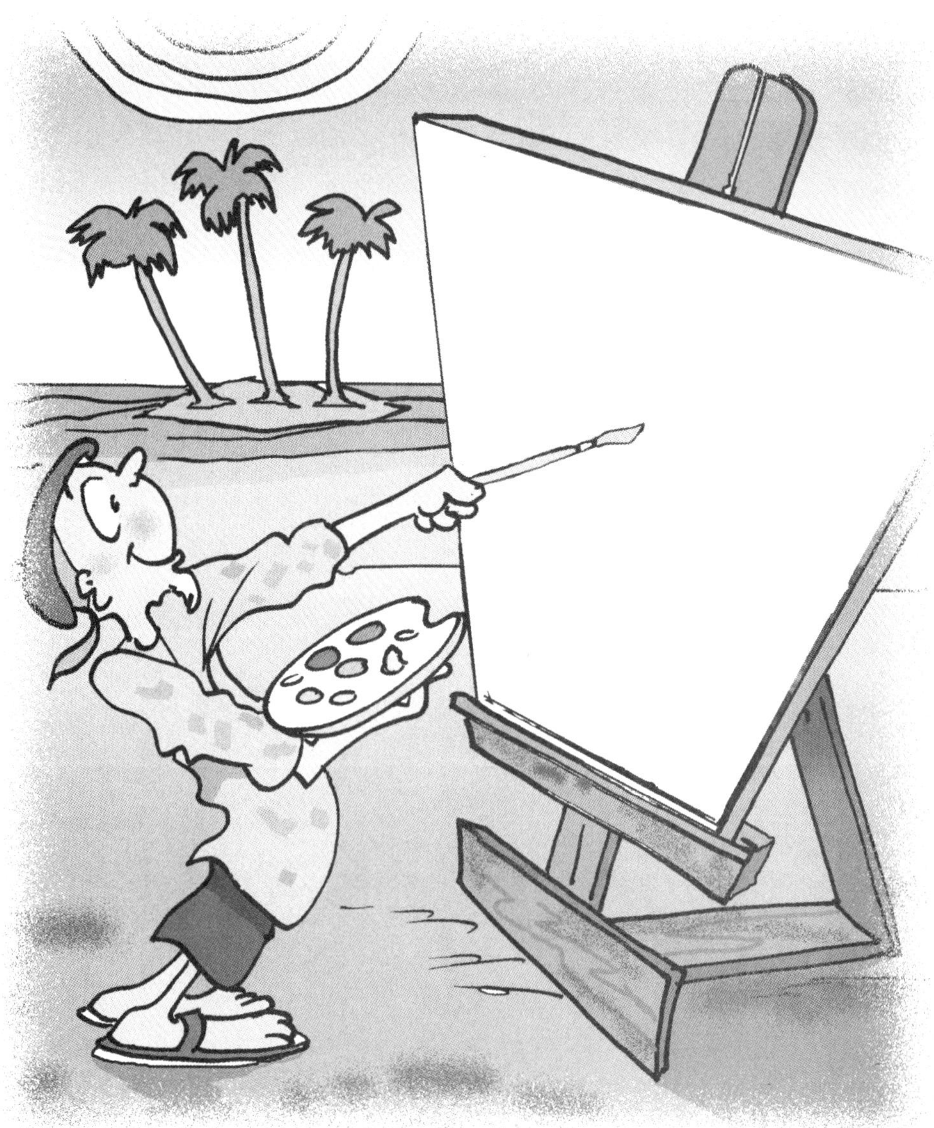

Turn your thoughts to a visual place. Picture yourself on a beach. You are taking a walk along the shore. There is nothing but sand, surf, sky and one other thing. There is an artist who has set up an easel in the sand. It is a very large easel and on it is a stark white canvas. The artist has left a table full of tubes of paint. There is also a palette, several paint brushes and jars of water on the table. The breeze is light, the canvas is ready, and the easel is sturdy. You are standing in front of it, staring into its blank space.

You can hear the surf and some squawking seagulls. You can smell the salty air. Yet, you continue to stare into the white space ahead of you. It is time to think of your favorite color.

"Nice Work"

You are drawn to one color of paint on the table. You pick up that tube of paint, open it and spread the paint onto a palette. You grab a thick brush and dip it into the paint. You feel the brush move across the canvas and watch the paint flow smoothly in one direction. You dip the brush in more paint and draw the brush across the canvas in the opposite direction. Then you find it necessary to change direction again, this time motioning across the canvas in a swoop of an arc. Again, you dip the brush in the paint. Feeling the canvas, you let the brush go where it may. You paint loops, swirls, dips, dots, curly-cues. No one is there but you, the sea, the sand, the sound of surf and the song of a seagull or two. You step back a moment to see the painting blend in with the sky. The color you chose is perfect for its surroundings. The brush strokes you've created mimic the cirrus clouds that rise above the canvas. Some brush strokes near the bottom flow in a similar direction to the horizontal waves of the water. The edges of the canvas seem to disappear as does the easel. Your painting is now floating. It lifts up and begins to receed away from your place in the sand. It drifts backward over water hovering a few feet above the waves. It gently retreats further and further until it meets the horizon. Now it is the size of a postage stamp. Now it is just a dot on an "i". It is your "i", and your eye that sees it. It disappears. You wave to it and smile.

The artist who left the canvas, table and easel appears again and stands next to your side.

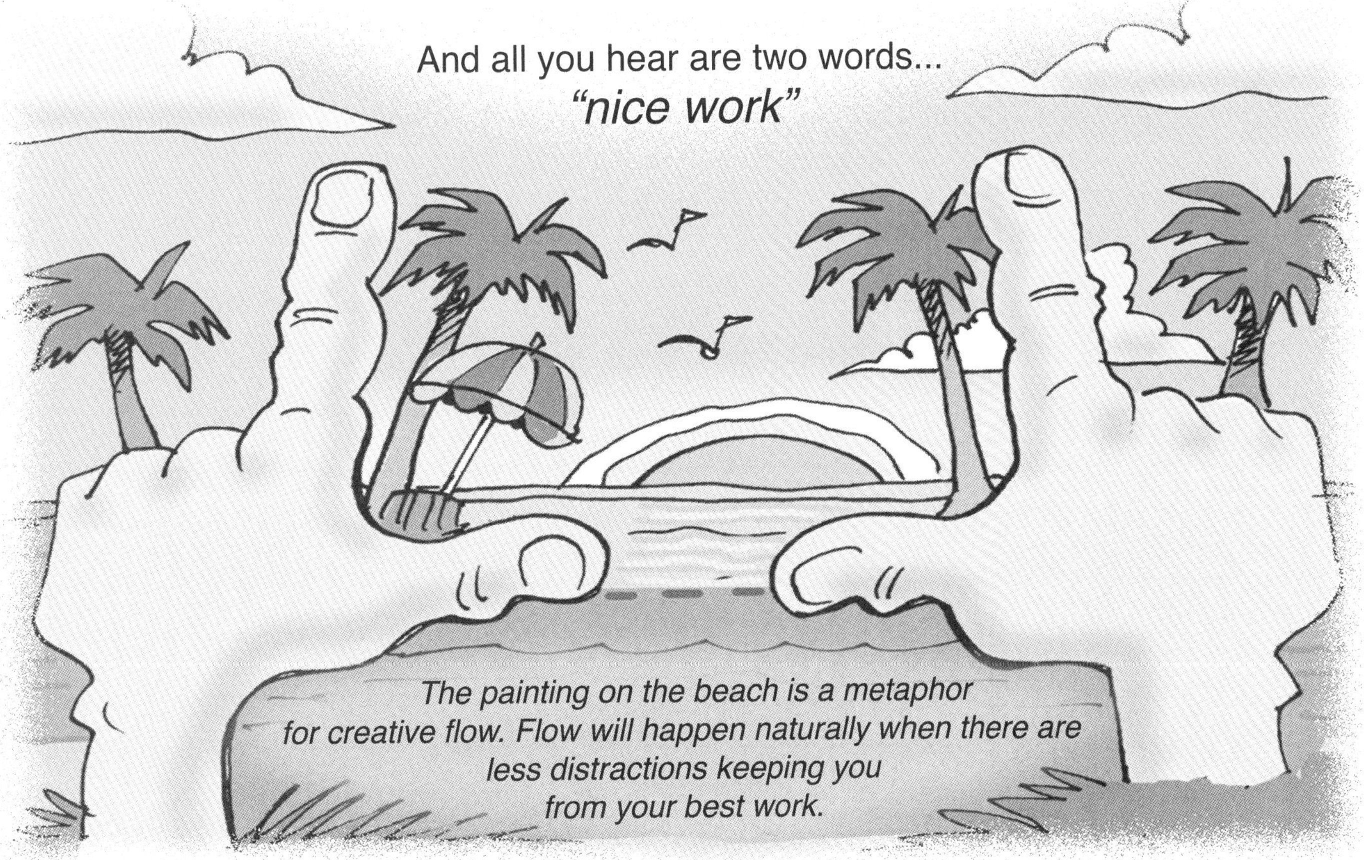

What's In Your Memory Bank?

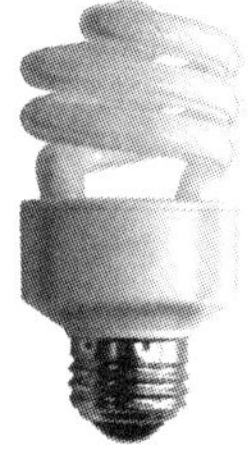

Idea Exercise: Recounting your good childhood memories

The memory brain bank below needs your help. In the empty spaces within the brain write in the things you remember as a child that made you feel comfortable and happy. See if you can fill the entire brain with *good* childhood memories. If you need more space, fill in the blank lines below the brain to list more memories.

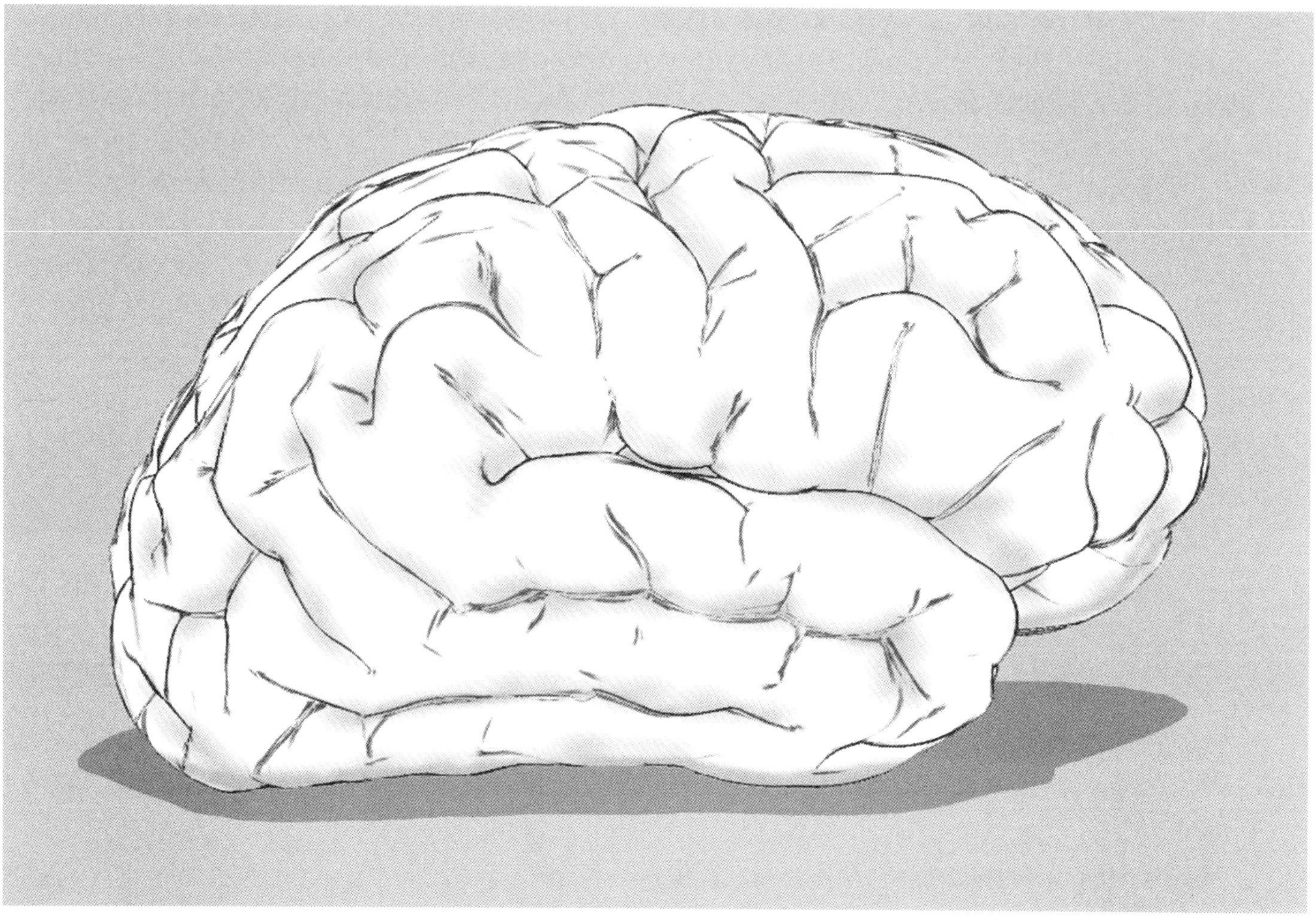

All Children Are Artists...

"All children are artists. The problem is how to remain an artist once he grows up."

- Pablo Picasso

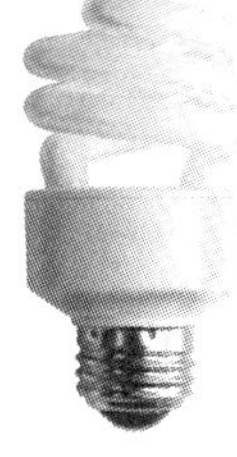

Idea Exercise: Tell a story with those good memories

From the filled in memory bank on the left, choose **five words or phrases** and write a short story about those good memories. Weave the words into the story so that the reader can feel, hear, taste and touch the good memories. If you don't feel like writing then try and draw those five elements into a picture story that takes us to that place and time of your childhood.

Float...

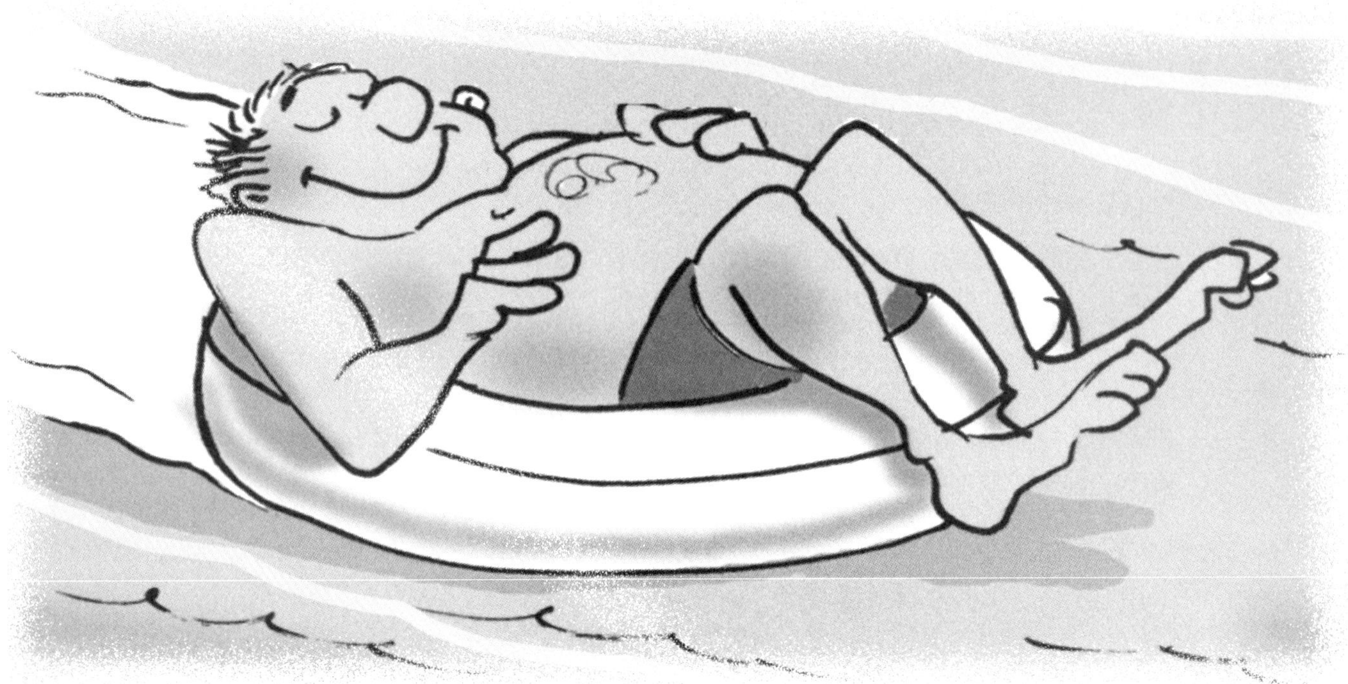

Idea Exercise: The Floating Chaise Lounger

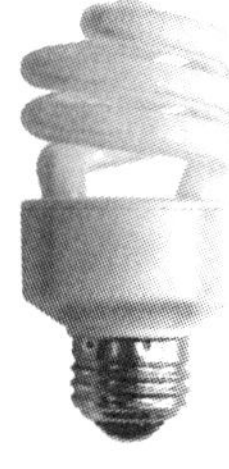

Find an indoor or outdoor pool. Outdoor pools are not necessarily temperature controlled so the time of year is crucial to your comfort if you step outside. Buy or borrow a floating chaise lounge. If you can't get to a pool, try this in the middle of your living room.Lay in or on your lounger face up. Float out to the middle of the pool. The less distractions the better. Try to make the pool as noise-free as possible. Lay there as motionless as long as possible. If you are outside stare at the sky. If you are indoors stare at one portion of the ceiling and stay fixed on it. Drift and allow your conscious mind to relax.

If you are staring at a cloud, watch it change shape. Be patient, wait...
Ask yourself what that cloud reminds you of.
Is it a person, place or thing up there floating?
Is it an animal shape, or maybe a profile of a person's face?
If you are indoors close your eyes and picture clouds hovering overhead.
Can you see the cirrus cloud wisping along high above all other clouds?
Can you see a stratus layer of clouds, or the cumulus clouds below them?
Make the clouds move in your mind. Allow them to dance, drift, and form images of wonder.
Can you visualize a cloud you can sit on?
Can you create a cloud shaped like your favorite recliner or sofa?
Can you sit in it and let the gentle breeze carry you where it may?
Where does it take you? Are you moving down the street in your cloud chair?
Are you out of your town now, or out of the state? Are you over water or land?
What can you see below? Are there mountain ranges, deserts, or forests beneath you?
Do you see the symmetrical shapes of farm fields being cross cut by meandering streams and rivers? Can you see the intersection of man-made structures and roads nestled among the green forests and blue-green ponds and lakes?

...In Space

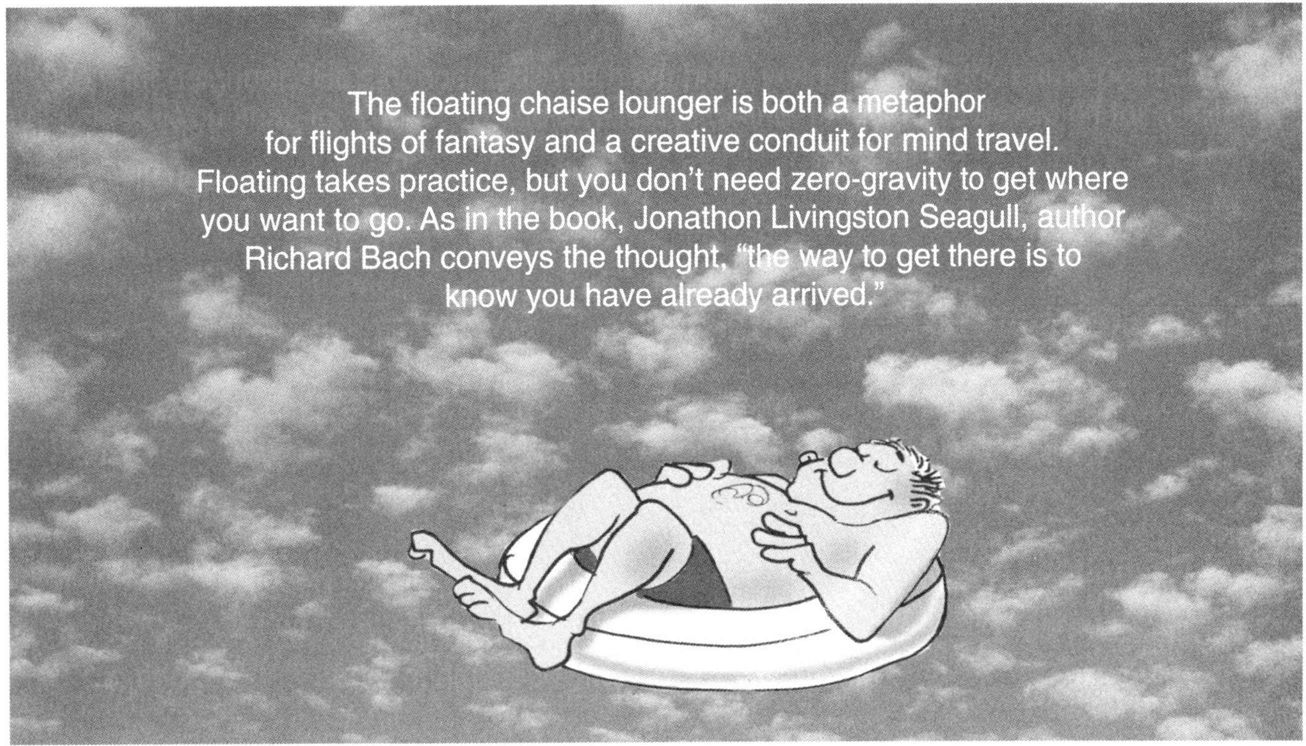

From the sky, can you see the bright blue square-shaped pools behind neighborhood homes? Go ahead and wave, if you look hard enough you may see yourself floating in one of those pools. Do you see yourself? You pass over your house and you look toward the horizon. Can you see that red hot-air balloon about eye level? You are closing in on it. Can you see some flames flashing and hear the whooshing roar of more hot air released into the balloon? Can you see the balloonist?

The balloonist is signaling to you to move closer. He's all decked out in a top hat and tails and you grab the cane he is holding. He greets you with a smile and says, "Welcome aboard there, sky sailor." You are amazed at how easy it is to get yourself on the hot-air balloon. The friendly balloonist ties your pool lounger to the balloon basket and asks you a question.

"Where would you like to go? The sky's the limit, you know"

You are not quite sure what to say. This is your first balloon trip. You ponder. You wonder. You ponder some more. You say to him, "You know, I always wondered what it would be like to be atop Mount Everest"

"Then Mount Everest it is," returns the balloonist with a heart-felt chuckle, "We'll be there before you know it."

Just then you hear a voice saying, "Hey are you all right, are you alive?"

It is your neighbor. He's concerned. You have been laying there in the same position, totally motionless. You snap to. You sit up and say, "Oh, I'm fine, I must have dozed off for a minute."

He says not really and claims you have been asleep over an hour.

Get Your Head In The Clouds

"Twenty years from now you will be more disappointed by the things that you didn't do than by the ones you did do. So throw off the bowlines. Sail away from the safe harbor. Catch the trade winds in your sails. Explore. Dream. Discover."

- Mark Twain

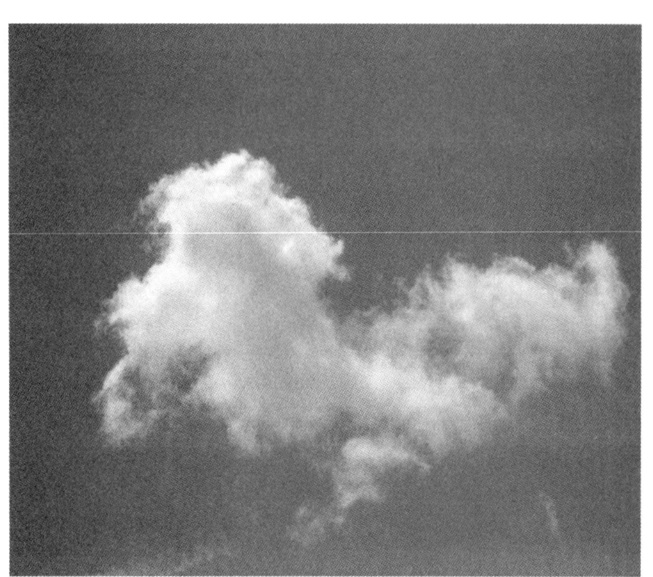

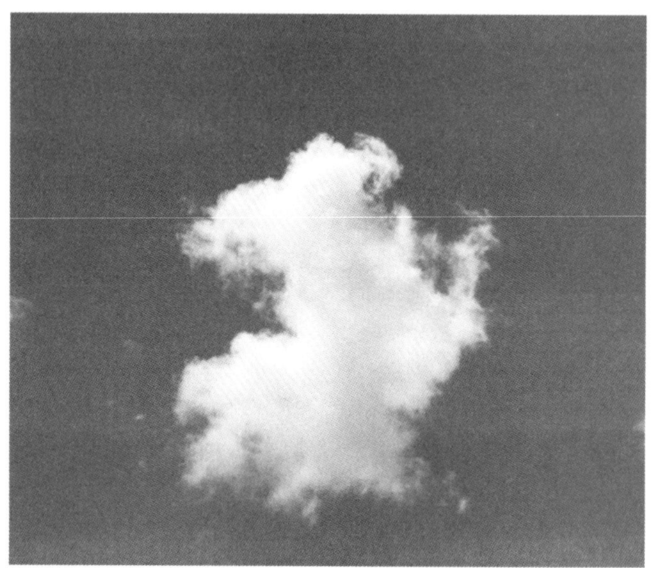

Idea Exercise: Get Your Head *in* the Clouds

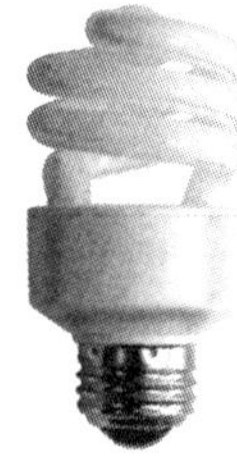

Clouds are a great way to free up the mind to see and wonder. Lying in a hammock, recliner or chaise lounge with an unobstructed view of the sky look into the clouds. The puffiest clouds generally provide the best opportunity to see shapes. Look at the two cloud shapes above. What do you see? Do they remind you of any particular animal? Do they have a human shape? Do you see a face? In the spaces below make a list of the images you see for each cloud. Now go outside and try the same exercise. Bring a camera or sketchbook and record your discoveries.

What Do You See?

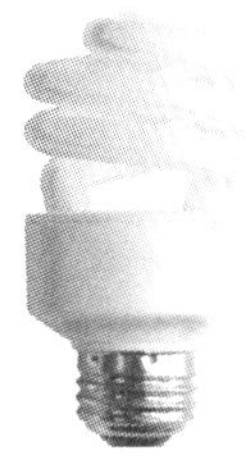

Idea Exercise: Keep Your Head *in* the Clouds

Here are four more cloud shapes. What do you see?
Write down the shapes these clouds bring to mind.

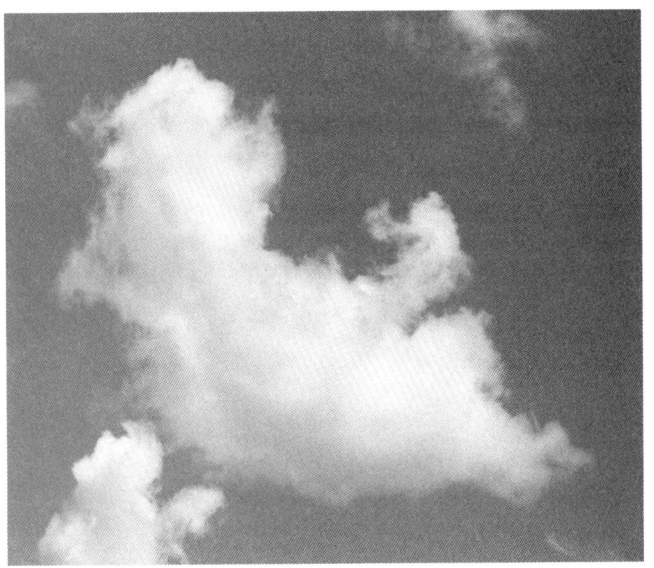

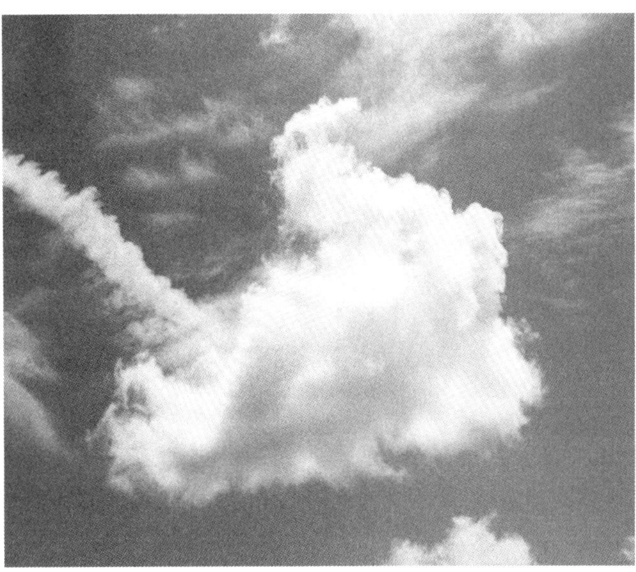

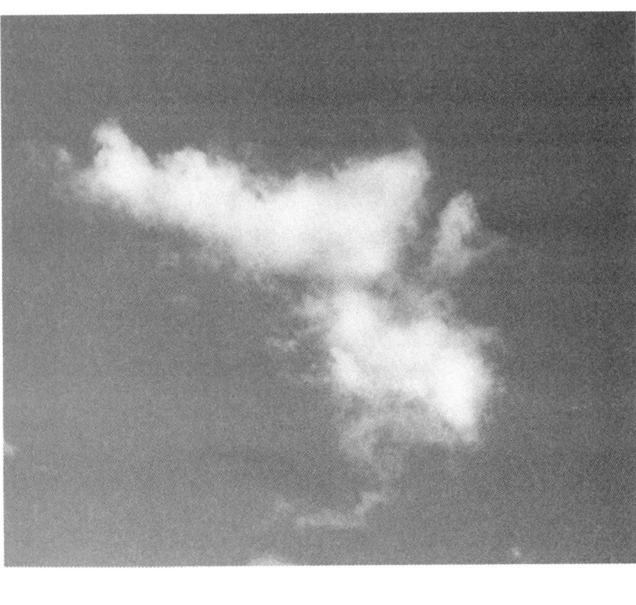

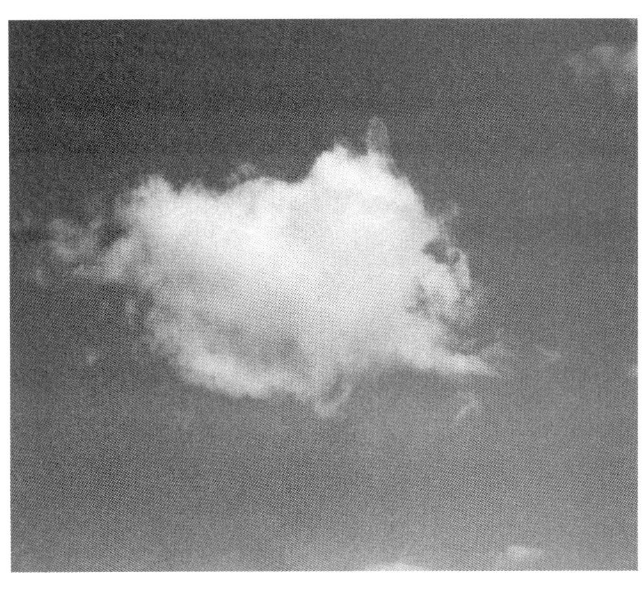

Don't Lose The Muse

O! for a muse of fire, that would ascend the brightest heaven of invention.

- William Shakespeare

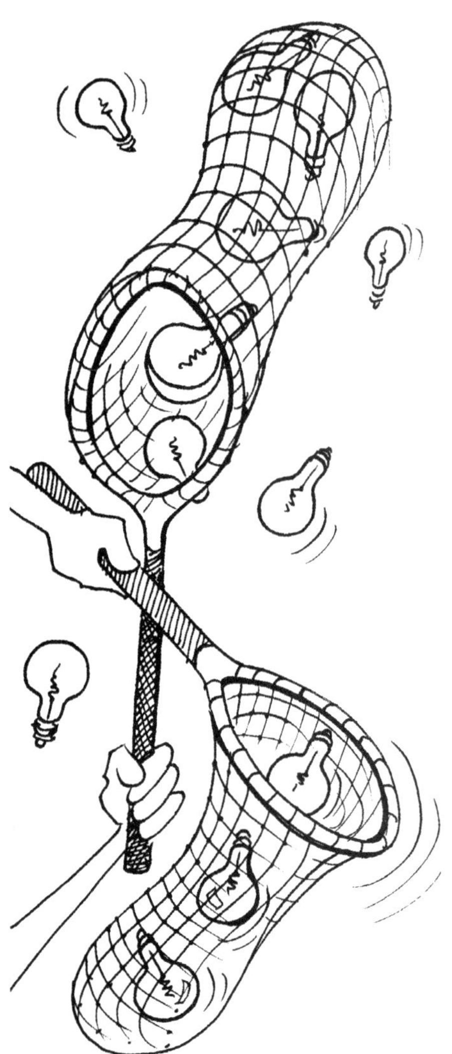

Ideas are fleeting. They pop in and out of our consciousness so quickly, it is really important to *write, draw and record* these ideas of inspiration immediately.

One of the easiest ways to grab an idea is to record it. Keep a digital recorder in the car, in your pocket on a walk or wherever ideas come to you. If you are driving it is unsafe to write holding on to a steering wheel. If you can't pull over at least with a digital recorder you can enter your thoughts with the push of a button. *Also, always carry a small note pad in the car with you so when you do pull over safely you can write your thoughts.*

Another way to store ideas is with journals. You may want to purchase more than one journal. Some journals are good for collecting random thoughts. Another journal could be used to chronicle dreams. Keep that one near your bed so you can write it down before the dream fades. Another journal might be for poetry, writing lyrics, or phrases that you have heard during the day. Some journals might be for visual use only. You might try doodling, drawing and sketching ideas. You can also paste photos, leaves and ideas written on napkins into your journal. Some folks might need one large book journal that houses all of these ideas in one place.

Whatever you decide, know *your* journal is your way to document, grab and grasp illusive thoughts. Also, keep it handy. If you choose to record your ideas digitally, it may be a good idea to transcribe those thoughts into your journals for back-up.

Try this exercise:
Write down several ways you can think of to **catch something**. Here are three to start with:

fishing with a pole		
setting a trap		
using a net		

Catching ideas and storing them is one of the biggest challenges to staying creative. Making a list will guide your mind's eye to see and seize ideas.

Build The Muse A Treehouse

Create A Tree of Ideas:

Another exercise to try is fun and challenges your free-flowing thought process. Find a blank piece of paper the size of a poster. Draw the trunk of a tree at the bottom and label it *ground zero*. Everytime you think of an idea, draw a branch. Instead of leaves draw words to describe your idea briefly (what we'll call "a brief leaf"). One idea should spawn another. Keep drawing branches and "brief leaves" to connect as many ideas as possible. Your **Tree of Ideas** should begin to take shape. Watching it grow is fun. Don't expect to fill the entire poster. Set it aside, then come back to it later when you have more ideas to make it grow. If your thoughts are scattered, place a brief leaf in a random area and attach your branches later. Look at the drawing below see how your **Tree of Ideas** might branch out and take shape. You might even build a treehouse in your tree so your muse can live feeling safe and secure.

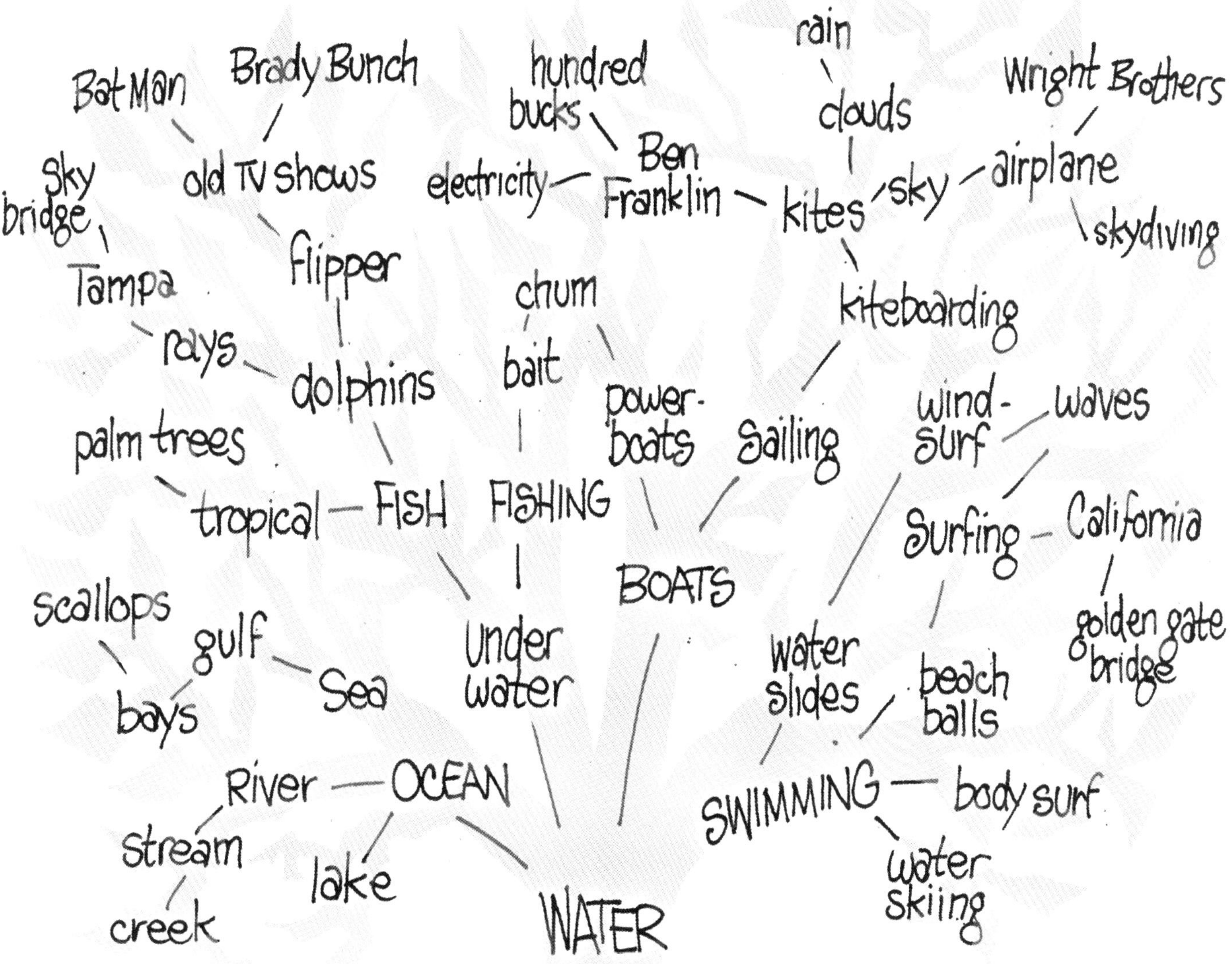

GROUND ZERO

Your Super Memory

"Another word for creativity is courage."
-George Prince - author, innovator

Idea Exercise: Superheroes to the rescue

Did you have a favorite comic book superhero when you were a child? Did you collect comic books? Did you watch superhero cartoons or real-life superhero shows? Did you ever come up with your own superhero? Did you ever give it a name and draw it? Here's a chance to remember those childhood heroes again. If you drew one when you were younger, try and draw them below. If you would rather write about your superheroes, go ahead and describe what you remember. If you never had a superhero, go ahead and create one now.

You Don't Scare Me

"Creativity requires the courage to let go of certainties."
- Erich Fromm - psychologist and humanistic philosopher

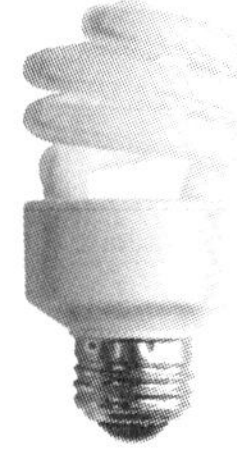

Idea Exercise: You don't scare me

What is the scariest story you remember when you were a child? Was it from a movie, a book or sitting around a campfire and hearing stories? Write a short story about your scariest memory. If you would rather draw your story use the space below:

Uncovering Household Treasures

"One of the advantages of being disorderly is that one is constantly making exciting discoveries." - A.A. Milne

You've heard the expression, **"One man's trash is another man's treasure."** Uncovering treasures in your house, attic, basement, car and your garage can be fun, profitable and most of all a source of creative fodder. It's time to put on your detective cap, your explorer hat and find surprises right under your nose.

•Your glove compartment: Let's start where you spend a lot of time, but forget about unless you are being pulled over by the police! A long time ago car companies invented glove compartments for just that, a place to store gloves. Now we store maps, insurance cards, the car registration and goodness knows what else. Take a few minutes to look through the glove box and find some surprises.

•Catch-all drawers: Everyone has one or two, maybe more. It's that drawer that catches all of the miscellaneous items around the kitchen, the garage, and laundry room. Time to seek it out, clear it out and find all kinds of knicknacks, pencils, screws, batteries, glue bottles, scissors and playing cards. Most likely you will hear yourself say, "I've been looking for that!" Well, now you've found it. Organize the drawer into "keep to use", "toss", and "save as art" for a creative project.

•Stash of books: No doubt you have collected scads of books over the years. Some may be in boxes, some are on your library shelf. Some you have read, more than once. Others you have never cracked open. Ask yourself why. It's time to go through them and consolidate. Make *two piles.* One to treasure forever in your own house, and one to send to Treasureville on the other side of town. Go through your books carefully. Sort by *books you will read and re-read* and the rest to *donate.* There are so many wonderful places to donate books. Think of retirement homes, libraries, homeless shelters, hospitals and churches. Make a list, box them up and send them to Treasureville.

•Stash of VHS Tapes: Do you still have home family videos on VHS? It's time to archive them onto DVD. You can still find VHS to DVD recorders at electronic stores or online. Preserve those precious VHS family moments by digitizing them to DVD. It is time consuming but you can re-live once in a lifetime moments and pass them on to your children and grandkids. It is well worth the time and effort.

How do I sort this stuff?: Sort it all in various piles or boxes. Make a sentimental save pile, a donate to charity pile, a re-gift to friends pile, give back to the family pile, a museum might want it pile, a creative keepsake art pile and finally the trash pile!

Sorting Trash From Treasure

"There comes a time in every rightly constructed boy`s life that he has a raging desire to go somewhere and dig for hidden treasure" -Mark Twain

•Wheelbarrow & Wagon Bound: So its Saturday morning and you are headed around the neighborhood looking for garage sales. It's a trip to the treasure trove and it's all within walking distance. Don't drive, take the wheelbarrow. If you don't have a wheelbarrow, bring a little red wagon. If you bring your car you'll end up tying patio furniture to the roof of the car and buying more than you need or have room for. A wagon or wheelbarrow makes it easier, economical and fun.

Now, what to buy? Depends on what you consider art. For a future project in this book find your treasure trove with art in mind. We are going to assemble a still life to photograph or draw. You'll need to find the fun, ridiculus, unusual, striking and conversational treasures. Don't go broke doing it. Just put them in your wheelbarrow or wagon to get them home and then store them safely for our rainy day project.

•Pantry Party: When is the last time you checked your pantry inventory? Look for perishable and outdated items. Toss those out first. Now look for the items that could go in a casserole, soup, crock pot, or tasty dessert. As you sort them out, also think about what would be good to take to the local soup kitchen. What's not in the donation pile is yours to turn into your own pantry party. Be creative. Make a dish with what you have, not what you need at the store. Make do and whip up a meal *without* using recipe cards. Use your imagination and your taste buds.

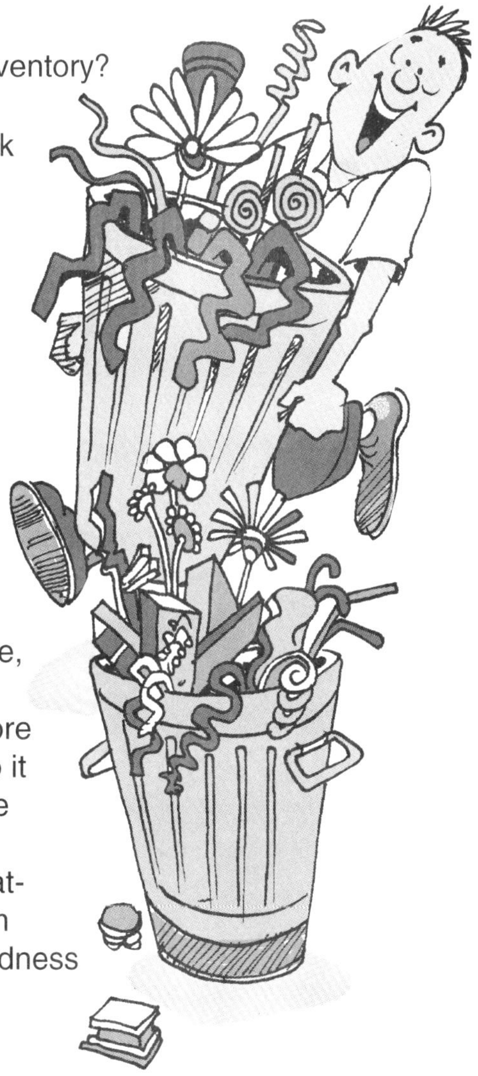

•Scan framed pictures: Over the years you have probably collected plenty of framed pictures of friends, family, vacation trips and special events. Those pictures may have been taken with an old camera and there is no digital record of them. They may be hanging or laying on shelves all over the house. They may be in boxes, hopefully dry and temperature controlled. Wherever they are, get them out and take them out of their frames. It's time to scan them. If you don't have a scanner you can take them to a photo store and pay to have them done. Or you can invest in a scanner and do it yourself. As with the VHS to DVD project you will preserve valuable memories by archiving them on a CD disk. It is worth the time and expense passing them on from generation to generation. Your great-grandchildren will thank you for them. By the time they look at them they will transfer those CDs and DVDs to a hologram format or goodness knows what else.

Rediscovering Attic Treasures

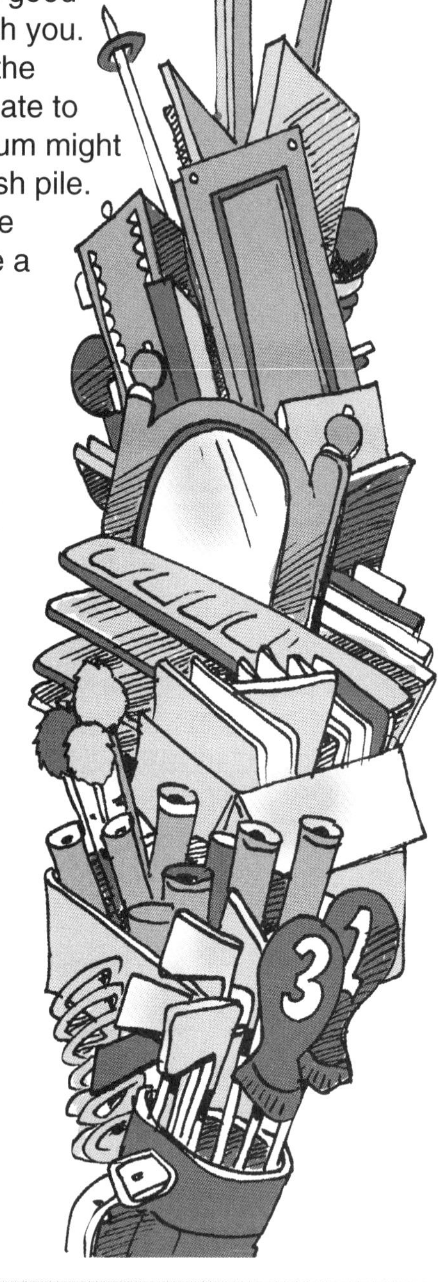

•Attack the attic: Afraid to go up there? Well, it can be very hot or very cold, so pick a day to go up and discover when it is most comfortable. Most likely you have forgotten what is up there. That is the point. You can re-live memories and have creative fun doing it. Make sure you can see well up there. Get a good flashlight or battery-powered storm lantern. Take a pad of paper up with you. Make a list of inventory. As we did on the previous pages let's sort out the attic clutter into various categories. Make a sentimental save list, a donate to charity pile, a re-gift to friends pile, give back to the family pile, a museum might want it pile, a creative keepsake art pile (see below), and finally the trash pile. Once you have made your list, decide how you are going to move these items around. Some items are coming down, and some will stay. Make a floor plan *and* a game plan to move items.

- ***Before you move anything ask for help. There's no sense getting hurt or stuck in the attic when you don't need to. Be careful up there.***

•Go on a sentimental journey in your journal:

Now that you have things sorted out from the attic take a look at your creative keepsake pile you brought down. Place the items near you; reachable from a comfortable chair. A suggestion might be to arrange them in chronological order. Place the oldest items on your left, newer on the right. Get your creative journal out and a favorite pen. Stare at the items and let the memory of that keepsake take you to that time and place. Recount the positive pleasure from that treasure. Then write about it. Allow the memories to wash over you and paint a picture with words. Write verbal postcards while you take a sentimental journey back in time. Let the journal be your creative passport. Have fun. (See the attic isn't such a scary place after all.)

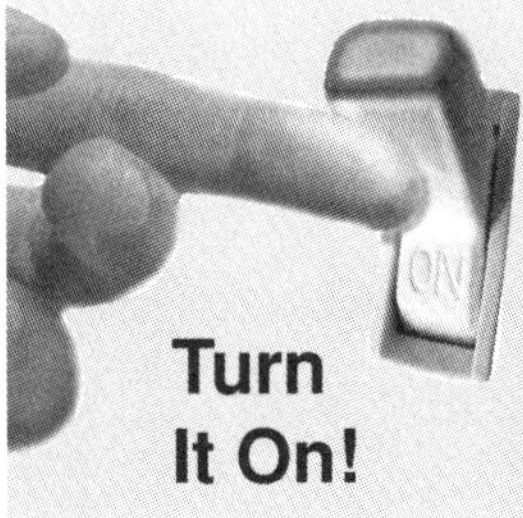

•Create a household treasure still life: Go one step further. Make your keepsake pile into a work of art. Assemble an interesting still life from framed pictures, tools, tape dispensers, cup full of pencils, knicknacks, and an array of treasures. Photograph, or draw it. It tells a story of who you are. Use the **next page** to draw, plan out or write about your life's treasure trove as art.

Your Treasure Trove As Art

my life treasure trove story:

Title: ____

Become A Wordsmith

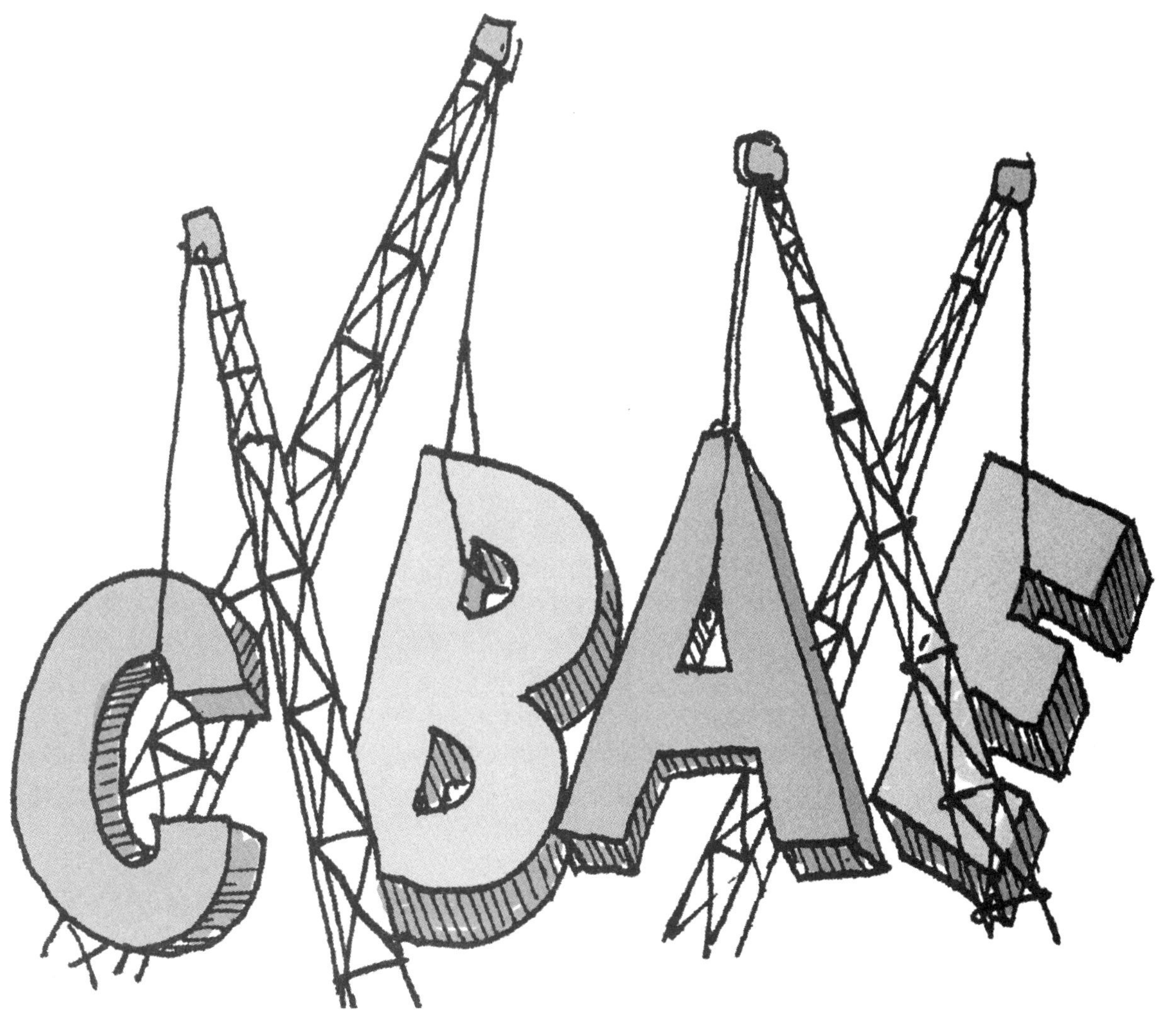

Word·smith: (w rd- smith - noun)
a person who works with words; especially a skillful writer

Can You Coin A Phrase?

Wordsmith exercise: Make up your own sayings

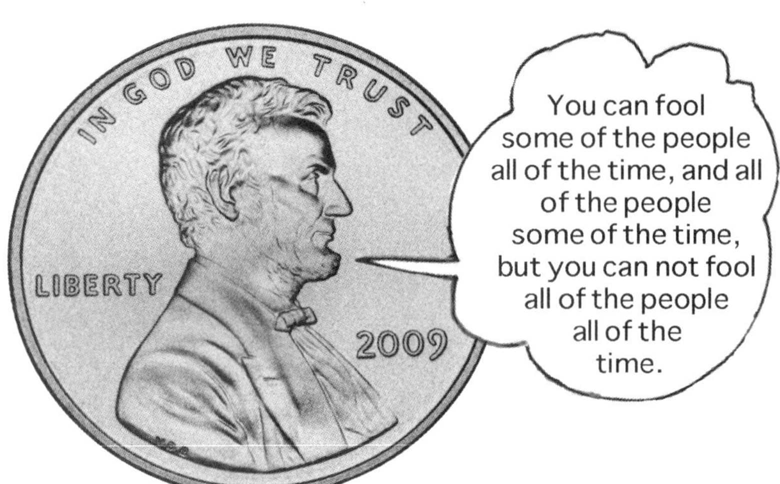

You hear wise and funny sayings all the time. Have you ever wanted to make up your own? Then it's time to coin a phrase. Speaking of coin, here is Abe Lincoln with a famous phrase of his own.

There are a few common sayings below to get you started. Have fun making up your own in the space provided:

"Money Talks ... but all mine ever says is Goodbye!"

"I saw Elvis. He sat between me and Bigfoot on the UFO."

"I'm in shape ... round's a shape isn't it?"

"I'm on a seafood diet...I see food and I eat it."

The Power of Visual Words

Wordsmith exercise: Memorizing words

First, cover the second list at the bottom of the page so you can't see it. Now, look at the list below for only **ten** seconds. Try to remember as many words on the list as you can in your head. Ready, go!

term	labor	same	send
comma	sequence	loss	quantity
about	set	certain	determine
appendix	vary	deficit	phase

How did you do? How many did you remember?
Now, uncover the list below and do the same test with this group of words. Look at them for only ten seconds. Ready, go!

wishbone	guitar	sunset	monkey
cow	wristwatch	mirror	pretzel
roses	pencil	brick	goblet
umbrella	oil can	diamond	castle

How did you do? How many did you remember this time?
These words were easier to remember because they are *visual* words. The right side of the brain *sees* these words and remembers their context by shape and color. It then tells the right side of the brain to process the list. With both sides of the brain working as a team more words go in the memory bank. Writing visual words always lights up the bright side of the brain!

In Your Own Words

"Creativity is the ability to see relationships where none exist."
Thomas Disch - American science fiction author and poet

Words are wonderful tools to help you become more creative. Using new words or creating a new word out of two words is not only fun, but can become part of our lexicon. Become a wordsmith and craft a language all your own.

The legacy of Dr. Seuss isn't just visual, it's verbal. Some of the words he invented are a part of our modern language today. He invented the word "nerd". He created "grinch" and "lorax". These words never existed until Seuss made them an everyday part of our language.

•**Make up nicknames:** We had them as kids, and many have carried over into our adult life. Write down all the nicknames you can remember from acquaintances you know to famous people in history. Then think of people you know that don't have a nickname and create one for them. Try animals. We do this all the time with pets. Look at pictures of animals in a zoo or in the wild and create a nickname to match their physique and personality. More on page 42.

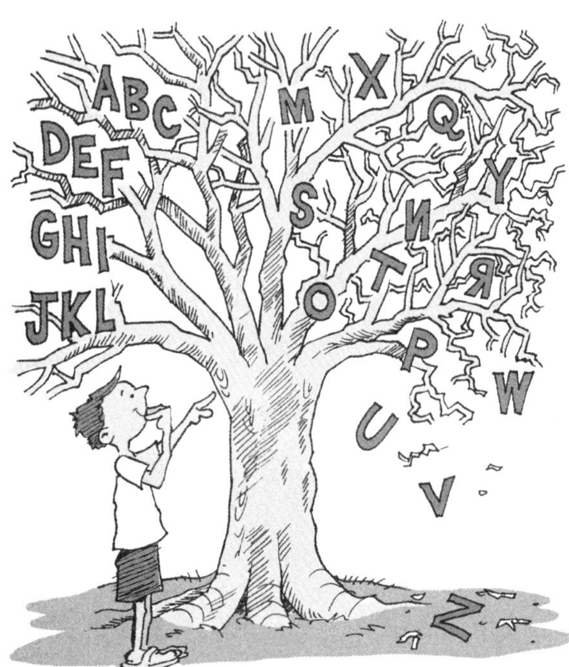

•**Make up words:** Don't just stop with nicknames, make up words to describe your job, your car, your house, your neighbor's house, lousy drivers, a brilliant sunset or maybe even your favorite food. Create your own superlatives, oxymorons, adjectives or adverbs. Create sentences with these words in them. Once you get hundreds of words made up, you may want to go the next level...

•**Create your own abridged dictionary:** Why not? Define your word and provide a pronounciation for it. Use them in a sentence so readers can better understand their meaning.

•**Create your own slogan:** Advertising is filled with catchy phrases and slogans. Create your own for your favorite team, squadron, club, musical group, business group, association, etc.

•**Re-Title It:** Make up new titles for nursery rhymes, fictional books, biographies, songs, TV shows, movies, famous paintings, toys, gadgets, food products and future cars. You name it! Get creative!

Wordsmith exercise: Create a name for a new:

Bowling alley	Candy	Spaceship to moon	Sneaker
Boat	Hardware store	Paint color (white)	Soft drink
Football team	New airline	Race horse	Record label

Create A New Species

You can combine two words to make one new word!

It is a lot of fun to make up new words by adding two words together. You can start by thinking of some animals. You can dream up new species of creatures on land, in the sea or in the air by combining characteristics. This is a cartoon of a dinosaur and a fossil fuel engine put together.

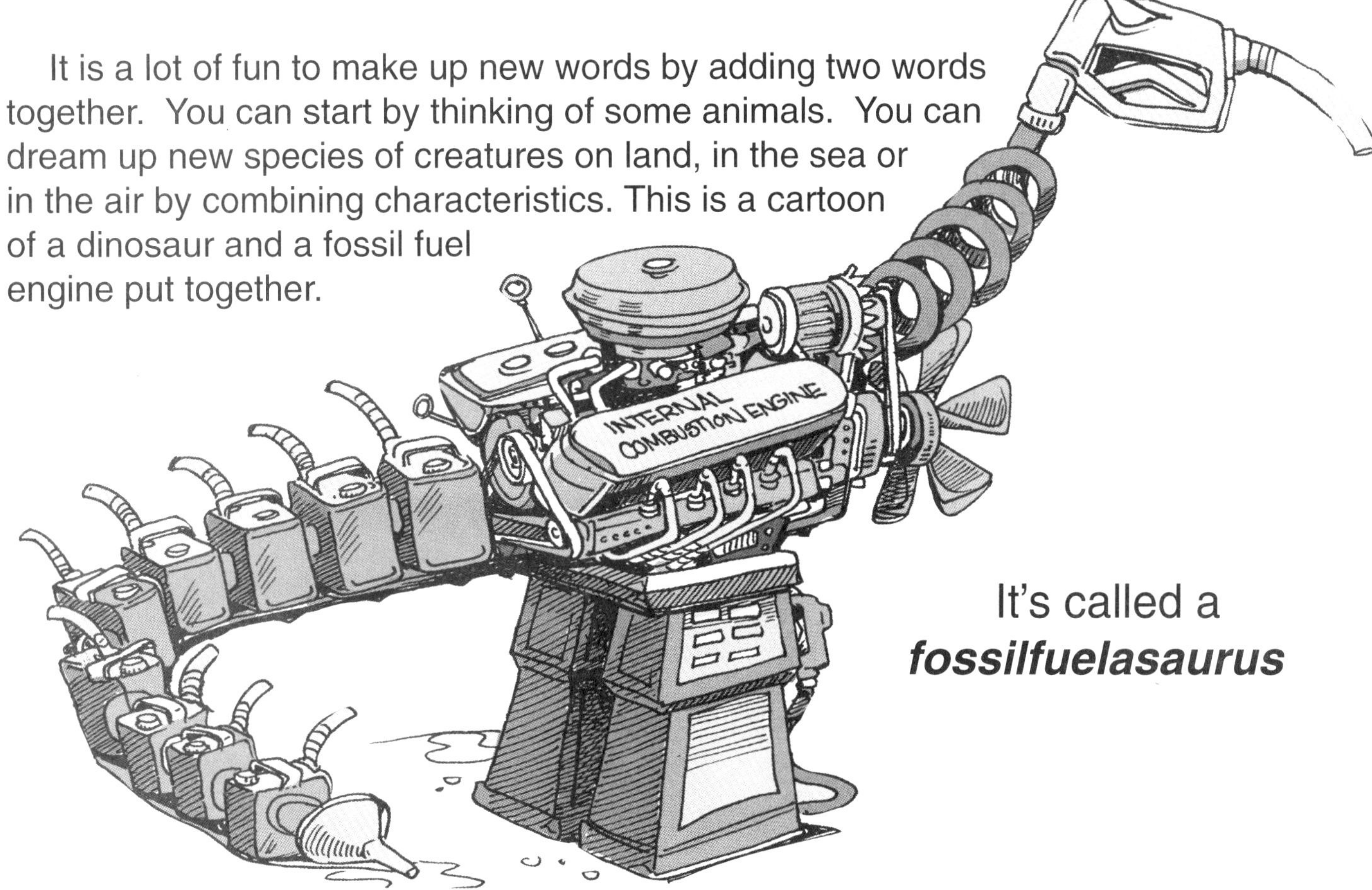

It's called a ***fossilfuelasaurus***

Start with		add		and you get
HIPPOPOTAMUS	+	PLATYPUS	=	**HIPPOLATYPUS**
GIRAFFE	+	RHINOCEROS	=	**GIRAFFOCEROS**
FUN	+	PHENOMENAL	=	**FUNOMENAL**

________________ + ________________ = ________________

________________ + ________________ = ________________

________________ + ________________ = ________________

________________ + ________________ = ________________

________________ + ________________ = ________________

Message In A Bottle

Wordsmith exercise: Stranded on an island

These two guys are separated by miles of ocean. The only way they can communicate is by a message in a bottle. What would they say to each other? Write their messages under the cartoons.

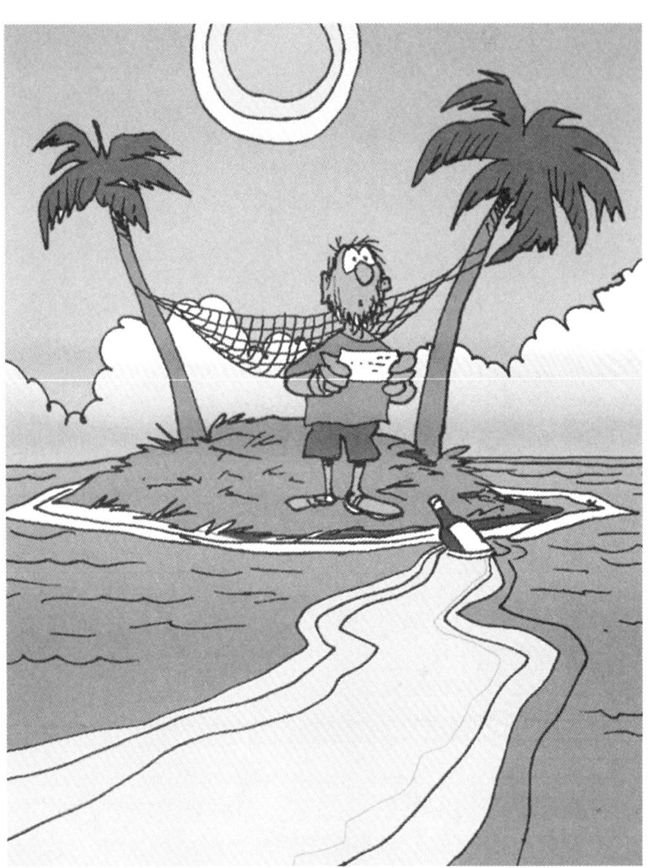

Bottle Message #1

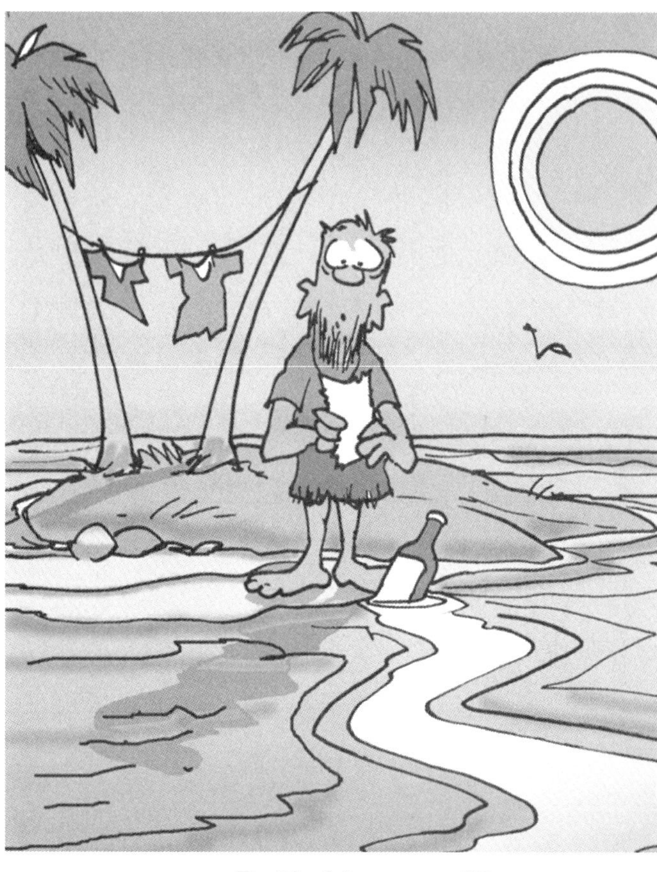

Bottle Message #2

Create A Caption

Wordsmith exercise: What is happening in each of these cartoons?
Create a funny caption underneath each cartoon in the space provided.

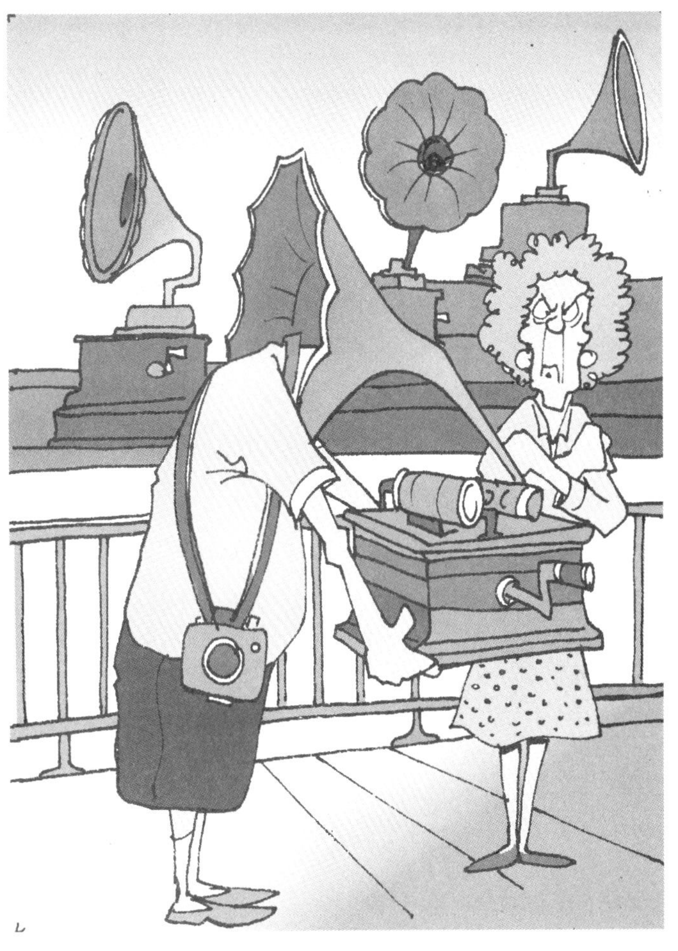

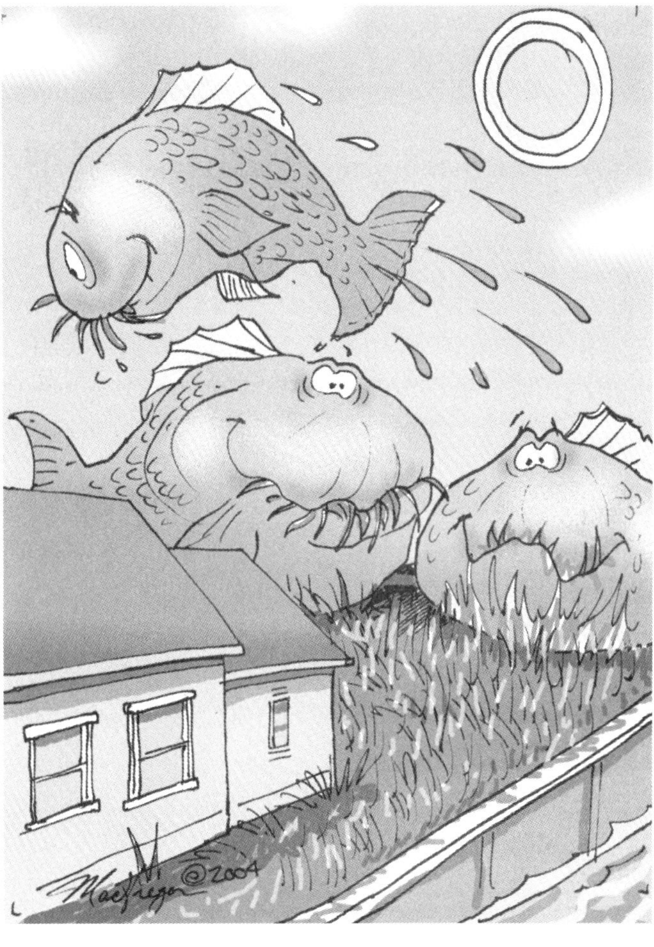

Wordsmith exercise: Make up some **oxymorons**:

an **oxymoron** is defined as a figure of speech that combines two normally contradictory terms.

Here are five examples to get you started:

dying to live **peacekeeping force** **sad smile** **small crowd** **jumbo shrimp**

Anagrams and Spoonerisms

Wordsmith exercise: ANAGRAMS

anagrams are words or phrases made by mixing up the letters of other words or phrases. Here are some examples. Make up ten **anagrams** below:

a decimal point (I'm a dot in place)

school master (the classroom)

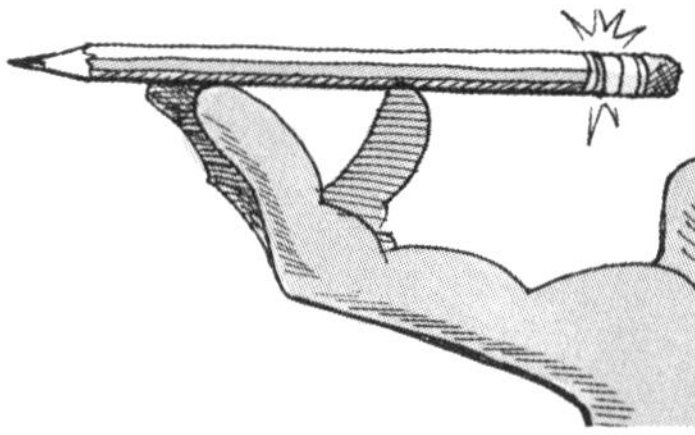

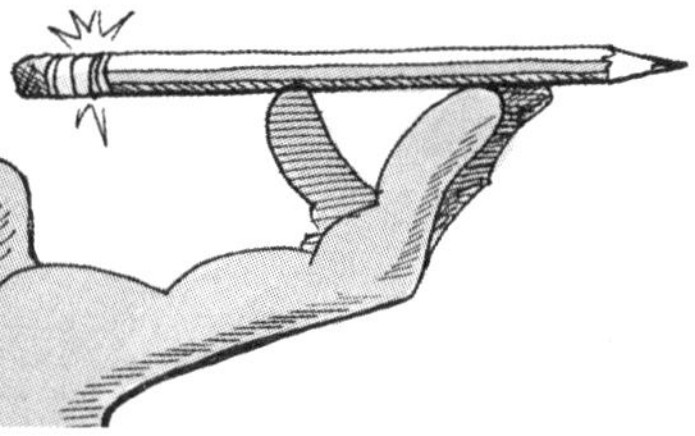

Wordsmith exercise: SPOONERISMS

Spoonerisms are a play on words or phrases in which letters or syllables get swapped. Corresponding consonants, vowels, or morphemes are switched to create a new phrase. Here are some examples. Make up ten **spoonerisms** below:

blushing crow (crushing blow)

fighting a liar (lighting a fire)

Palindromes and Pangrams

Wordsmith exercise: PALINDROMES

Palindromes are words or phrases that read the same backwards or forwards.
Here are some examples. Make up ten **palindromes** below:

Race car

Never odd or even

Wordsmith exercise: PANGRAMS

A pangram is a sentence using every letter of the alphabet at least once.
Here is an example that uses 35 letters.
Make up five **pangrams** below with less than 35 letters if you can:

The quick brown fox jumps over the lazy dog.

Word Picture Puzzles

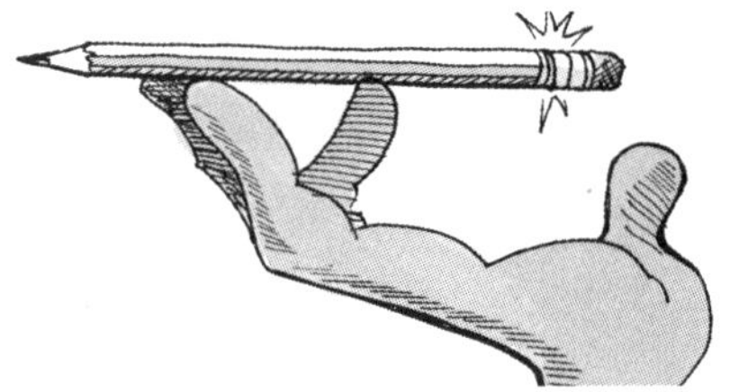

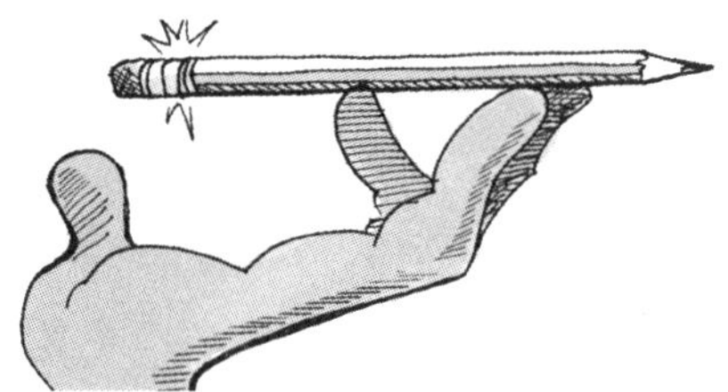

Wordsmith exercise: Word picture puzzles

Try and solve these picture puzzles. Answers are below.

MILL1ON

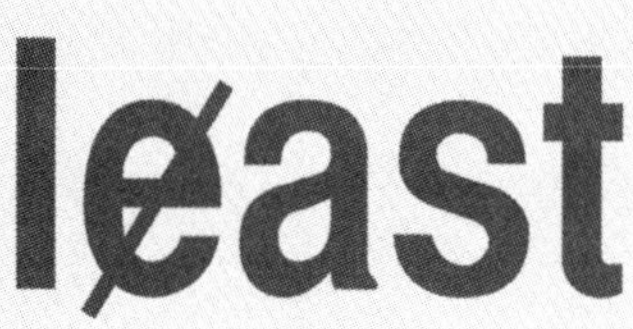

par
two

another one thing

but
thought thought

After you have solved these six puzzles try and create your own word picture puzzles. How many can you invent?

From left to right: one in a million, last but not least, two under par, one thing after another, but on second thought, the long and the short of it

What In The Word Is A Rebus?

Wordsmith exercise: Solve a rebus. Create a rebus.

A **rebus** is a puzzle that consists of pictures of objects, signs, etc, which by the sound of their names suggest words or phrases. Try this one..

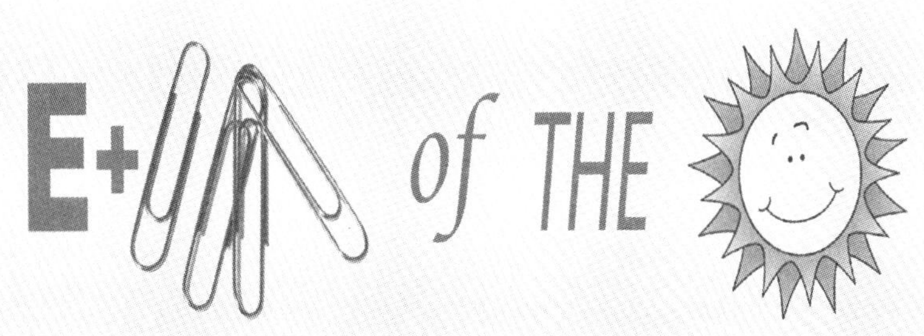

The answer to the rebus puzzle to the left is:

ECLIPSE OF THE SUN

Try and solve the three below. Answers are at the bottom of the page.

1

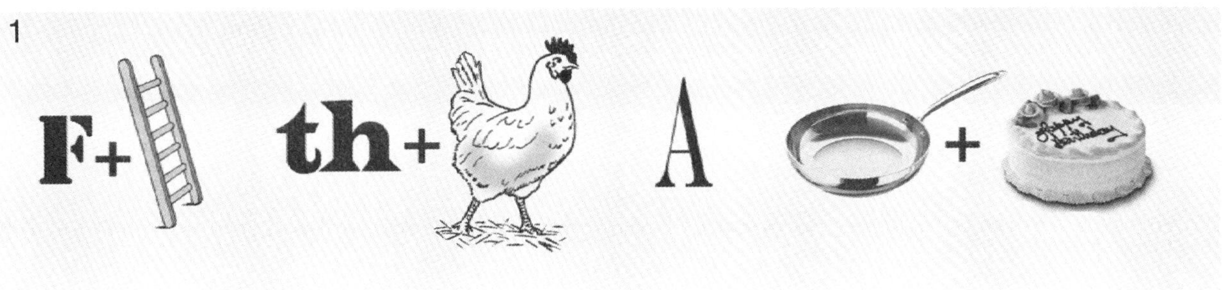

2

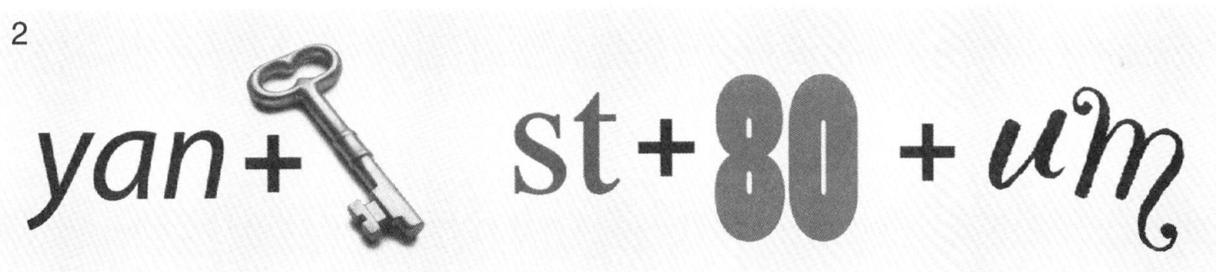

3

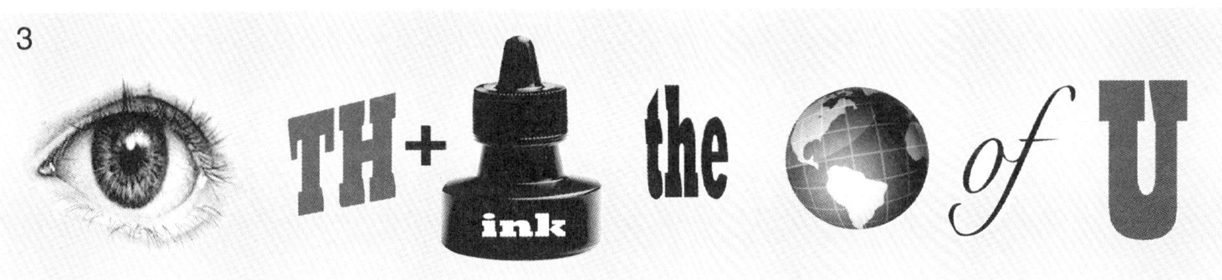

Did you solve all three? Now, try and create your own. How many can you invent?

Answers: Flatter than a pancake, Yankee stadium, I think the world of you

Solve The Rhyming Puzzle

Wordsmith exercise: Find the puzzle words that rhyme

This puzzle has 29 words that rhyme. They are listed under the puzzle below.
Words may be found forwards, backwards, diagonally, upside down, and reversed.
Try and find them all by circling them.
The first word, "chute" is already circled for you.

U	T	E	E	T	U	H	C	A	R	A	P	T
F	C	H	U	T	E	M	F	L	U	T	E	S
O	R	U	O	O	T	H	C	O	O	T	T	A
E	O	U	T	S	H	O	O	T	H	R	L	L
T	S	H	I	E	U	D	N	O	A	I	O	U
U	B	O	O	T	R	I	S	O	S	B	O	T
L	S	O	S	U	B	S	T	I	T	U	T	E
O	H	T	H	P	M	P	I	E	U	T	O	T
S	N	C	O	M	M	U	T	E	T	E	O	U
B	E	R	O	O	T	T	U	M	E	M	C	L
A	W	O	T	C	T	E	T	O	S	Q	S	I
C	T	R	I	B	U	T	E	T	U	O	R	D

chute • flute • coot • attribute • cute • fruit • outshoot • hoot • boot • compute • astute • substitute • commute • root • tribute • toot • moot • shoot • suit • constitute • dispute • loot • newt • route • salute • absolute • parachute • dilute • scoot

Draw Your Name!

Wordsmith Drawing Exercise: Make a picture with your name

Write your first name big across the page. Leave some space between letters.

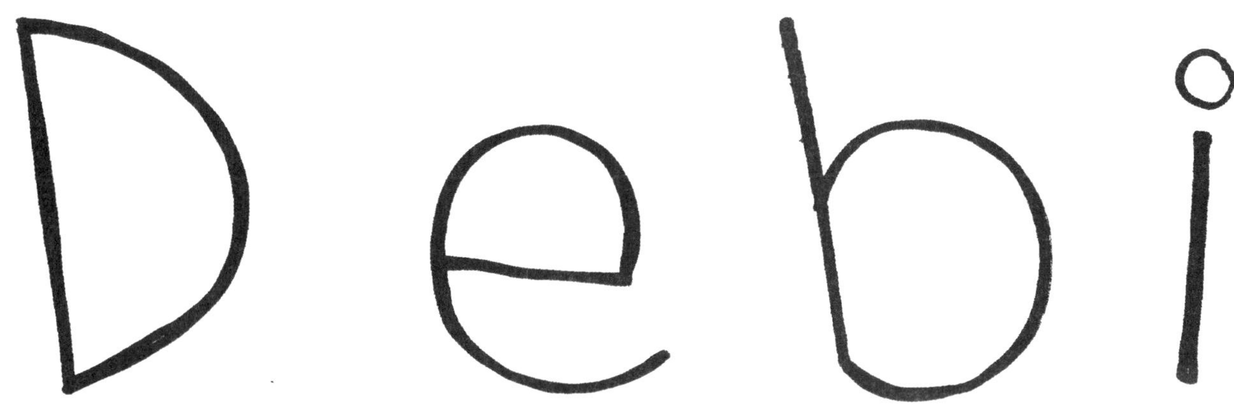

Make the letters into pictures. Look for spaces inside, outside and around the letters to draw what comes to mind. The shape of the letters can give you picture ideas too. Fill up the entire page if you can. See if you can find your name when you are done. It is highlighted in light grey. See it?

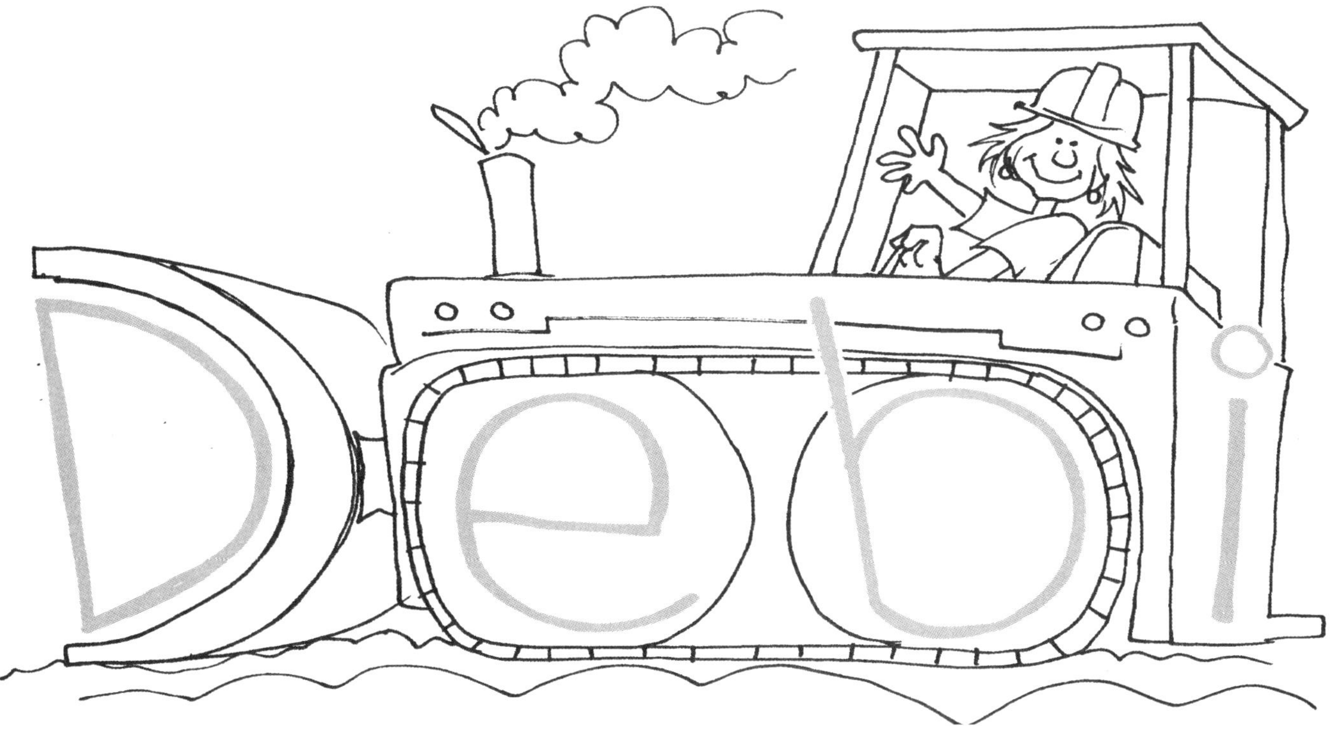

What's In A Name?

Wordsmith exercise: Make up your own nicknames

We all had them as kids, and many have carried over into our adult life. In the space provided below write down all the nicknames you can remember. They can be acquaintances you know or famous people in history. Then think of people you know that don't have a nickname and create one for them. Try animals too. We do this all the time with pets. Look at pictures of animals in a zoo or in the wild and create a nickname to match their physique and personality.

Thomas Edison	**Wizard of Menlo Park**
Wilton Chamberlain	**Wilt the Stilt**
William F. Cody	**Buffalo Bill**
Charles Lindberg	**Lucky Lindy; Lone Eagle**
James Butler Hickok	**Wild Bill Hickok**

NAME	NICKNAME

What's In a Family Name?

Wordsmith exercise: Make up your own family sport nicknames

You have heard of the Jacksonville Jaguars, New York Yankees, San Francisco Giants, Toledo Mud Hens and the Chicago Cubs. But, what about making up a name for a family sports team? Look at the examples below and think of some team names you can attach to families you know. How about relatives and neighbors? Use the space below and get creative!

The Jones Family	**The Jones Bonecrushers**
The Smith Family	**The Smithereens**
The Jackson Family	**The Action Jacksons**
The Bingham Family	**The Big Bad Binghams**

FAMILY NAME	TEAM NICKNAME

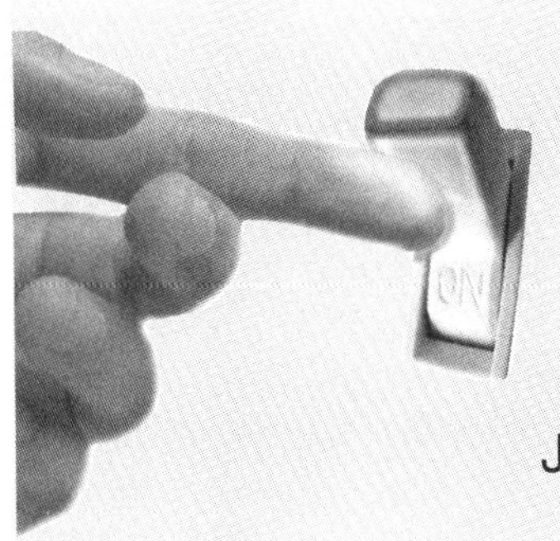

Here's another bright idea

Now that you have a fun list of team names, try drawing mascots for the nicknames. You may want to come up with a logo and a slogan for each team. Design a t-shirt, flag and a bumper sticker. Go all out and create a family food dish for a tailgate party. What would The Action Jacksons love to chow down on before the big game?

Staying Indoors On A Rainy Day...

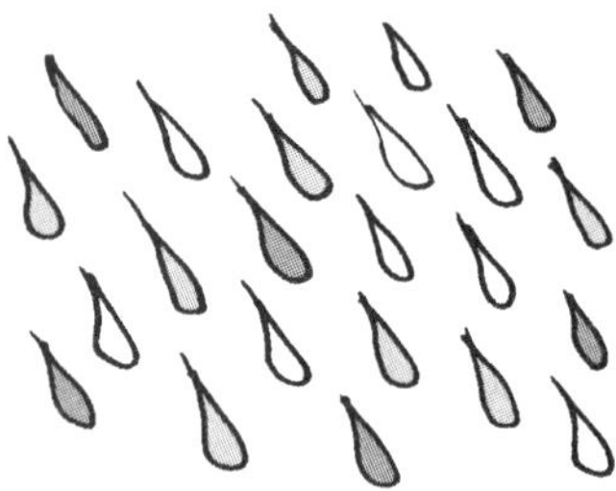

"The sun did not shine.
It was too wet too play.
So we sat in the house
all that cold, cold, wet day."

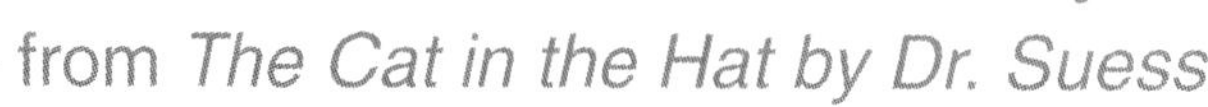

- from *The Cat in the Hat by Dr. Suess*

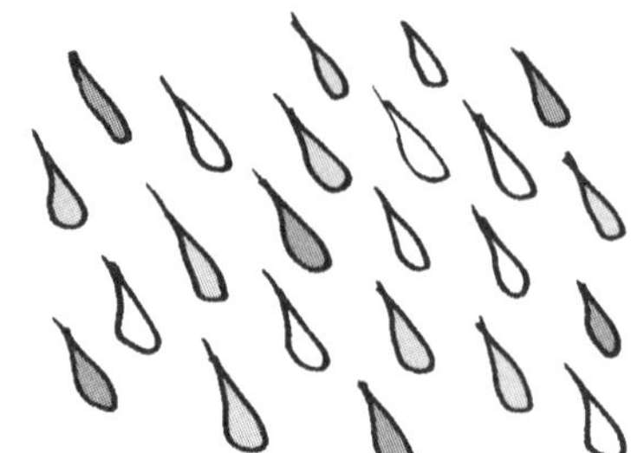

You're trapped. It's raining outside. It's wet and you can't go out and play. Not to worry, there's plenty to do inside your house and inside your head. How can you be bored? Your imagination will allow you to go anywhere and you don't even need an umbrella, unless of couse you are Mary Poppins or the Cat in the Hat. Here are a few rainy day diversion excursions you can take on the next four pages...

•City of Happenstance: Get out an old rotating globe. Place it in front of you, close your eyes and spin it. Let your finger slowly touch the globe as it spins. When it stops your finger is pointing to a random city of chance. If you don't have a globe use a world map atlas. Open it, close your eyes and point to a city on any page. Now go online and google the name of your *city of happenstance.*

What are the people like that live there? What do they wear? What do they eat? What do they drive? Where do they work? What do they produce? What do they do for fun? What languages do they speak? What does the music sound like in the town? Are there any famous places nearby? What is the city's nickname? Write ten things you would like to do if you visited this far away city. Do you have your ticket to visit yet? Bon voyage!

•Where's Bigfoot?:

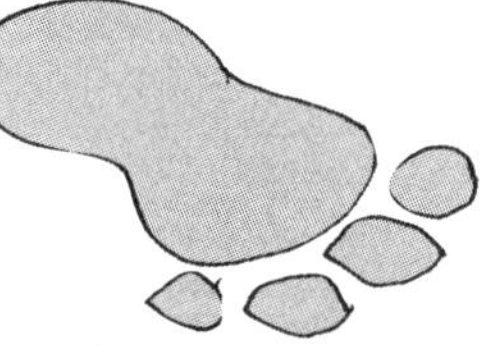

Find some poster board or cardboard. Make cutouts of some really big feet. Create a foot trail for everyone to follow. Where does it lead? If the trail stops, place a clue there that will lead to another trail of footprints. Somewhere in the house Bigfoot is hiding. Where could it be? You may want to write or draw about the adventure further. Do the footprints stop at the front door? Did Bigfoot just stop by to get a drink out of the refrigerator? If he is out in the rain, where would he go? Write and draw a story about Bigfoot's visit to your house and where he might be headed. Did he take a nap? Where?

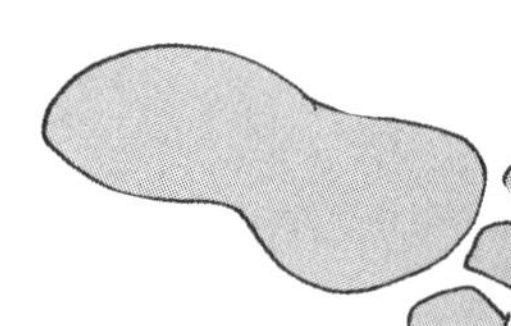

...Can Be Fun And Entertaining!

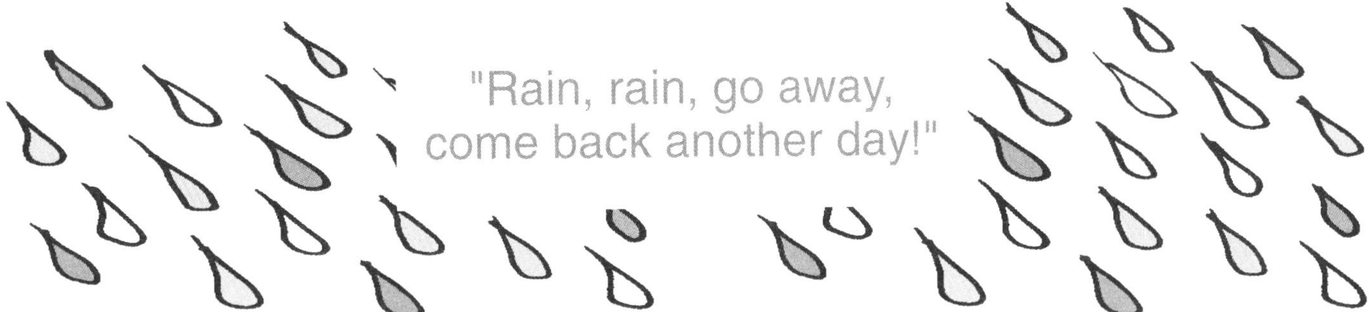

•Make a Ten Million Dollar Movie: You don't have to be Steven Spielberg to make a movie people can enjoy. Use your own family and friends. A digital video camera is all you need. You can just sit around a table taking turns in front of the camera. Need an idea? Pretend you just won ten million bucks in the lottery! Now, try acting out what it would be like if you just discovered you won. Would you scream? What would you do with all that money? Would you share it with the folks around the table? How would you spend it? Would you donate some of it, all of it? Get in front of the camera and tell the world what it would be like to be an instant millionaire! Wow!

•Make a Family Treasure Movie: Nothing can be more valuable than treasuring the life experiences of your family. Produce a video interview with them. Ask them to share their most memorable experiences growing up. What new inventions have they seen in their lifetime? What presidents do they remember? What big events in world history did they live through? What was their happiest moment? Their first love? What was their toughest time? Do they have any regrets? What were their proudest moments? Share all memories. Having a video recording for generations to watch is priceless.

•Create a Wall of Claim: Find a hallway in your house that needs changing. Paint it a favorite color or colors and create your own "my space" on it. Fill it with framed photos, pictures, awards, favorite momentos and things to be proud of. Then declare it, "My Wall of Claim"

•Top Ten Lists: By yourself or with friends and family create your own "top ten" list. Use categories like best TV shows, best hotels, best vacation spots you've been to, best songs, best commercials. Keep them to yourself or share them with the world.

Are You A Shutterbug?

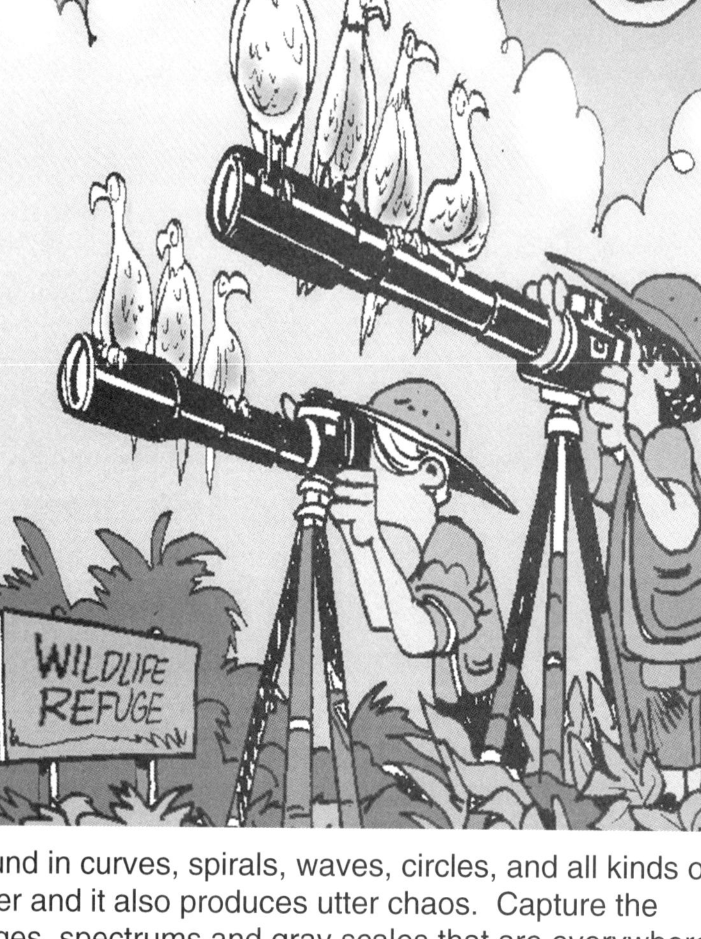

Do you like photography? Do you have an eye for capturing a moment in time with a camera?

Most people love to shoot the usual stand and pose photos. Or, if they are outside most people will take the obvious sunset shot.

It is tougher to look for uncommon subject matter. If you are photographing people it is more challenging to be more artistic with expressions, poses, lighting and composition. If you are outside, find an unusual setting. It may seem more of a risk and a clean break from conventional thinking. The common, predictable shots get boring real quick unless you *shake up and shift the shutterbug.*

Try seeing through the lens in several different ways. Try shooting something upside down. Try looking up at the object. Then try looking down on it. Changing your perspective will creative more varied results.

Grab your camera, get outside and focus the lens on natural life. Look for repetitive patterns. Nature's design can be found in curves, spirals, waves, circles, and all kinds of geometric shapes. Nature creates perfect order and it also produces utter chaos. Capture the complexities and simplicities, rhythms and edges, spectrums and gray scales that are everywhere.

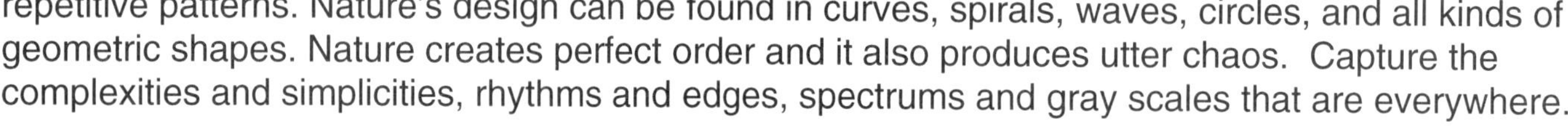

To sharpen your sight, *listen* more closely. Hear nature from its stillness to its thunder. Turn your ear inward to hear the slight, nearly inaudible sounds. Get up close. There is a whole world inside a flower or a seashell. Be patient. If you want that magic shot to happen, you'll have to wait. It will come to you. When you; feel a chilly breeze, walk along a winding brook, run through a giant meadow, climb a sprawling tree, jump in a mud puddle or lay on your back and make a snow angel, your mind's eye will come alive. Photographing for fun and exercise sometimes produces your most creative moments.

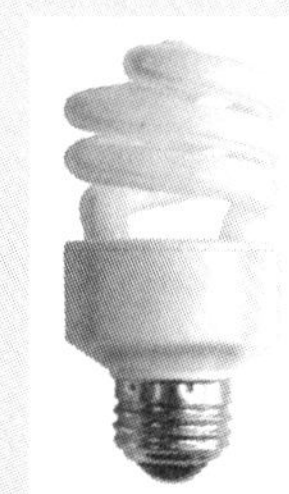

Idea Exercise: OK shutterbug, get outside and photograph nature!

Get a digital camera and a digital recorder. Go out to a park, preserve, refuge, beach, forest, meadow or swamp and take lots of pictures. Record your thoughts as you walk between shots. Keep your voice low. Take deep breaths. Look at every angle possible. Shake and shift the shutterbug. Be patient and ready to shoot at a moment's notice. Try this exercise often. Change venues. Your mind's eye will sharpen more and more on each excursion. Have fun and enjoy the physical exercise.

Super Bowl Ad Campaign

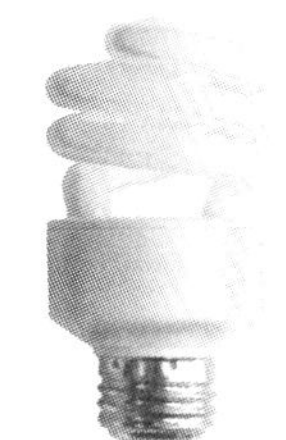

Idea Exercise: Plan a Super Ad

Let's create a pitch for a 60-second TV commercial on Super Bowl Sunday. Millions of viewers are going to see it, so let's make it great!

What are we selling? The make believe company is called **Brain X**. It is inventing a new search engine for the internet. Using this search engine we can look up anything and get an answer instantly.

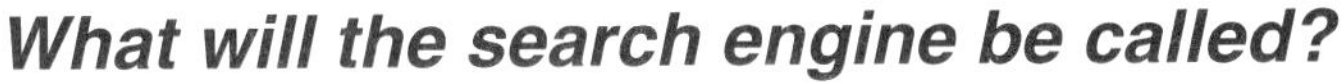

What will the search engine be called?
Sorry, *Google, Bing, AltaVista, Lycos, and Ask.com* are already taken. Think of a clever new search engine name.

We'll need a character to sell it: We have one! "It's" right here, but "it" doesn't have a name. Can you give 'it" a name? "It" is very fast and smart. "It " can find the answer to any question you ask it.

What is our catchy slogan and jingle? We will also need a slogan, or catchy phrase viewers will remember. Maybe the slogan can be musical. Can you write a jingle? We want this ad to be the one people remember after the game is over. Remember what we are selling.

Create a storyboard: This character will be animated. It will speak and move across the screen. We'll need to design a storyboard. Can you write a script for our 60-second ad? What will "it" say? What message do we want to bring to millions of viewers? How can we demonstrate the power of our internet search engine? Remember, we need to tell a story in 60 seconds. When we have written our script we can draw our storyboard. In large panels, sketch the character in the position it will be on the screen for each five second intervals. Write the words "it" will say underneath each panel.

What will the character sound like? Can you make up a voice for our character? After you have created a storyboard and written a script it is time to record it. See if the words you are speaking stay under 60 seconds.

Time to make a pitch: Can your character get up in front of the CEOs of Brain X and answer these questions? What will it say, how will it sound? How will it look? Who will it attract? Will people remember it? Will people want to use the product? What makes it different than the other search engines on the internet?

Make it a Super Bowl ad for the ages!

That's So Random!

Random thought is both common place and practical. When random thought is allowed to take place without constraint or expectation, ideas begin to flow. You'll be surprised at how coincidence and serendipity play a role in random creative thought. Making connections and establishing patterns in totally unrelated elements can be both fun and phenomenal.

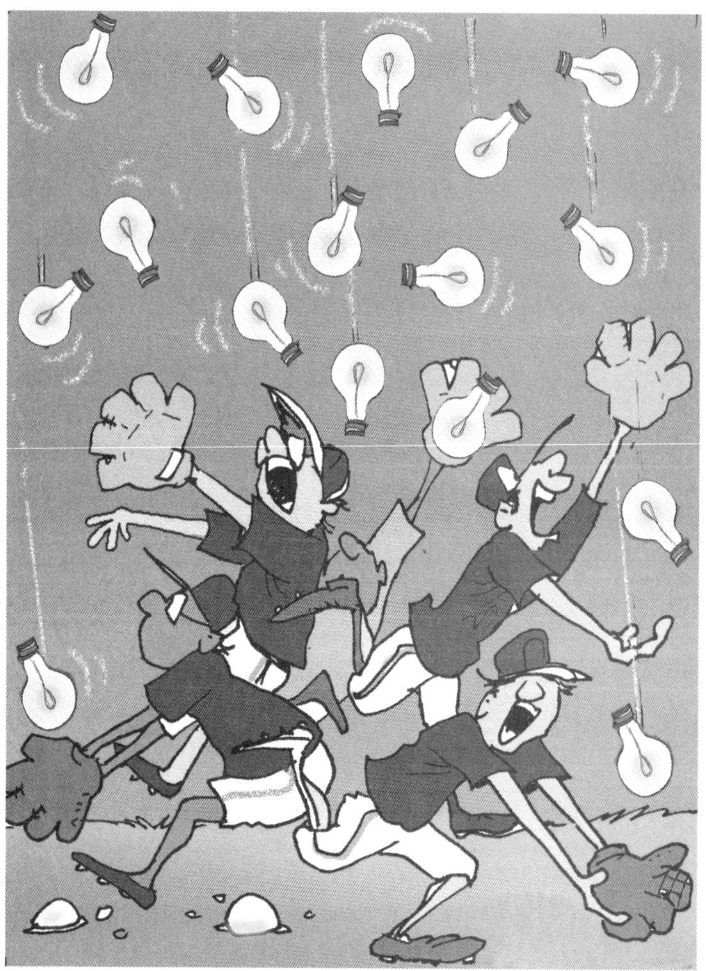

Let's start with a couple of idea exercises to get started on random creativity.

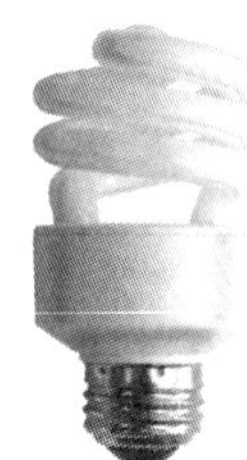

Idea Exercise:
Where in the World is Charles Atlas?

Find a large travel atlas. Place it on a table or on your lap. Go to the page with the first map, don't look at the title or map, but glance down and find the page number. Now go to the last map in the atlas and find the page number. Now think of a random number between those two page numbers. Turn to that page. Close your eyes and point. Where are you pointing? Write down the city, town and country you are in. Now think of another number randomly. Find that page in the atlas, close your eyes and point. Write down that city, town and country you are in. Now the fun begins.

Go online and find all you can about the town you picked first. What language do people speak there? What do they eat, what do they wear, how hot or cold does it get? Write down a couple of dozen questions and research the answers. Do the same research for the second town. Ask the same questions as you did before.

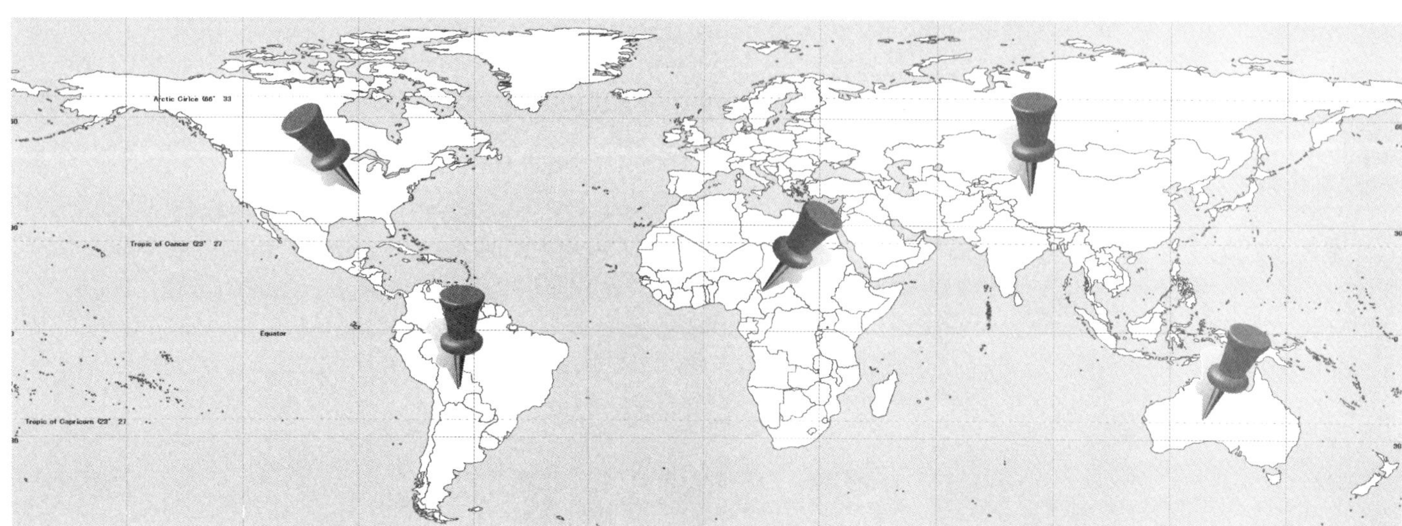

Create A Randomscape!

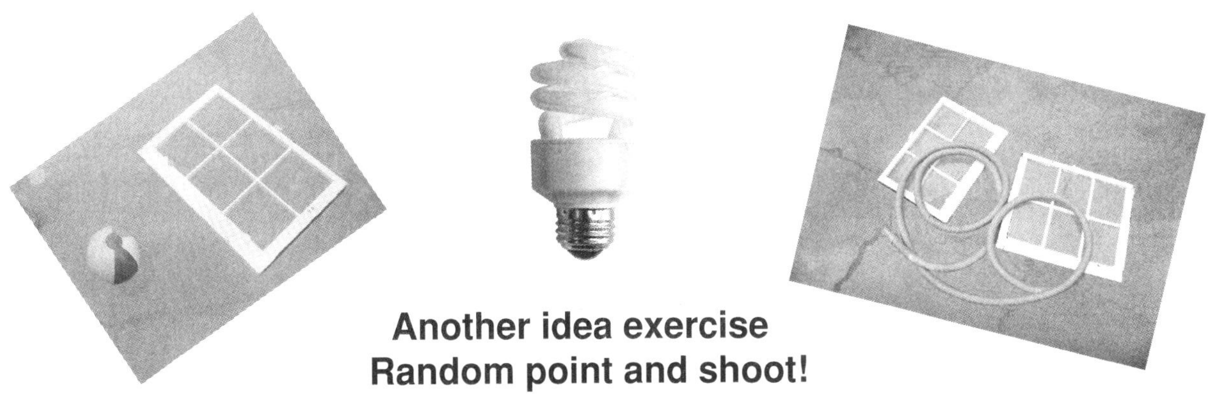

Another idea exercise
Random point and shoot!

Close your eyes and hold a pencil in your hand. Place this page in front of you. Randomly scatter ten small "x" s around the **words below** without looking. Once you have done ten, open your eyes. Write down the words that the "x" is touching or is nearest. Once you've got your words, you have a choice of doing **photography, writing or drawing**.

• Try and find all ten words in real life. Look around the house, scan the neighborhood. Get in the car or on your bike and go on a scavenger hunt. **Photograph** each word as you see it. • You can use those words to tell a short story. Weave the words into sentences that create a **word picture**. Make sure all the words you chose randomly are used. • If you feel like **drawing**, use those same words in a dreamscape, (or randomscape), still life or abstract illustration. Let your imagination run loose.

tea bag • pears • mittens • stove • battery • telephone booth • bedspread • picture frame • visor
book shelf • paper clip • tape dispenser • pipe • rubber band • cord • scoreboard • chairlift • car
cookbook • old movie projector • scissors • apple • butter knife • rotary phone • calculator • plug
yellow crayon • eraser • fire hydrant • pennant • glass ornament • wooden chair • silk scarf • tie
newspaper • lamp • cotton balls • watermelon seeds • old bicycle • earrings • manila folder
empty coke bottle • hand saw • piece of rope • handful of nails • piggy bank • shoe • lake • coin
empty picture frame • button • frying pan • clothes pin • old credit card • fifty-cent piece • bark
desk calendar • stereo speaker • telephone cord • light bulb • roll of duct tape • shoe box • river
drill bit • umbrella • flower vase • sheet music • old transistor radio • tea cup • library book • kite
map • postage stamp • bracelet • planet mars • a spice • needle and thread • quilt • index card
cigarette lighter • ski pole • golf ball • can of bug spray • hot pad • ash tray • bottle cap • pen
ink bottle • nut and bolt • telescope • bridge • blade of grass • red caboose • bar bells • glass
kitchen sink • butterfly • paper weight • tire pressure gauge • baseball cap • mailbox • wallet
hub cap • gas can • sling shot • cigar box • toilet plunger • tire iron • horseshoe • garbage can
extension cord • space ship • microscope • traffic light • ice cream cone • bowl of fruit • stapler
prism • jar of pickles • beaker of water • picnic table • trail map • old album cover • salad bowl
toothbrush • pail • acorn • chalk • popsicle stick • checkered flag • fortune cookie • china • ruler
shovel • gloves • stick of gum • sun • chop sticks • wire • syringe • door bell • peace sign • door
wax • perfume bottle • cannon • diamond ring • cloud • oak tree • bowling ball • goal post • sea

Look Near, Look Far...

A major force of creativity is observation. Being more observant in everyday life takes practice. Some people are naturally more observant, others of us are oblivious to what is in front of us.

Train your mind's eye to wander and wonder.

Idea Exercise: Look to the small!
You can start by looking through a microscope. If you have access to one, look at all kinds of things under the scope. Look at samples of hair, onion skin, soapy water, small insects, fabric, spores or whatever you want to see more of. Notice the design and structure of cells and the building blocks of nature. Nature makes patterns. Study them. Keep a sketchbook or journal of what you see. Try and draw your discoveries from what you are observing under the microscope. Describe in words what observations you have made.

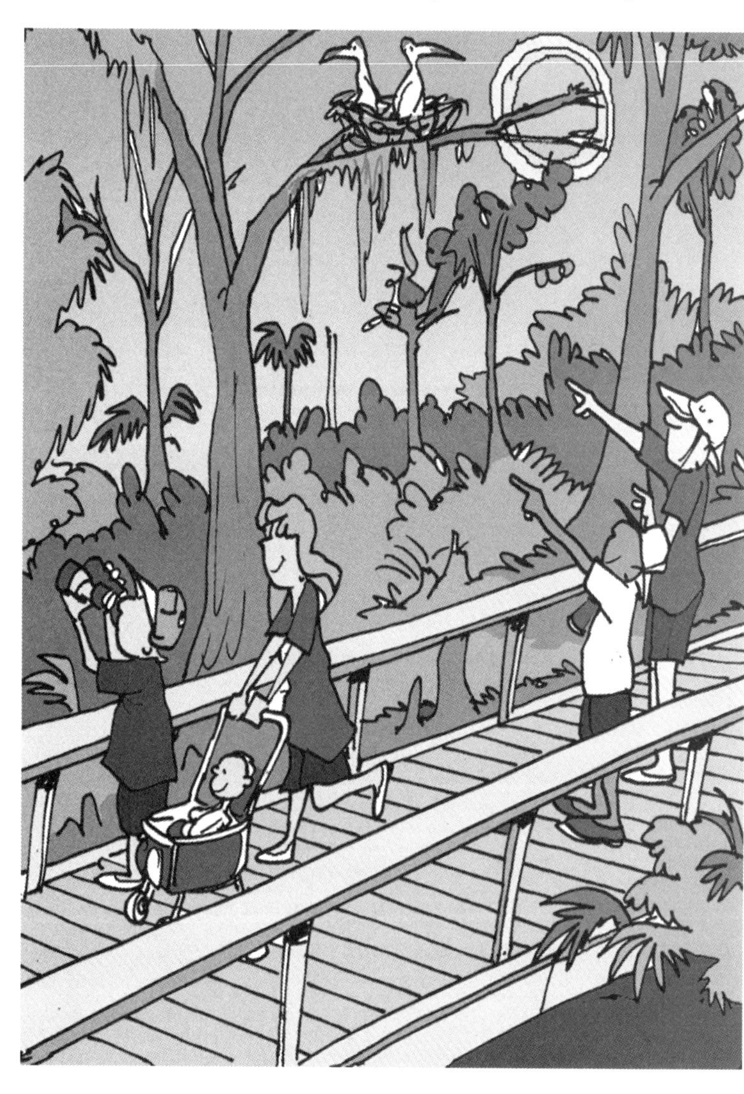

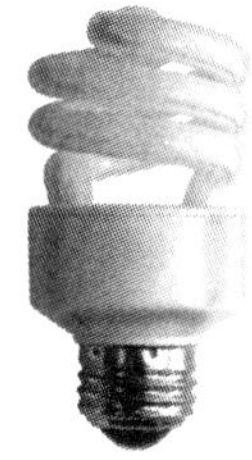

Idea Exercise: What is hiding?
Once you have explored the smallest of things, now it is time to wonder about what nature is hiding in your backyard. Do you have access to a pair of binoculars? If so, set a time to explore nature from a park, refuge, forest, beach, or preserve. There are so many places to visit for free. Research your area, design a game plan and go. Bring a small notebook with you. If you have a camera with a powerful zoom lens, bring it along. Create your own field day of discovery and journal what you see.

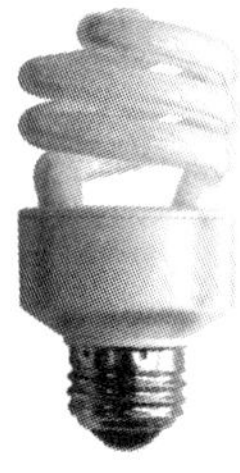

Idea Exercise:
Look into the universe!
Now, for discovery of the vast and infinite. Do you have access to a telescope? If not, it would be a good idea to visit your local planetarium. On special occasions the public is invited to see through a telescope when there is a lunar eclipse, or possibly a rare comet is in the sky. Treat yourself to the adventure of wonder through the lens of a telescope. Ask yourself how many light years away the nearest star is from earth. Remember a light year is equal to 5,865,696,000,000 miles. Wow! That's an amazing distance. Journal your thoughts, your dreams, your wonder and amazement.

...and Listen Closely

Have you ever closed your eyes and just listened to what is around you? Have you ever tried to see with your ears? Visual cues are a huge part of the creative process, however, listening is fast becoming a lost art. Plugging in your iPod uses auditory cues to stimulate the brain. But, mostly the sounds you hear daily are background noises. Try truly LISTENING.

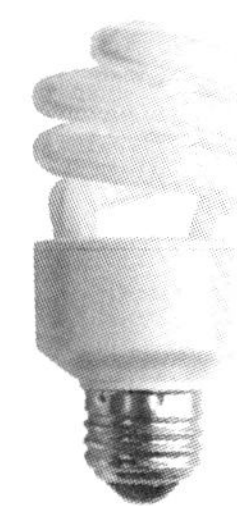

Idea Exercise: Gimme some of that ol' time radio

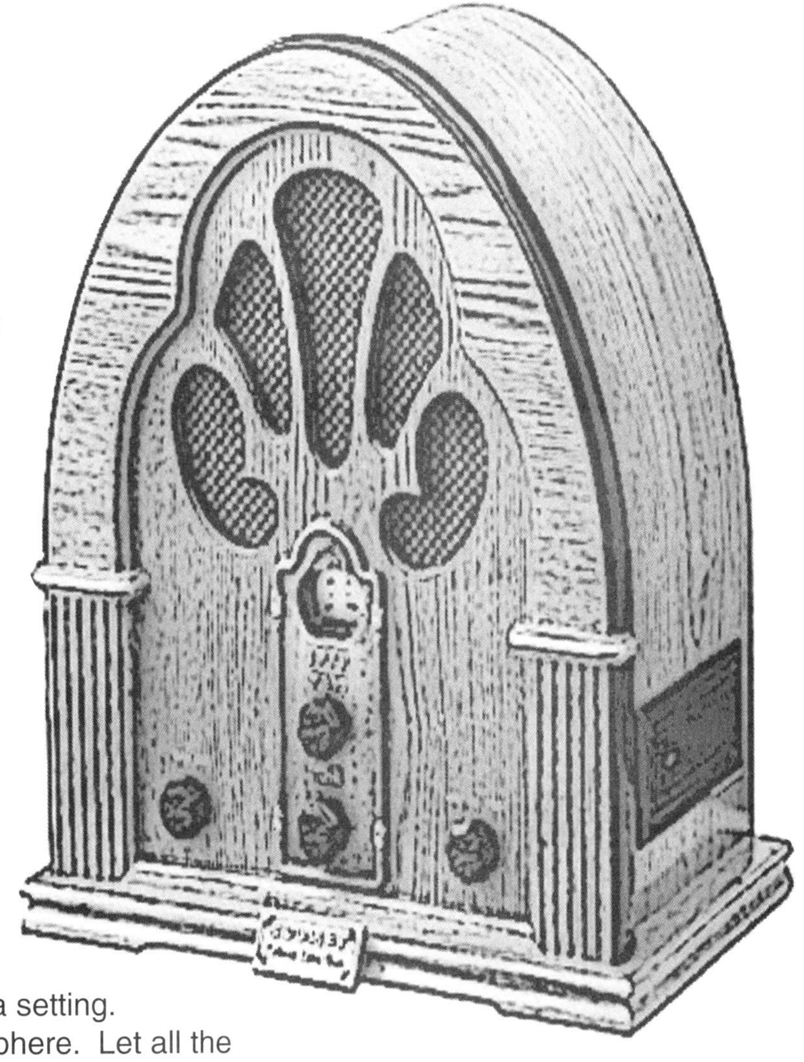

If you have a grandmother, grandfather or great-grandparents living, ask them to help you. Ask them what was their favorite radio show was as a kid or as an adult. Was it a comedy, an adventure series, a mystery?

Research some of the old shows online if you don't have a family member you can ask. These shows are available on CD and online.

Now, sit in a comfortable chair in the living room. The only sound you should hear is from the radio show coming to life through your speakers. Try not to hear through headphones or bugs.

Now listen to the show and picture the characters talking, moving through the action. Listen as the sound effects create a setting. Let the music of the show create an atmosphere. Let all the sounds tell the story. Let your inner ear light up the room with images. Stare at one object in the living room and let the show come to you. Let the sound permeate your body; feel it in your bones.

After the show is over remember that millions of people worldwide listened to radio as their major source of news and entertainment for over 35 years. Families sat together and listened hour after hour. There was no TV, video games, iPods or cell phones. Listening was revered and elevated to an artistic form. Hearing was a premium component of creativity.

Now ask yourself how much do you really hear during the day? How much of it is a distraction? How much of the noise pollution can you really tune out? When it is time to listen intently, can you hear clearly?

Much of being truly creative involves listening. Being able to listen closely and use your **"inner hear"** takes practice. Learn to tune in to what you really need to hear.

Sound Signatures

Sound is such a vital part of our lives. We spend a good portion of our day *missing* sounds that go on around us. We only hear them when we are distracted by them or when those sounds make us pay attention to them. The *sense of sound* can be an amazing creative tool for all walks of life. Those folks who have an active talent to sing or speak and make a living using their voice know the importance of focusing on auditory stimulus and reaction.

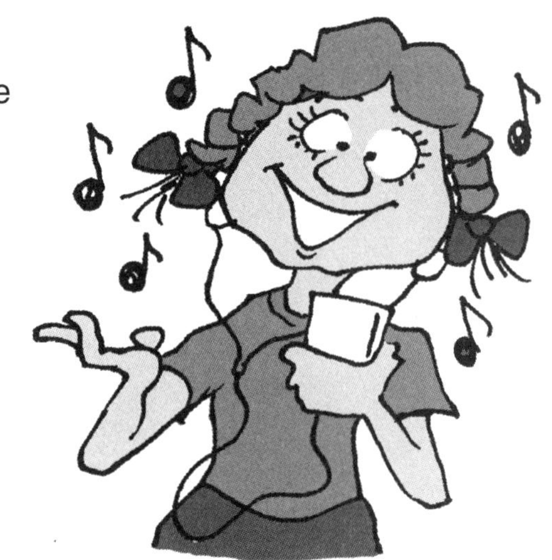

The rest of us hear daily sound as human conversation, music, and mechanical noise (which is mostly indoors) on a bus, or in a car to work. When we are at home sound could also be more conversation, media or entertainment driven or noises from household appliances or motors. If we took the time to **write down every sound we hear all day long** the results might be interesting. How much of it did we generate ourselves from our mouth? How much of it did others generate by speaking or singing. How much of it was mechanical? How much of it came from nature? Noise pollution has been around since the beginning of the Industrial Age. It wasn't until recently with the invention of iPods and personal listening devices that we have tried to shut off the outside stimuli and control what we hear.

The big question is how creative have we become at generating our own sounds. As kids we use to make up sounds or imitate the sounds we heard. We could do that by throwing our voice, impersonation, cupping our hands, whistling with our fingers and hands, or we used a myriad of silly exercises. Some of us even got called to the principal's office for disrupting a class. It is some of those kids that are now working for animation studios doing voices for cartoon characters or voiceover work at radio stations.

Sounds emanate from thousands of sources. The creative trick is to hear them more as auditory resources, than just noise in the background. It's time to take off your headphones. Listen to the world around you and wonder about sound. Every sound has a signature. Find the ones that are unusual and ask yourself, **"what would the sound signature be?"**

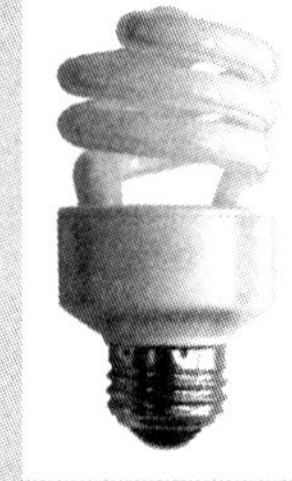

Idea Exercise: Record a Hundred Sounds

Why not? Get a digital recorder and listen for sounds around the house; man-made or mechanical. Record the ceiling fan that is out of balance and is making that annoying clicking sound. Record the startup chime of a personal computer. Go outside and record the splash of someone doing a cannonball in a pool. Record the scraping sound of snow being shoveled, a car horn blaring or people yelling. Look around, listen. Capturing a hundred sound signatures is really just the beginning.

Follow-up exercise: Digitize Those Sounds and Store Them In A Computer

Now that you have them, store them. Transfer those sound files into your home computer. Then what do I do with them you ask? Archive your sounds by type, location, time, how it was made, and how long it lasted. Be as specific as you want. These sounds will come in handy in a project we will mention in a later chapter. And don't forget to back up your files.

Do You Hear What I Hear?

How many different sounds can you make from ordinary or recycled items around the house? If you have ever been to a Blue Man Group concert you have seen and heard the sounds generated from ordinary construction material and household items. Hollow PVC pipe, plastic swimming pool pipes and tubes are a regular part of their routine. Taking the ordinary and turning it into the exraordinary is pure genius. Half the fun is discovering sounds you may not expect right under your nose.

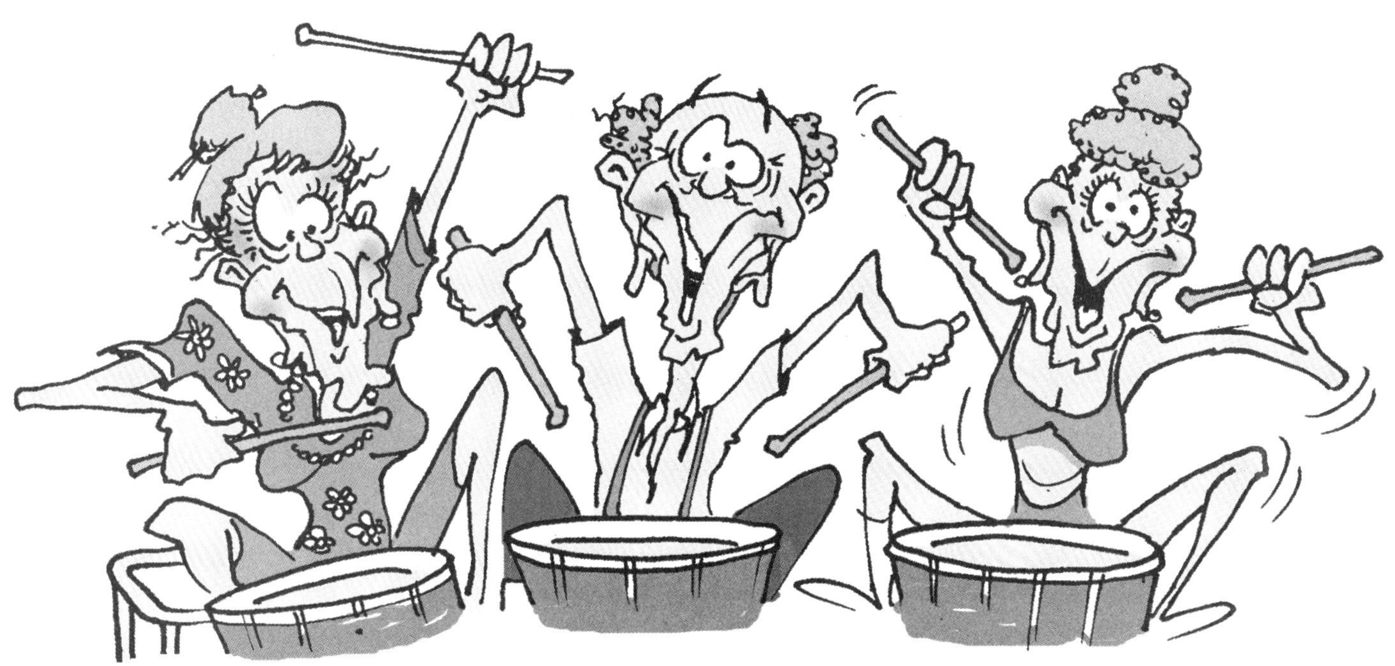

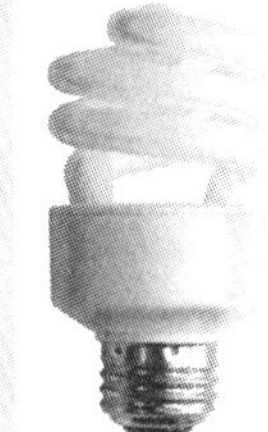

Idea Exercise: I Don't Want To Work I Just Want To Bang On Things Around The House All Day

Find an unsharpened pencil or a drumstick. Get a stack of small Post-it notes. Now go around the house and tap, bang, clang, rattle, jab, ding, whack and womp on everything that won't break. Be smart. Be careful. You don't want to try this on an old florescent tube, your Waterford crystal, or your grandma's best dishes. Find interesting sounds from plastic, metal, stone, wood, cardboard and glass. Tea kettles, coffee cups, pots, and pans are obvious. Find the odd, the obtuse, the weird, the whacky, the mysterious places sounds might be hiding. Use your pencil or drumstick and set the vibrations loose. Tack those post-it stickies to the items to help you remember where they came from.

Follow up exercise: Digitize Those Sounds and Store Them In A Computer

Now that you found them, record them. Go around the house, find the stickies, make the sound again with one hand and record in the other. If it takes more than two hands get a helper that doesn't think this is crazy. Transfer those sound files into your home computer. Do as you did on previous page, archive your sounds by type, location, time, and how it was made, and how long it lasted. Be as specific as you want. You can use these sounds for background special effects in home movies or video slideshows.

Get Out The Brainstorm Umbrella

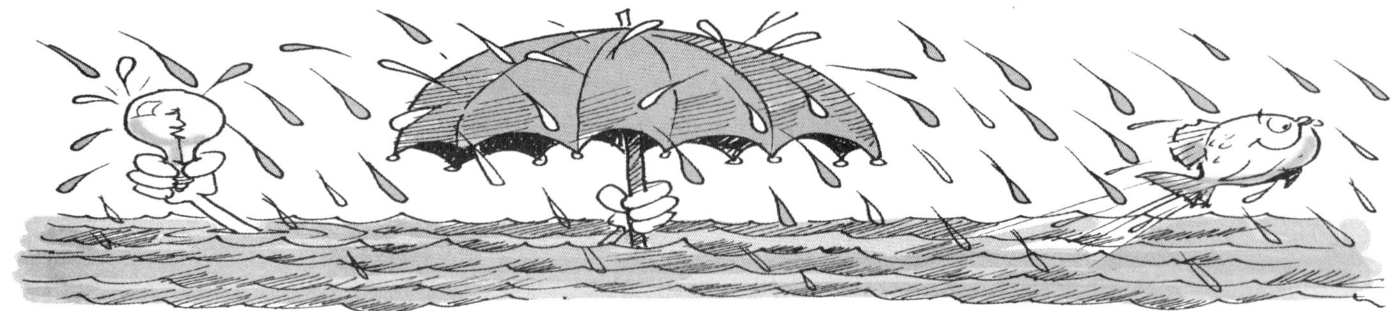

Thinking up ideas by yourself is challenging. Many times it is better to involve many people to keep the idea bulb moving around the room. A group gathering of ideas can take shape in a variety of ways. One way is to have the participants in the room work individually, then collaborate and share their ideas later in a group setting. Another way is for the participants to "brainstorm" in a more spontaneous fashion.

Let's try the first method:

Get your group of ten or more to sit around a table or in a circle of chairs. They need to be far enough apart to have some privacy. Next, you will pass out ten pieces of paper, one to each person. Each piece of paper has one word at the top of it. Each participant gets 30 seconds to write what comes to mind when they think of that word. After 30 seconds the person passes the piece of paper to his or her right. This continues until the original list rotates back to the first person. Tack up the results on a board, then discuss the results.

Try these words for starters or make a list of your own:

- theater
- City of Buffalo
- Christmas
- insect
- chess
- sunrise
- sailboat
- refrigerator
- carpet
- spinach
- soldier

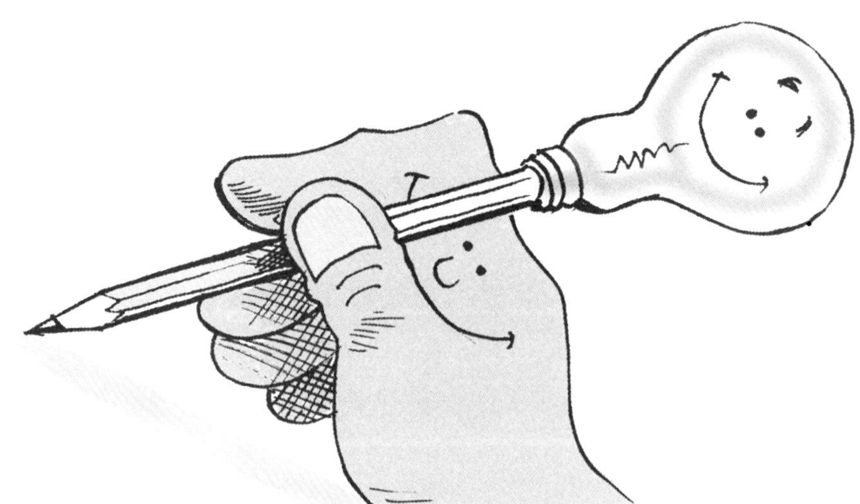

A second variation of this method is to use *free association* and brainstorm as a group. Start with the word "theater" and throw it on the table. Have someone record the words that people come up with when they think of that word. You don't have to go around the table in order. Let the words flow out spontaneously. One word might spawn another association. Be careful that the original word "theater" is not lost to "off on a tangent" thinking. The facilitator needs to keep the group focused on the word at hand. Go down the list of ten words one at a time. Tack up the results on a board for all to see. You may hear very interesting concepts from just one word.

...It's Raining Ideas Indoors

Brainstorming exercise: Let's open a restaurant!

Get your group to brainstorm ideas related to these questions:

- Where is it **located**?
- What is the **cuisine**?
- What is the restaurant's **theme/decor**?
- What is the **specialty** dish?
- What type of **entertainment**?
- What is the renowned **dessert**?
- What is the restaurant's **name**?
- What is the **slogan**?

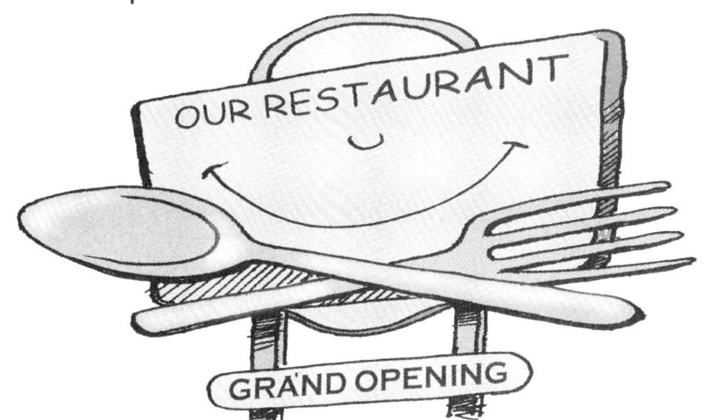

Here are some ground rules when you are holding the brainstorm umbrella:

- **Make sure that everyone understands the idea or issue.**
  - Tell them why we are doing this
  - Try to keep everyone engaged
- **Use Idea Etiquette**
  - Avoid criticizing ideas or judging their validity.
  - There are no bad ideas
- **Think Quantity, Build Quality**
  - Initially, a large number of ideas is the aim. If you limit the number of ideas, your group will start to judge the ideas and only put in their 'best' or more often than not, the least radical and new. (Ideas that are identical can be combined).
- **Be Free-wheeling:**
  - Don't censure any ideas, keep the flow going. Listen to other ideas and try to piggy back on them to create *more* ideas. Avoid any distracting discussions as they tend to stop the flow.
- **Use a Facilitator:**
  - Have someone facilitate to keep the group on task
  - Write down the ideas as they occur (the scribe can be a second person)
- **Build consensus:**
  - It is helpful to get a consensus of which ideas should be looked at in depth. Make a list, set a time table and action plan.

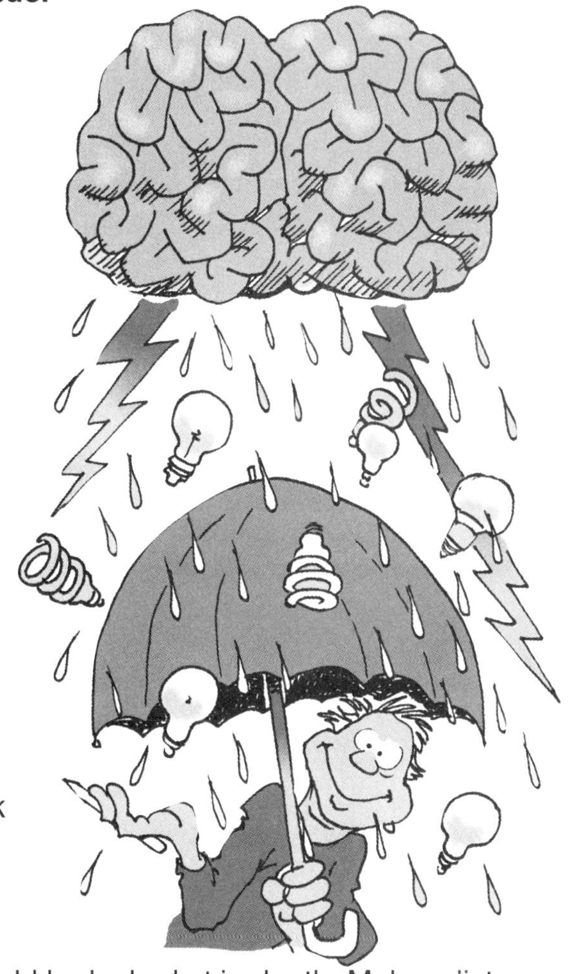

- **Clarify and conclude the session with an upbeat attitude. Everyone contributed. Nice teamwork!**

Are We There Yet?!

"The creative is the place where no one else has ever been. You have to leave the city of your comfort and go into the wilderness of your intuition. What you'll discover will be wonderful. What you'll discover is yourself."

-Alan Alda

Travel games, ideas for the road trip:

•Play by Play Driving Commentary: So you think you are an expert driver, then say so and record it. Keep a digital recorder in your car. While you are driving comment on what you see. Pretend you are a commentator on TV or radio and give us your viewpoint of the road. While you are being more aware as a driver you are also creating a humorous, satirical dialogue on the driving techniques of others.

•Make up a Road Song: Like to sing while you drive? Well take your driving commentary one more step. Make up a song about it. Stuck at a light? Make up some lyrics about the long light that won't change. Make up lyrics about the driver ahead of you. You know, the one that is on her cell phone and not paying attention to his driving. If you run out of ideas or lyrics turn the mirror on yourself and write a song about your driving.

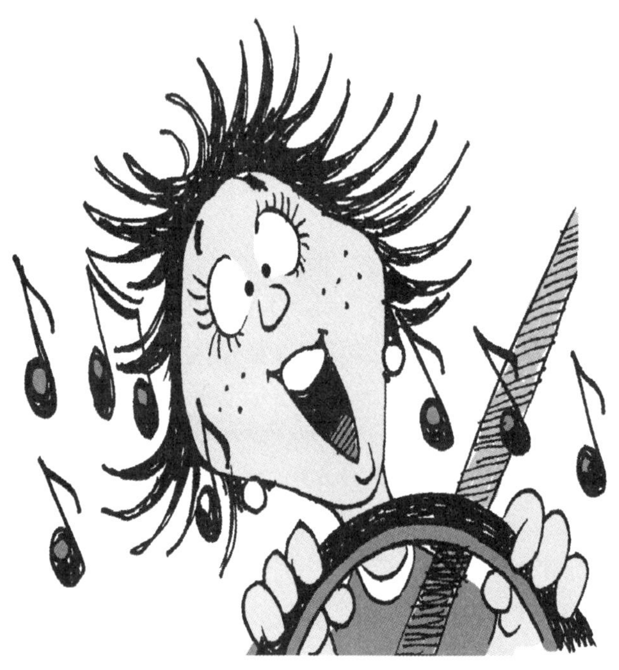

•Make up a Road Map: A hand-made map is easy to make and is easy to follow. Instead of a map with just roads and highway names, draw a map with bridges, landmarks, lakes, rivers, golf courses, parks, fast food restaurant signs, big buildings and airports. Draw what you see out the window along the road you are traveling.

•Bubble Blowing Contest: Pass out the same amount of bubble gum to everyone (but the driver of course) and see who can blow the biggest bubble. (Take a picture before it bursts).

•Travel Scavenger Hunt: The first one who sees each one of these items below out the car window gets to circle the word. The person with the most items wins. Impose a time limit.

- rainbow
- someone on a bike
- hardware store
- old Model T
- picnic table
- windmill
- cement truck
- person walking a dog
- church
- bingo hall
- post office
- statue
- boat on top of a car
- antique store
- license plate with a "Z"
- railroad tracks
- sign in a foreign language
- ice cream stand... STOP! let's eat
- white picket fence
- football field
- hay bales in a field

Road Signs From A to Z

Here's another road trip game for the entire family. Going through the alphabet, find words on road signs that begin with each letter. Keep score for fun. Write your discoveries for each letter below:

	What did you find?	Who found it?	Score
A			
B			
C			
D			
E			
F			
G			
H			
I			
J			
K			
L			
M			
N			
O			
P			
Q			
R			
S			
T			
U			
V			
W			
X			
Y			
Z			

Total Scores: ________________

Through The Window Of Imagination

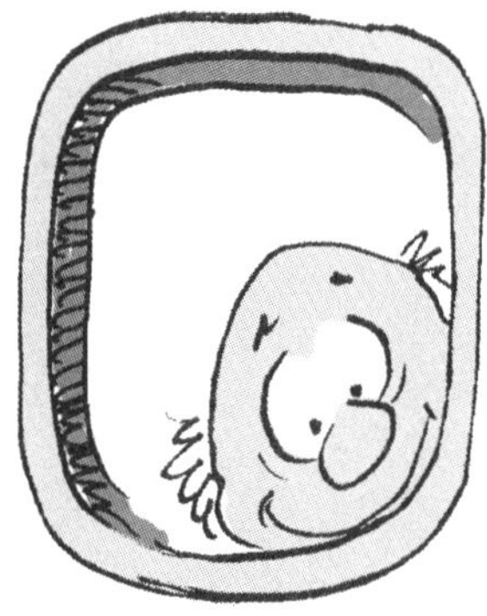 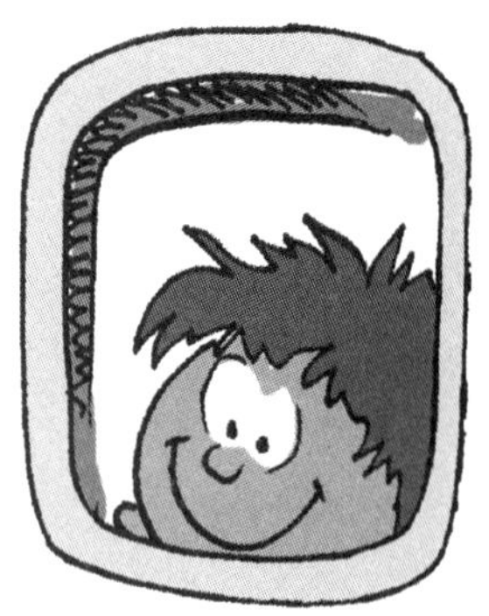 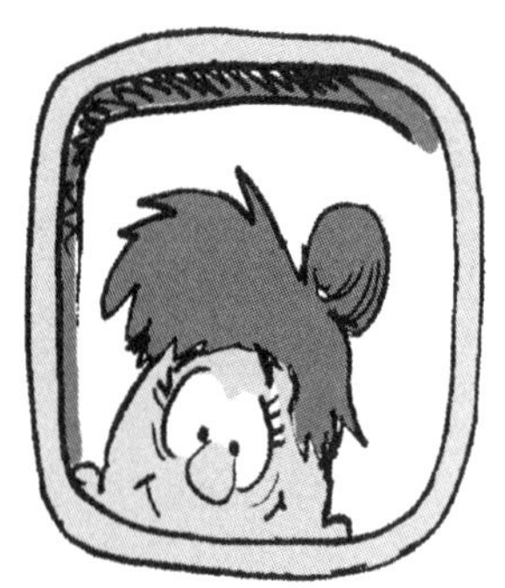 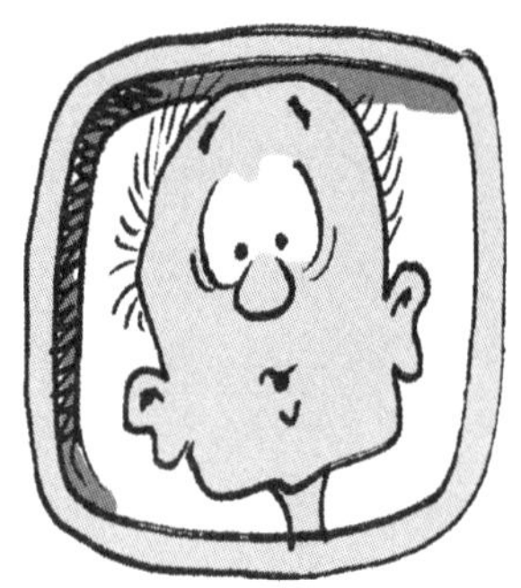

Idea Exercise: Looking Out Your Airplane Window

The next time you fly, book a window seat. With good luck the weather will be clear and you will be able to clearly see the landcape below. Unless the pilot tells you what state, city and town you are are flying over, most of the time you would have to use visual clues to guess where you are. It doesn't matter, you can use your imagination.

With the tray table down, place a pad of paper in front of you. Look out the window below. What do you see? Is it a city or town? Is it a small or giant farm field? Do you see a meandering river connecting many cities, towns and farms? Does the river run into a bigger body of water? Do the farm fields form geometric shapes? Draw the shapes you see. Does the city have tall buildings? Do the homes have backyard pools? Can you spot a golf course? Ball fields? Do you see the schools, parks, and churches?

When you pass over a town, city or farm, write down what you see through the clouds. Give the place a name. Imagine who lives there. Find one house in the city, town, or farm and write down who lives there. What are their names? What do they do? Where do they go for fun? Once you have asked enough questions, try and write a one chapter story about the place you just flew over.

If you have a longer flight and the weather stays clear try writing about more than one place. Maybe it is an island on a giant lake. Maybe it is about working on the top floor of a giant skyscraper.

Once you have written about your places, it is time to draw them. Try the idea exercise below.

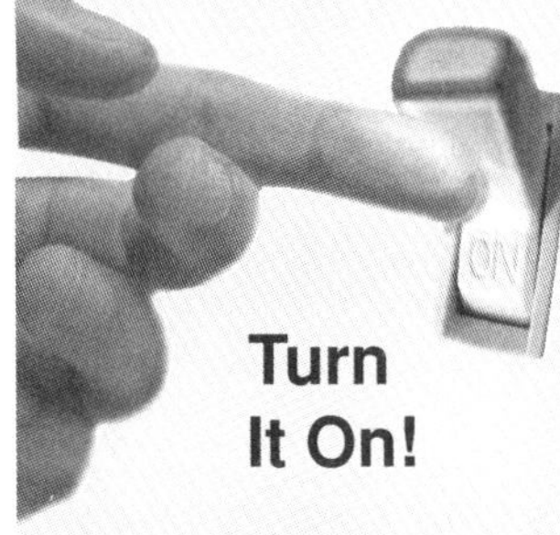

Go One Step Further: Draw your imaginary place

If the weather is lousy or gets too cloudy, create your own imaginary town, city or farm below. What would it look like from 30,000 feet? Does it have a river running through it? Is it on a lake, or a beach. Is it in the middle of a desert? Are there mountains around it? Do the town streets go in every direction or are they running parallel? Are there factories, golf courses and bridges? Use your imagination and name the place you are drawing. What is the area's population? What is the weather like? Draw your imaginary place. Start with the features of the land and build a town around that. You don't have to draw every house, street or waterway. Plan the city of your dreams. When you are done give your place a name. When are you going to move there?

Make A "Happening" Happen

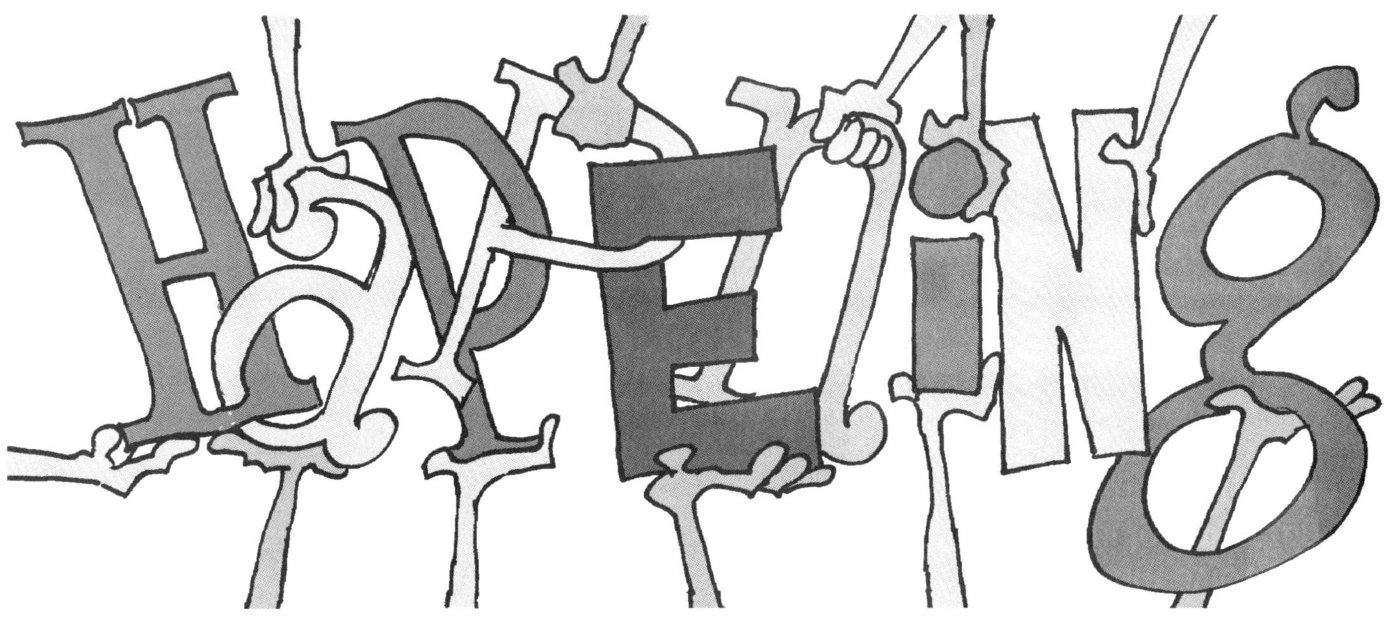

A **"happening"** is a performance, event or situation meant to be considered as art. Happenings take place anywhere; are often multi-disciplinary, often lack a narrative and frequently seek to involve the audience in some way. Key elements of happenings are planned, but artists sometimes leave room for improvisation.

In the later 1960s, perhaps due to the depiction in films of the hippie culture, the term "happening" was used much less specifically to mean any gathering of like interests, from a pool-hall meeting to a musical jam session of a few young people, to a fancy formal party.

Having a theme party is a planned event, it's staged and somewhat predictable. A "happening" is more spontaneous. You can plan a happening, but it is hard to plan what will happen once it's started. Here are "happening" ideas to get started...You may be called upon to be a ringleader...

Old Album Swapping Party Guests bring a handful of favorite old vinyl albums and everyone takes turns playing their favorite songs on a turntable. Make it casual, leaving enough room to dance. Sing songs, laugh and walk and dance down memory lane.

Standing in Line "Sing-A-Long" Who wants to be stuck in a line getting bored and frustrated? Try starting a song everyone can join in on. Watch the shy people get involved. Make up lyrics. Don't let it die. Keep the energy of the crowd moving. Keep them engaged. This is especially fun at the holidays

Make it "happen" Think up your own theme and invite friends. Tell your friends to invite more friends who will in turn invite their friends. You can even set up the event on Facebook or Twitter and watch the numbers grow. Have fun and remember your "happening" is a form of art.

DRAW! DRAW! DRAW!
(everyday)

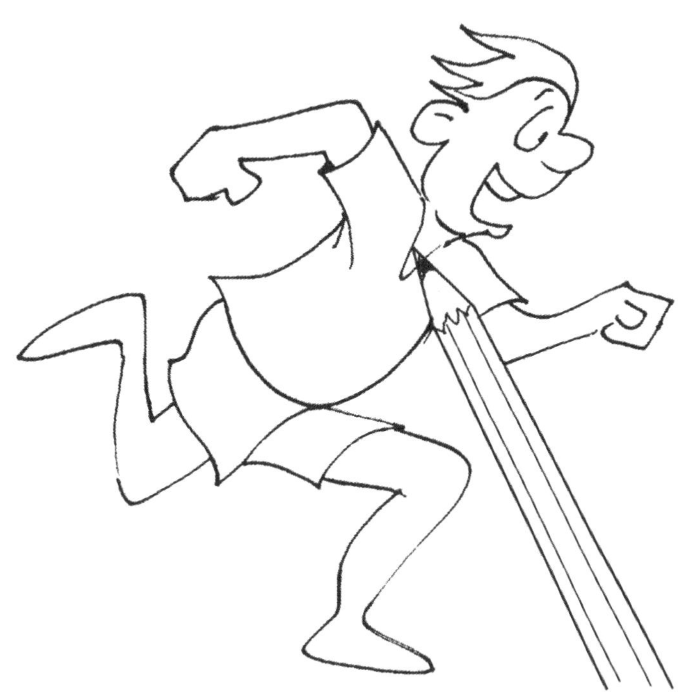

"Observe Everything.
Communicate Well.
Draw, Draw, Draw."

-Frank Thomas, Disney Animator

Doodle To Loosen The Noodle

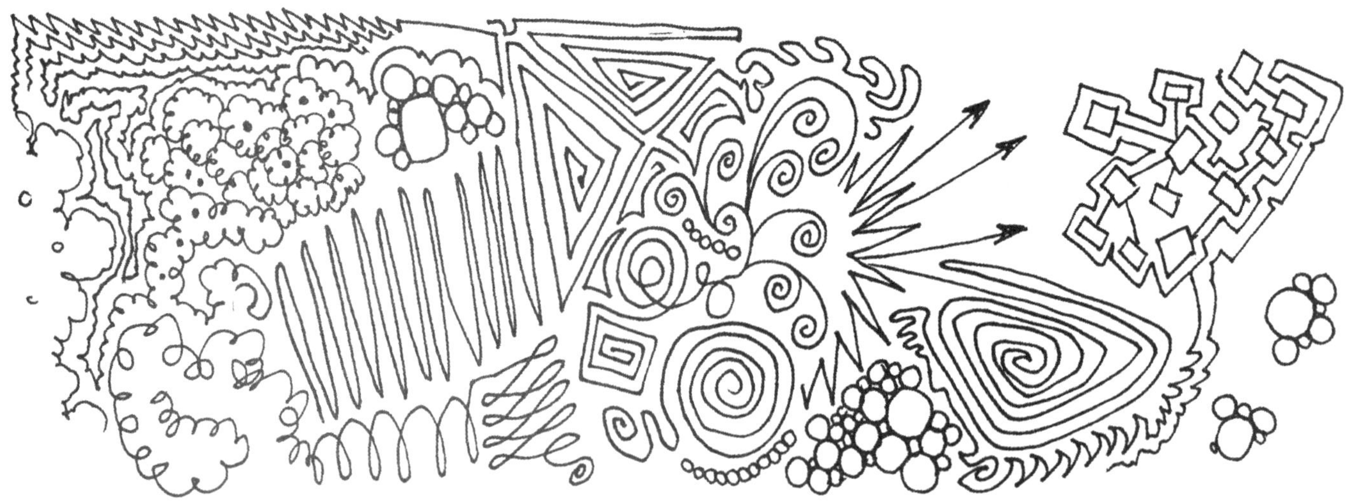

What you can do to loosen the right side of your noodle is to just doodle. Doodling can be an art, but the best thing about doodling is you don't have to be an artist to doodle. Doodling is really a way for the brain to relax.

Ask yourself these questions:

Is doodling nothing more than kid's stuff? Is doodling silly?
Is it fun? When do you doodle, if you doodle at all?
When was the last time you doodled? Do you doodle in shapes?
Do you draw squares? Do you draw circles, stars, triangles, and squiggly lines?

Doodling Exercise #1: Doodle listening to TV

Have you ever had the TV on, listened to it, but not watched it? You were just using TV as background entertainment. What a great way to doodle.

Get comfortable at a desk, kitchen table or just sitting on a couch. Get a pad of paper or use the next page of empty space. Turn the TV on and force yourself not to look up and watch it. Keep the volume soft. Also, keep the remote handy as you may want to change channels.

Start to doodle in the middle of your page. Concentrate more on the paper and not the characters you hear on the TV. You can doodle with letters and words too, not just shapes. Doodling has no rules at the moment. No one will judge your drawing ability, your silliness, your penmanship, your neatness or your sloppiness.

Let your pen or pencil go where it wants to. Fill up the page. Go back over areas. Repeat movements and patterns. Spend as much time as you like until doodling becomes boring or uncomfortably redundant.

Once you have filled the page try to remember what TV shows were playing while you were drawing. Did any doodles reflect what you were hearing from the background sound of the TV? Did you completely block out the sound? Did you change channels? What is your favorite doodle?

Here's Space To Noodle Doodle

my doodle masterpiece

Doodle To Bach And Rock

I know only two tunes: one of them is "Yankee Doodle," and the other isn't.
– Ulysses S. Grant

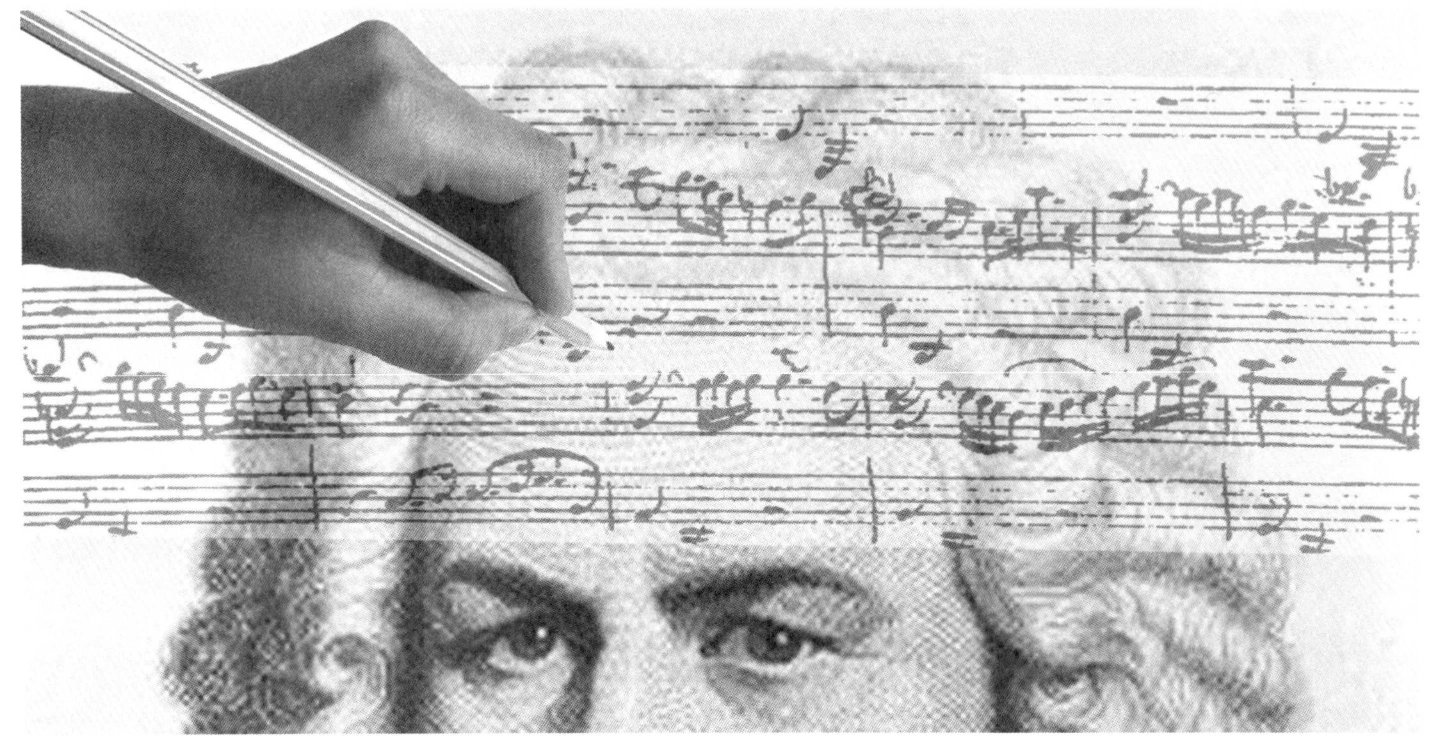

Doodling Exercise #2: Doodle to Bach

Have you ever doodled to music, specifically classical music. Have you ever doodled to Mozart? Find a CD of Johann Sebastian Bach's music. If you don't have a CD, go buy one. It's worth it. Find a comfortable environment to doodle. This time turn off the TV and just hear sounds from the CD.

Soften the lighting in the room to a comfortable level. Play the CD and settle in. You can use the empty page to the right as your doodle space. Don't draw right away, let the music tell you when you are ready. Let the music carry your pen or pencil around the page. Hear the symmetry. Hear the pulses. Listen for inflection. Sense the mood. Draw what comes to mind.

Doodling Exercise #3: Doodle to Rock

Now change the pace and the pulse. Put on your favorite classic rock album. Try the same method only let the energy of the music dictate the intensity of your doodles. Be as prolific as you can. Draw to the entire CD or change pages for each song.

Get out colored pencils and draw back over your black and white drawings. Hear the color of the music and use a palette that reflects what sounds you are experiencing. Stay with it as long as it is fun and interesting. Compare your Bach Art with your Rock Art. Are there any similarities? Are there any differences?

Doodle To Bach 'n Roll

Dive Into The Drawosphere

"Drawing is putting a line around an idea."
-Henri Matisse

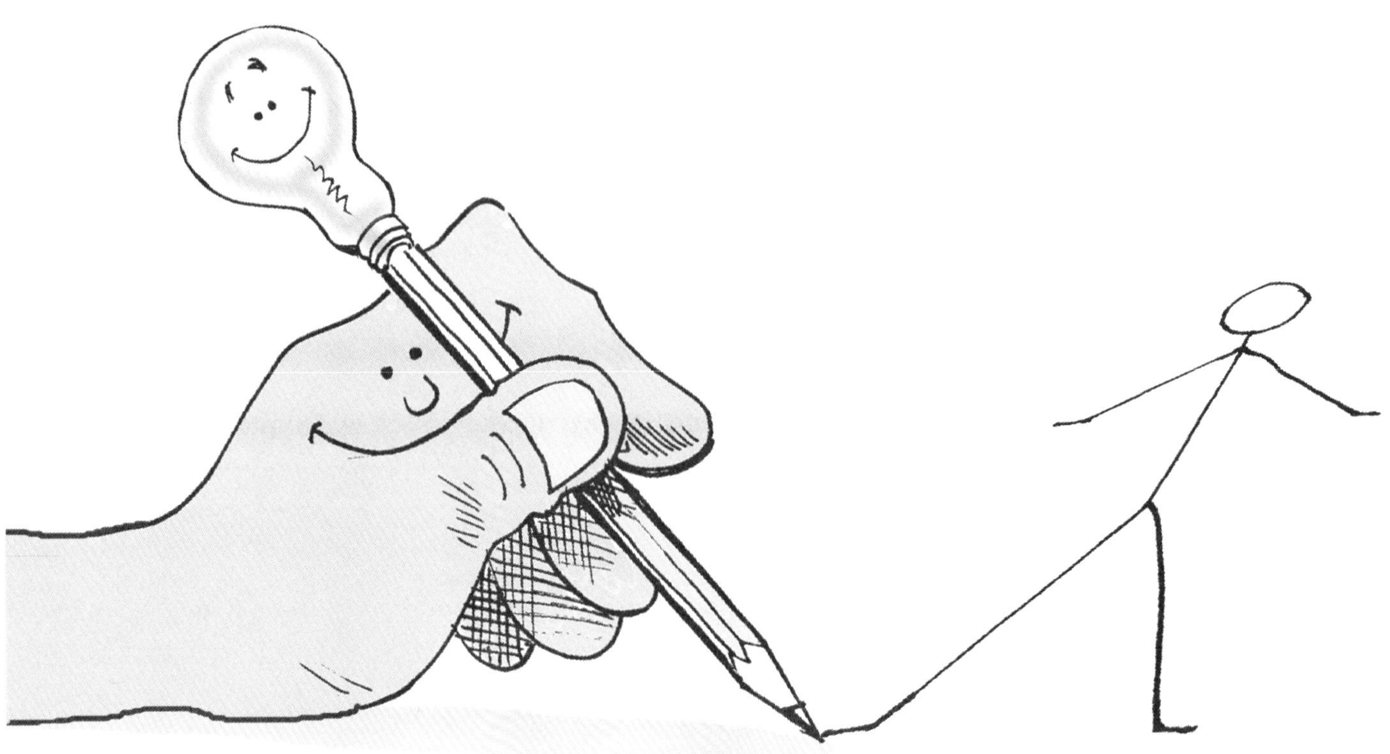

A lot of people say, *"I can't draw, I can only draw stick figures"*. Great, you can draw then! Stick figures were your earliest attempt to draw when you were a child. What happened is you probably stopped drawing at stick figures and never developed your abilities any further. Then you said, "I didn't have any abilities beyond that". So what you did, is you talked yourself out of drawing.

Someone may have made fun of one of your earliest drawings and you got upset, discouraged and quit. Or it is possible that no one was there at a young age to nurture, coax and guide you to continue. Or perhaps you were too hard on yourself, expecting perfection too soon. You probably got frustrated and quit.

There are any number of reasons why young people stop drawing, the least of which is ability. It is fascinating to watch children 3 to 7 years old sit and draw. Their minds are void of most constraints on creativity. They have no reason to be intimidated, no expectations have been placed on them. They dive into drawing like they were diving into a pool after they learned how to swim. Fear to them is not a factor.

If you are the stunted stick-figure-drawing person who is lost with a white piece of paper in front of you, welcome to class. Have no fear, these are fun exercises to try. There is space to the right to draw some stick figures. The lesson on the next page will be your first attempt to spread your wings and leap into the **drawosphere**.

Dare To Draw Stick Figures!

Drawing Exercise: Creating stick figures for fun

So all you can draw are stick figures? Great! Then draw some. Draw yourself as a stick figure. Drawing yourself thin is good for the ol' self image. (Besides, you can show that the diet you've been on is really working!)

Let's draw you in more than one place and in several positions. There is a stick figure to the right to get you started. Your drawing doesn't have to be any more complicated than that.

Draw yourself as a stick figure in the boxes below...

This is me

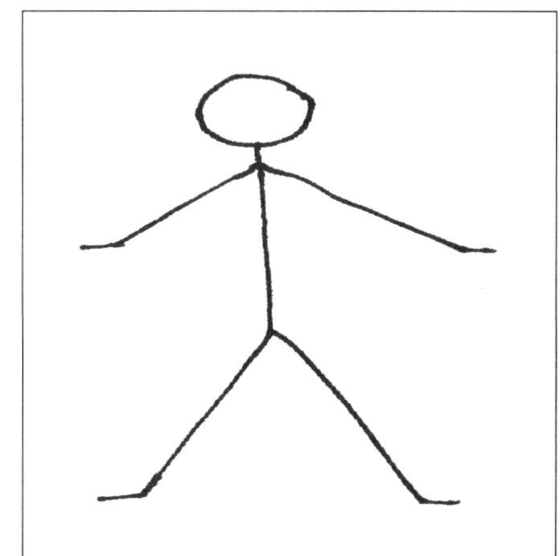

This is me standing

This is me in front of my house

This is me waving hello

This is me jumping for joy

This is me doing cartwheels

This is me flying

You Can Do It, Stick To It!

Drawing Exercise: My day as a stick figure...

So what was your day like at work? At school? How was your weekend? Cave men would document their day of the hunt with drawings on cave walls. With flame as a light source and colored clay and charcoal as their drawing medium, they left behind some of the oldest images of creative thought. (And they did it without art lessons!)

OK, it's time to come out of your creative cave and tell us about your day. You can create a stick figure storyboard or drawing diary. Start by writing a sentence about what it was like getting out of bed. Then write a sentence or two about getting ready for work, school, eating breakfast, driving the kids to school, driving to work, or however your day began. Next to your sentence, draw yourself as a stick figure doing the things you described. Use labels and arrows if you need to help the drawing tell your own story.

This is what it was like getting out of bed...

Once I got up I did this...

Then I did this next...

My Day As A Stick Figure

(draw your stick figure in the boxes)

Then I did this next...

After that I did this...

Then I did this next...

After that I did this...

Good night!

Draw...A Happy Face Man!

1. Start with the nose

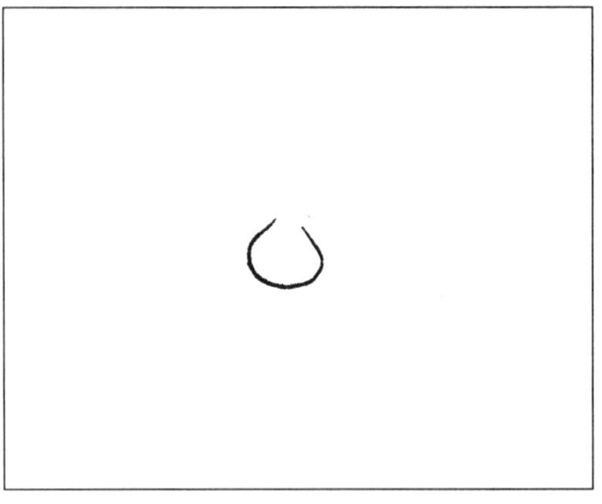

2. add two eyes and two eyebrows

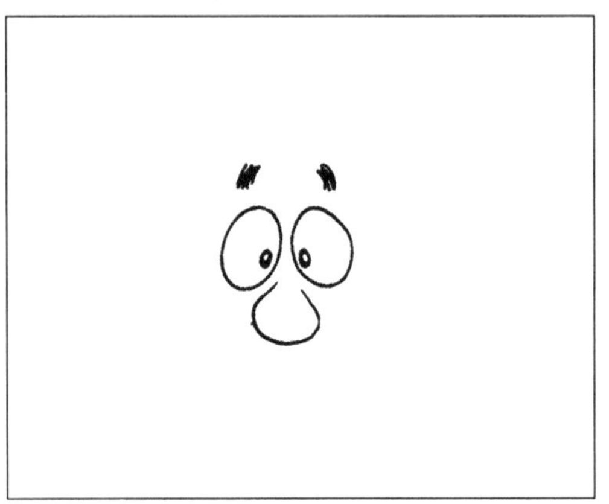

3. add a giant smile

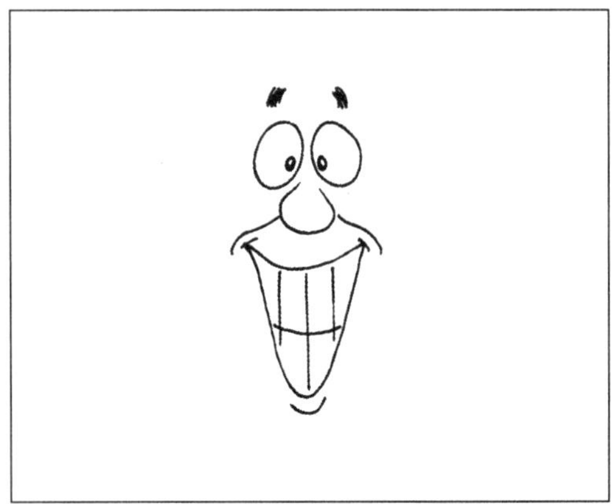

4. draw a circle to outline the face

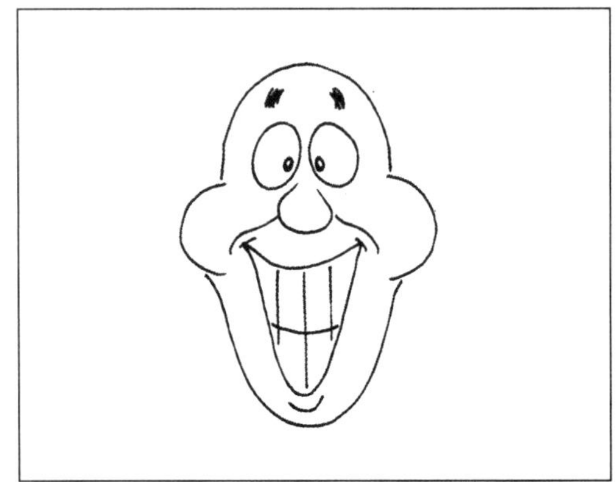

Drawing exercise:

Look at the drawings in each column of this page. Follow along and create a happy face in the space provided on the next page. Remember the drawings on this page are smaller. Draw your face much bigger. Try and fill the entire page with one big happy face.

1. Begin with the nose then add two eyes and two eyebrows
2. Remember that a happy face has eye brows that are raised so place them high on the forehead.
3. Add a smile drawn as a giant “U” shape and add the upper lip
4. Draw a large oval shape for the outline of the face. Remember when you smile big, your cheeks will get puffy. So add some fat cheeks.
5. Then add some ears
6. Take this character to the hair stylist and give him some hair.
7. Add a neck and a shirt
8. Finally, name your character.

Does that look like someone you know?

5. add some ears

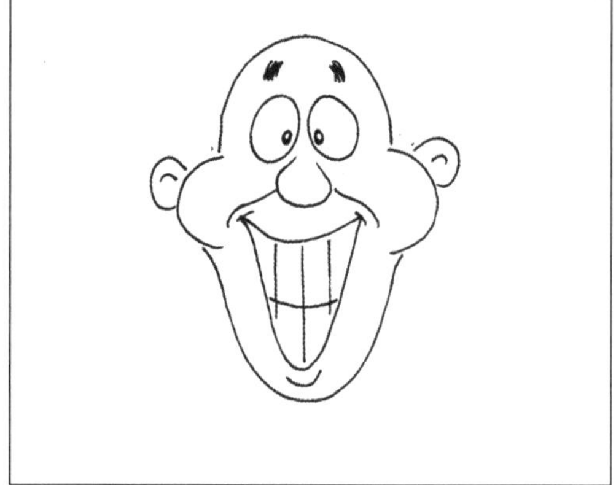

6. add a hair style

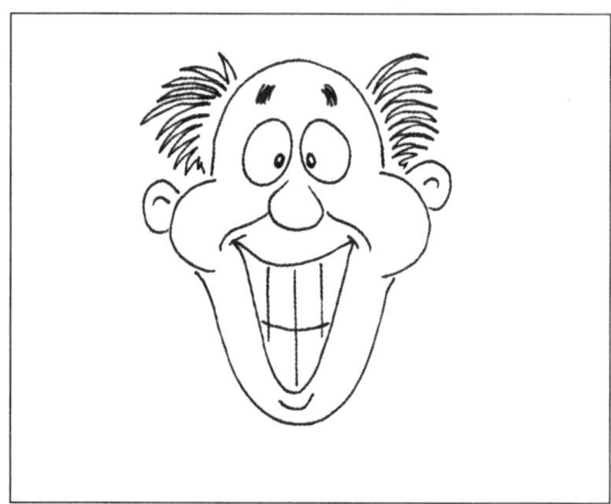

7. add a neck and a shirt

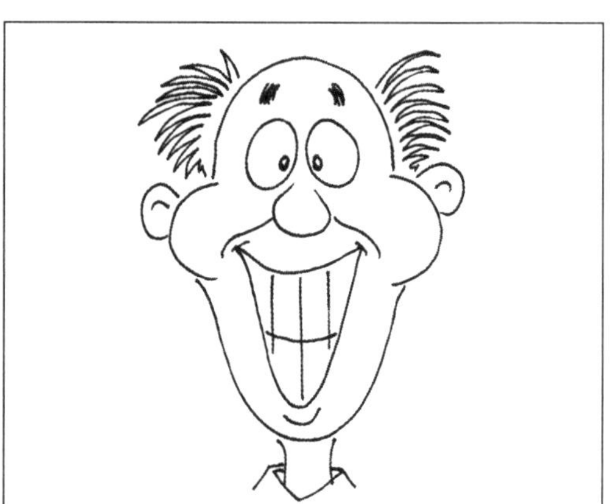

8. Give him a name

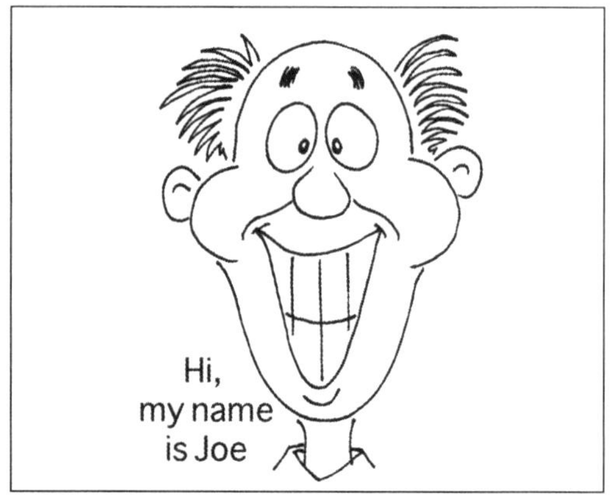

You Can Do It!

Draw big and try to fill the entire page with one face.
The nose is already drawn for you. You draw the rest of the face.

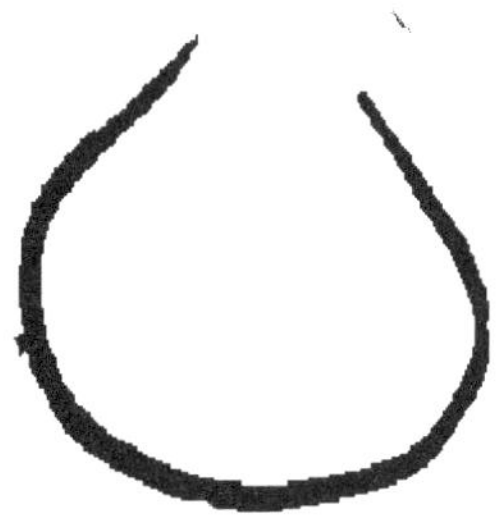

Draw...a worried cartoon face!

1. Start with the nose

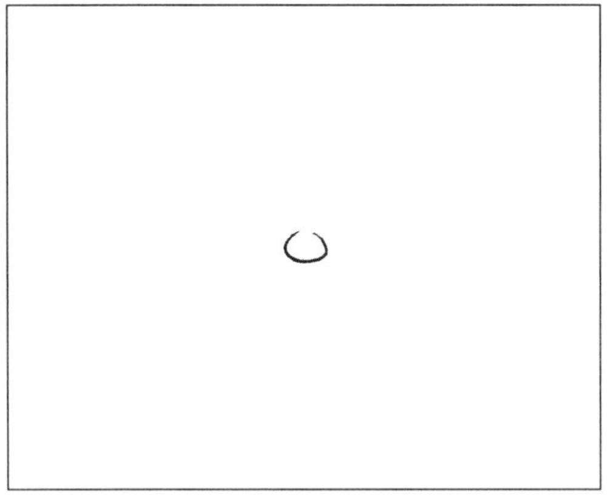

2. add two eyes and two eyebrows

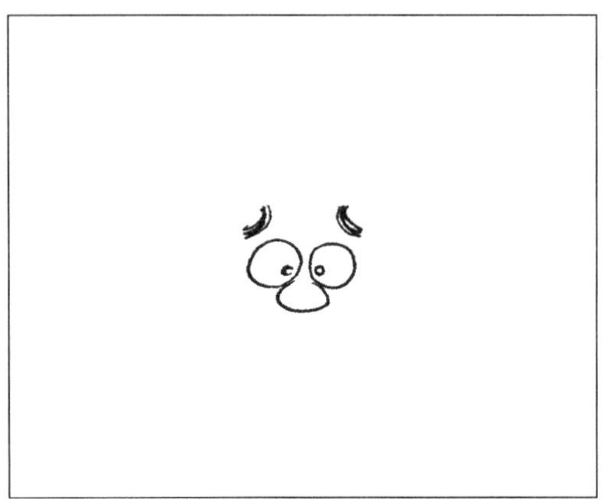

3. add a peanut-shaped mouth

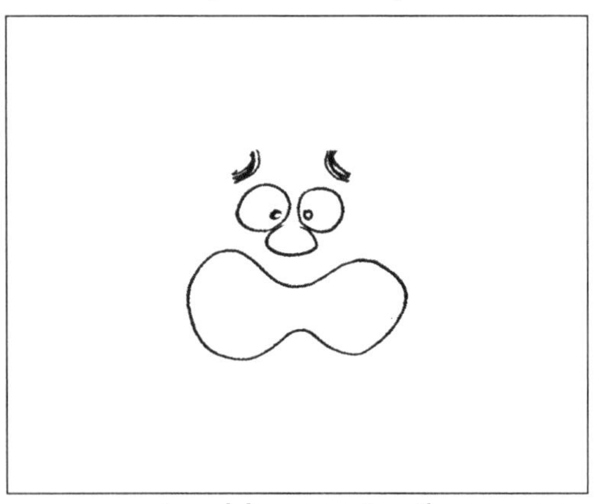

4. add some teeth

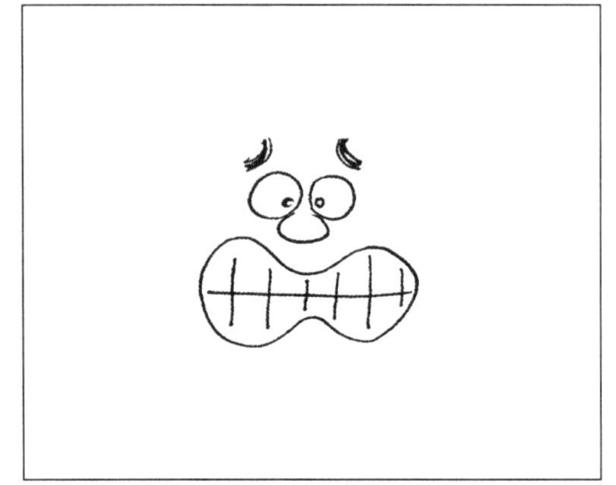

Drawing exercise:

Look at the drawings in each column of this page. Follow along and create a worried face in the space provided on the next page. Remember the drawings on this page are smaller. Draw your face much bigger. Try and fill the entire page with one big worried face.

1. Begin with the nose
2. Then add two eyes and two eyebrows. Remember that a worried face has eyebrows that curl inside out. Place them on the outer corner of each eye.
3. Add a worried mouth shaped like a peanut.
4. Show some teeth.
5. Draw a large pear-shape for the outline of the face.
6. Add some ears.
7. Give your character worried hair and perspiration.
8. Add a neck and a shirt and name your character.

Now, who is so worried?

5. draw pear-shaped face outline

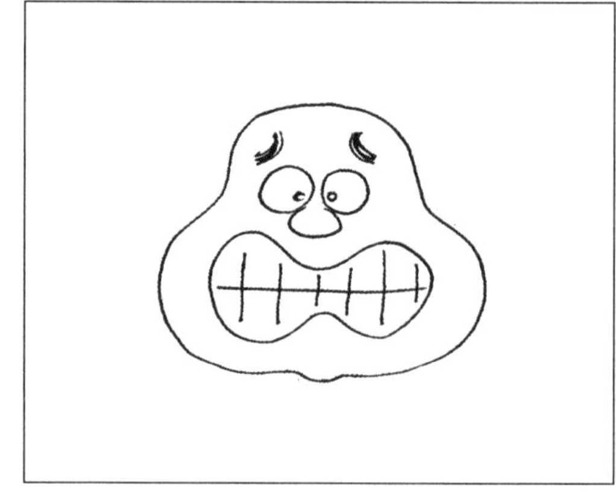

6. add ears

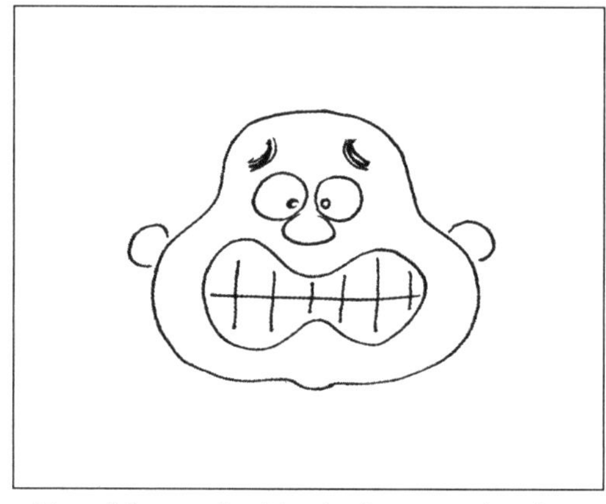

7. add worried hair & perspiration

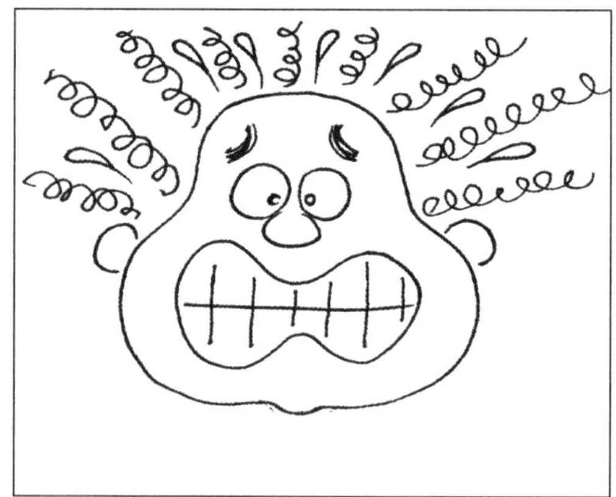

8. add a neck and shirt and name it

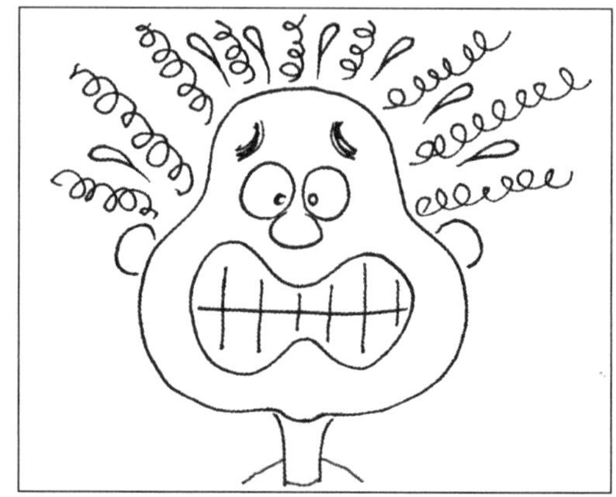

You Can Do It!

Draw big and try and fill the entire page with one big worried face.
The nose is already drawn for you. You draw the rest of the face.

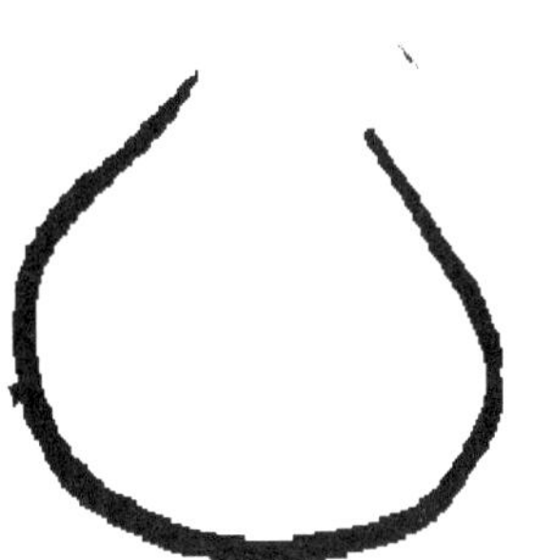

Draw many different moods

Sad

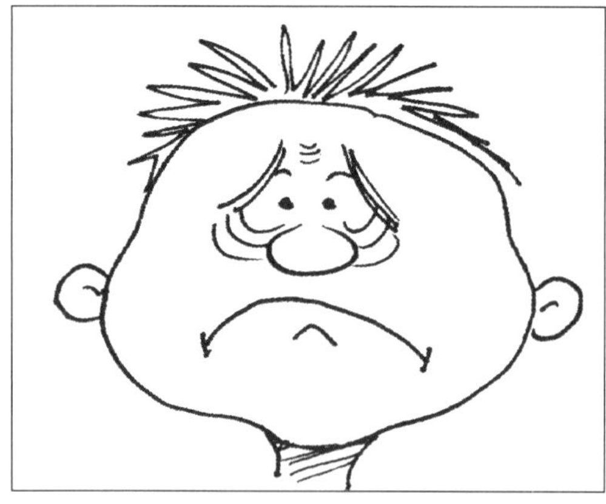

Ecstatic

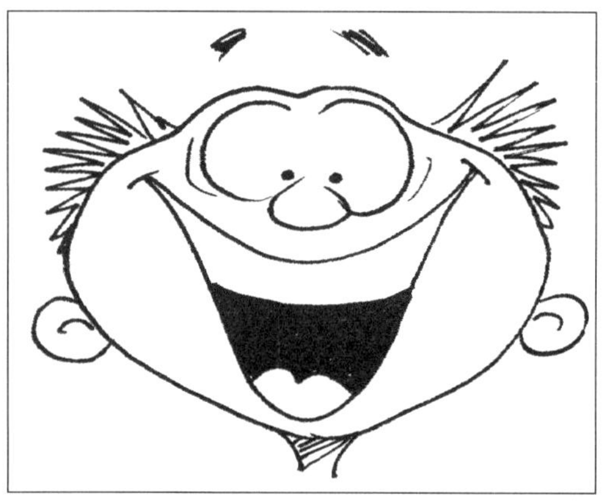

Even more worried!

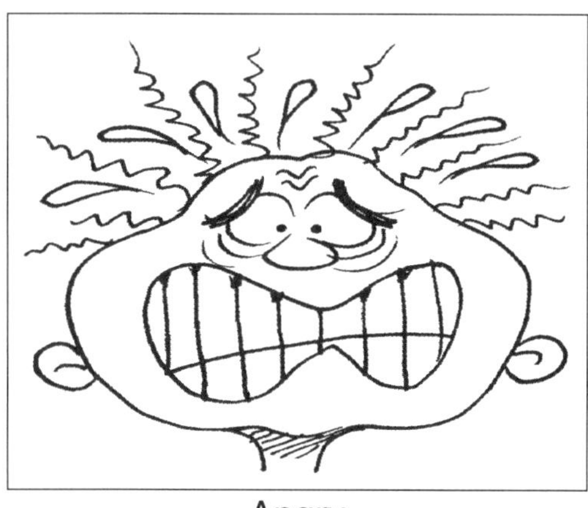

Angry

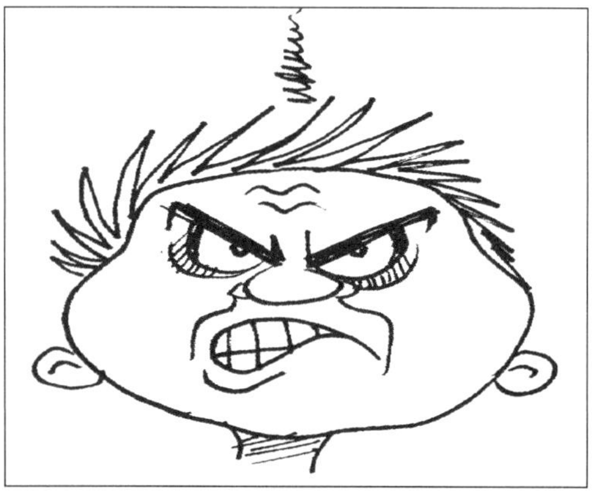

Drawing exercise:

Look at the drawings in each column of this page. The eyes, eyebrows and mouth all have different shapes depending on the mood of the character.

Try drawing as many as you can in the space provided on the next page.

Add some special effects (see even more worried) to give exaggeration and extra personality to your character.

Don't stop there. Draw more than just these faces. Make up many more.

Remember to study the eyes and mouth shapes when drawing and changing your character's mood.

Unconscious

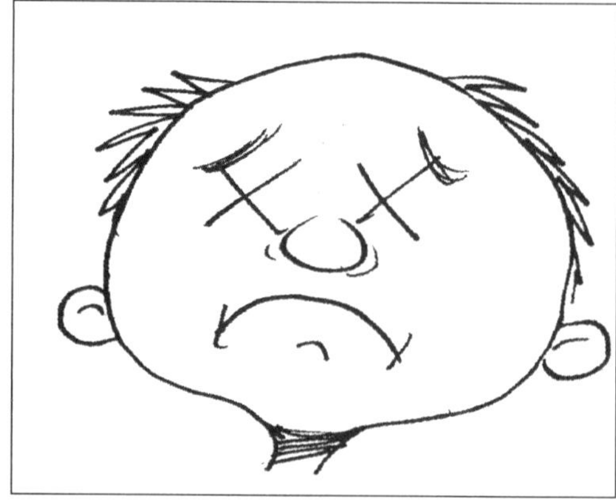

Tired

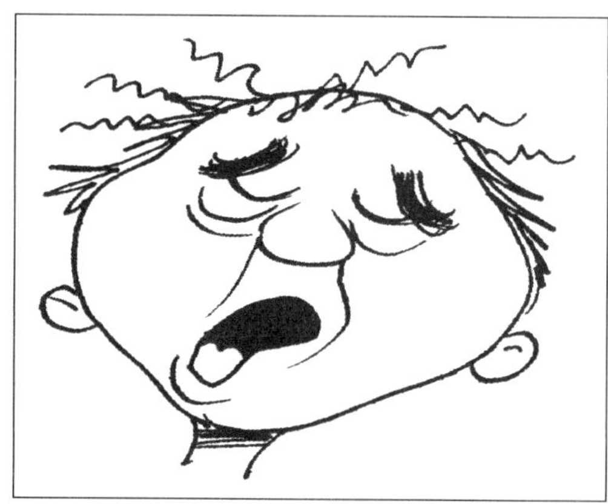

Confused

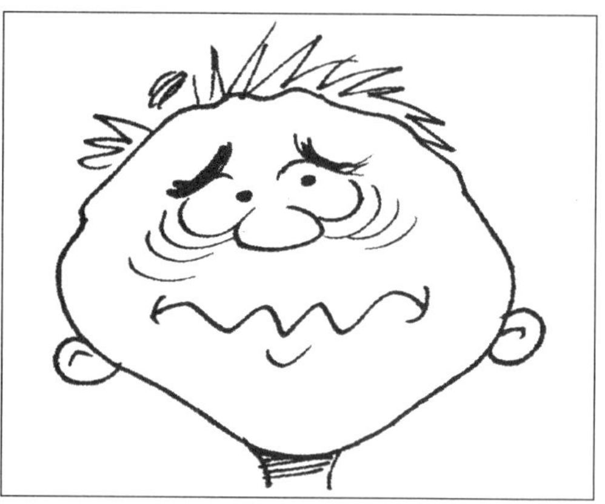

Singing

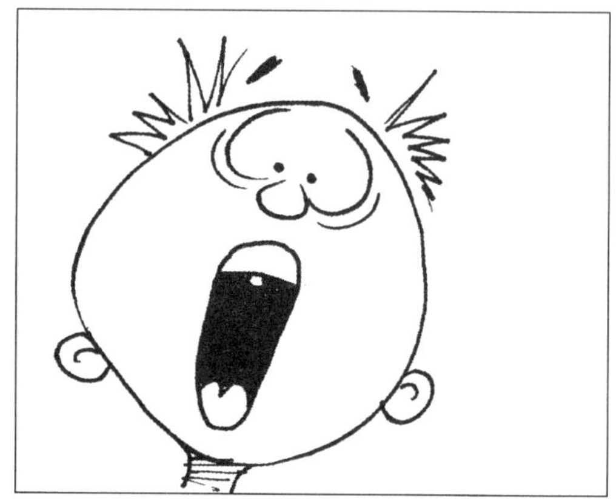

Face It, You Can Do It!

Draw each face smaller this time and try and fill the entire page with as many different faces as you can.

ACTION!

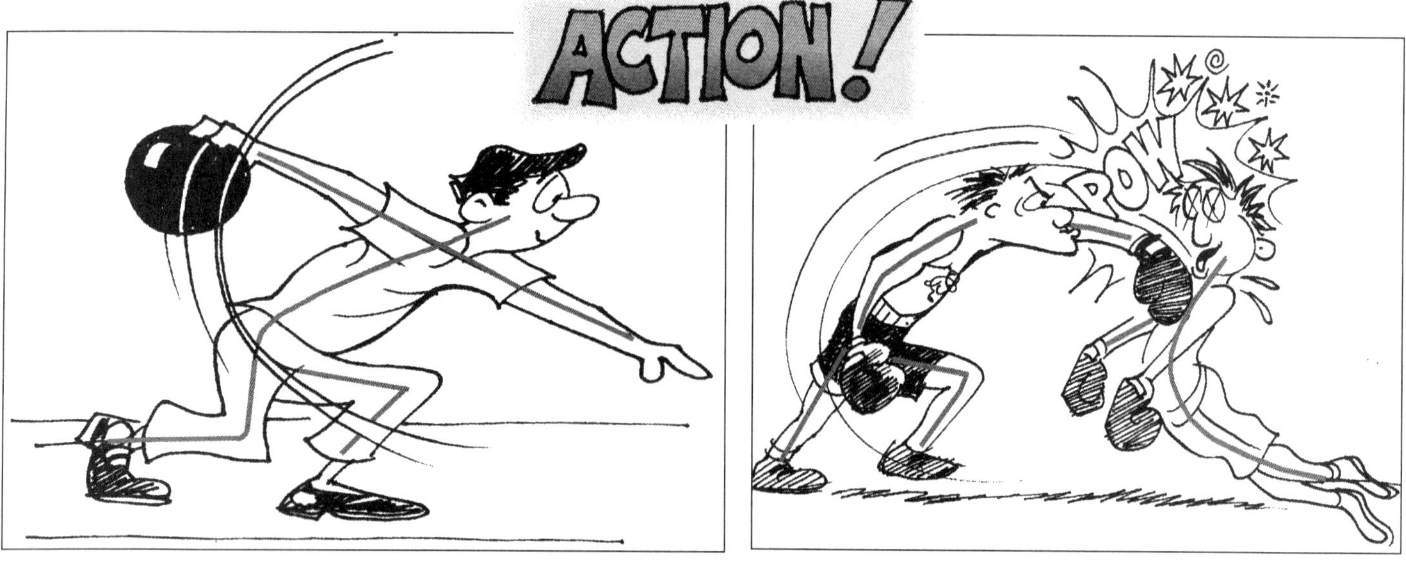

When drawing characters with a lot of action you need to begin with action lines. Capture the motion by drawing lines through the character in the direction of the action. Then draw the character over the lines.

THE BODY TALKS

Body language is important in telling the reader what a cartoon character is thinking.

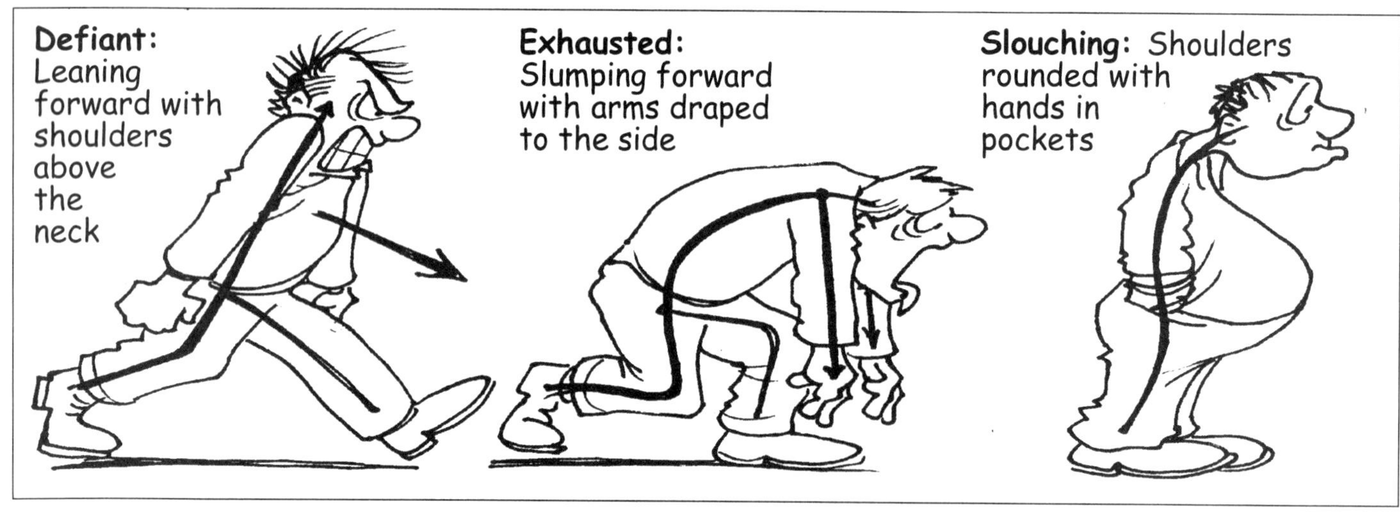

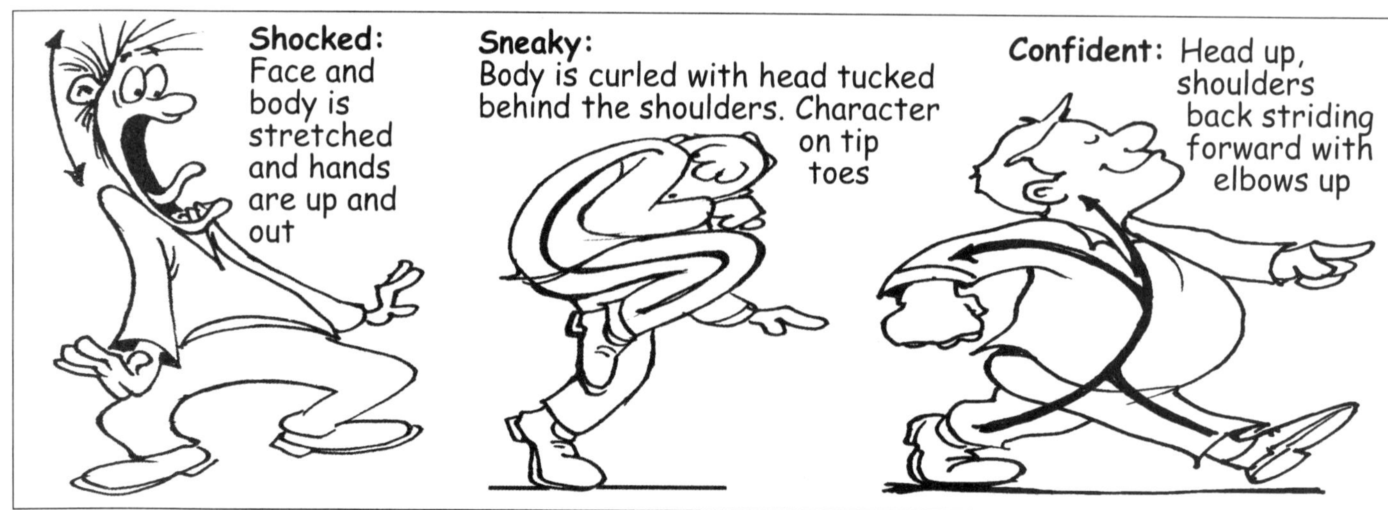

STICKS & CIRCLES

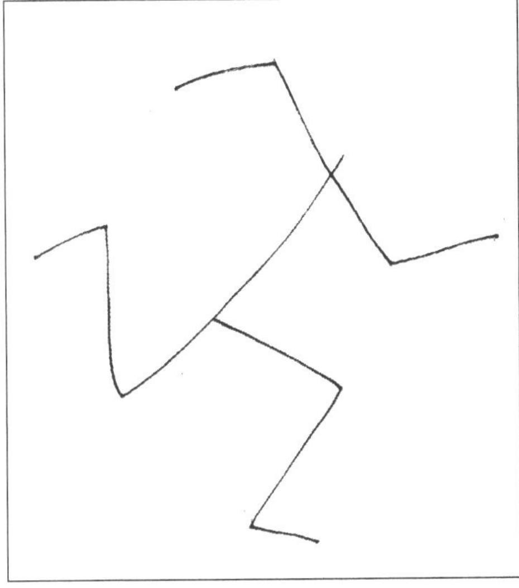

1. With pencil capture the action line by drawing a stick figure in motion.

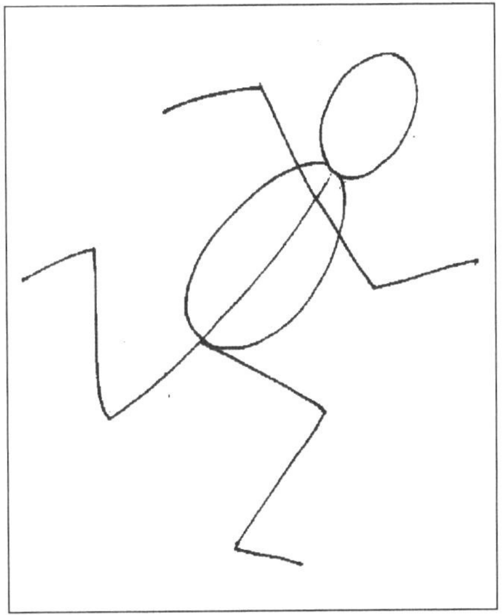

2. Begin to fill out the stick figure with ovals and circles to give the character shape.

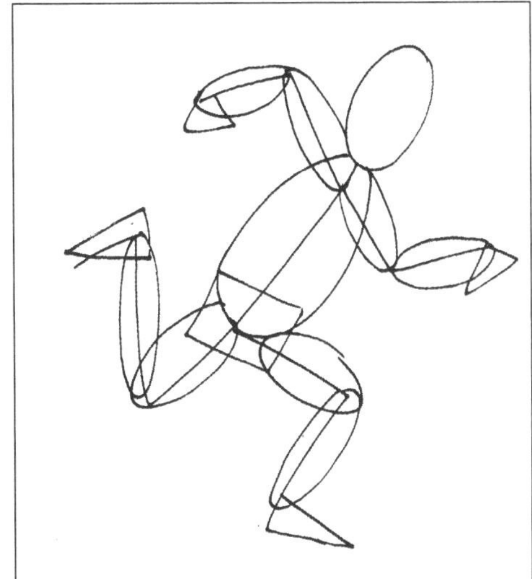

3. Finish filling out the stick figure with a square for the torso. Add ovals and circles for body, arms and legs. Add triangle shapes for feet and hands.

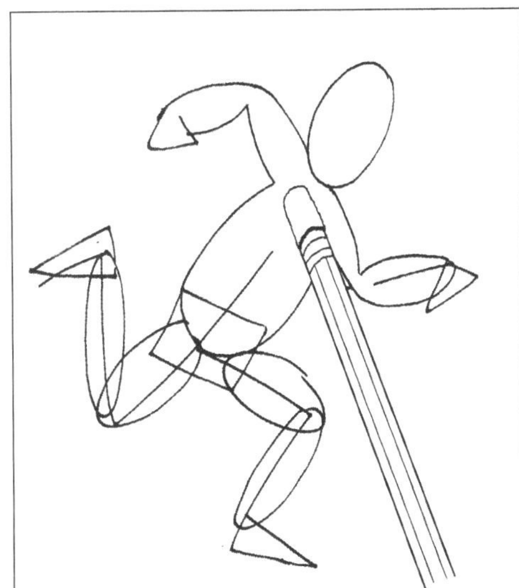

4. Begin to erase the inside lines so you can draw the clothing and face.

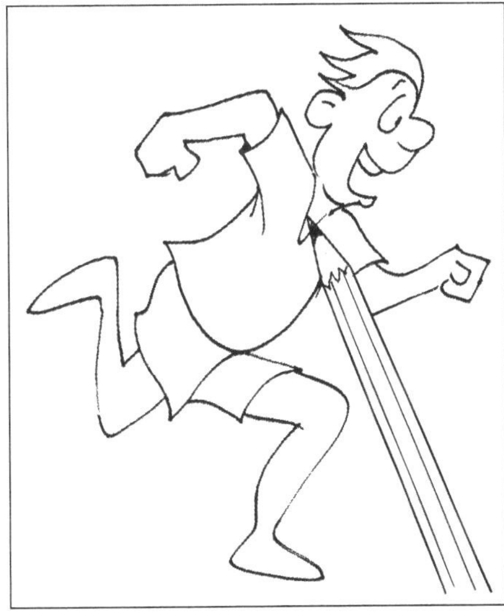

5. Finish by erasing all sticks and ovals. Add details to clothing and face.

You can create shape, motion and structure for your cartoon character by starting with a stick figure and adding ovals and circles on top. Then by erasing the inside lines and adding clothing, hair and facial features, your character is ready for action!

FOUR HEADS TALL

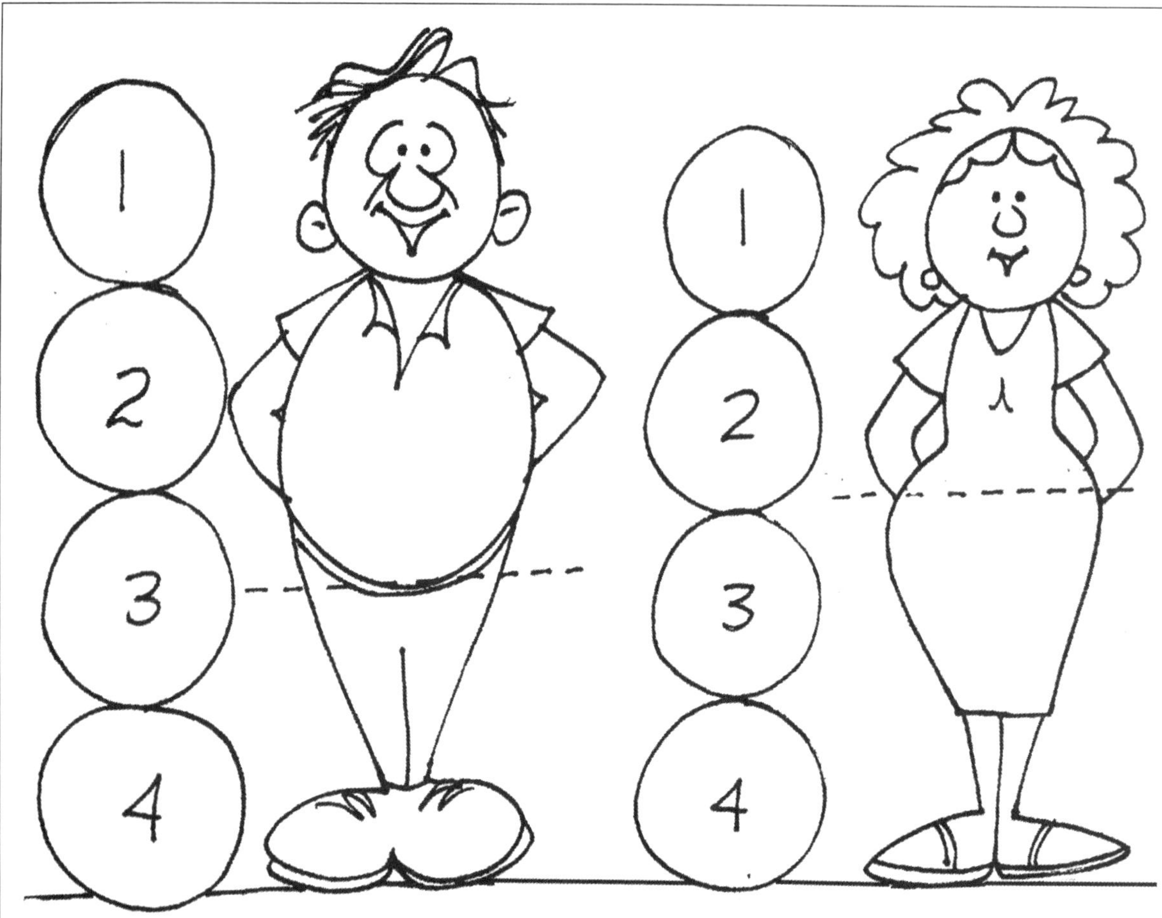

Most human forms are **seven to eight heads tall.** But, cartoon characters are shorter. They are about four heads tall.

Male characters are slightly taller, their waist is lower in proportion to their body.

Female characters are a little shorter and the waistline a bit higher.

BACKGROUND ART

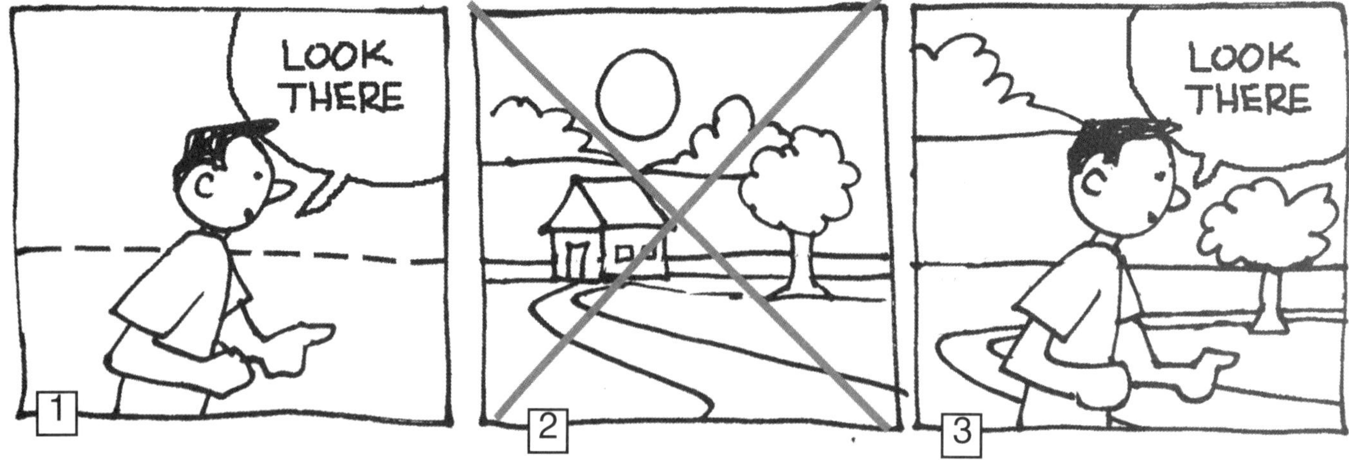

Once your character or characters are placed in the foreground and the dialogue balloons have been drawn in, it's time to draw in the background. First, draw a light dotted line to show the horizon. It's important to draw only background art that is necessary. Panel two shows that putting in a lot of detail in the background won't fit. So just draw a tree, a road or a cloud to finish the background setting.

MODEL SHEET

In order to keep your character drawings consistent you will need to create a **model sheet**. Draw your character from all sides and all angles. Refer to it when you place your character in the strip.

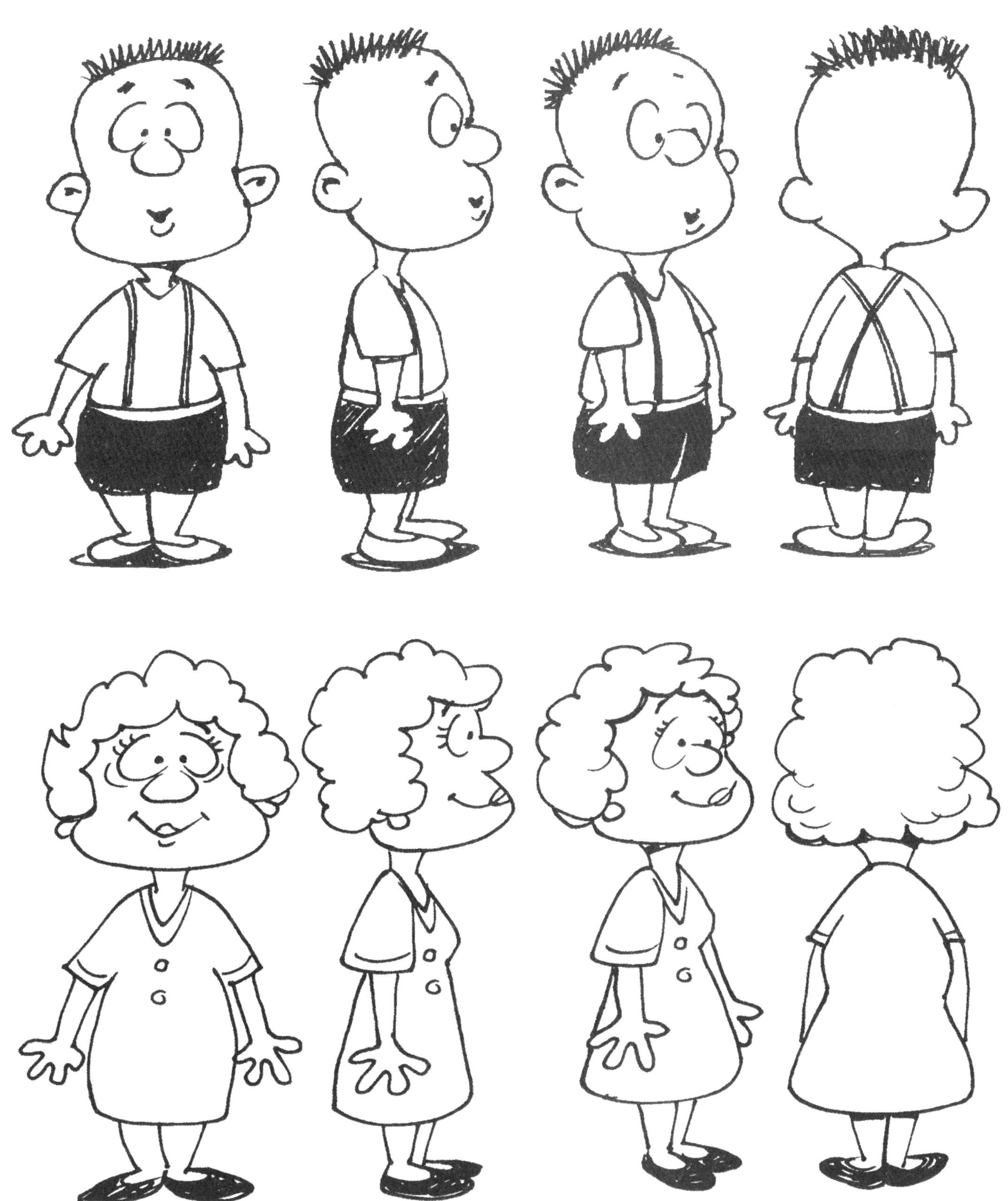

SILHOUETTE

Use silhouetted figures to give your strip a different look when laying out your panels.

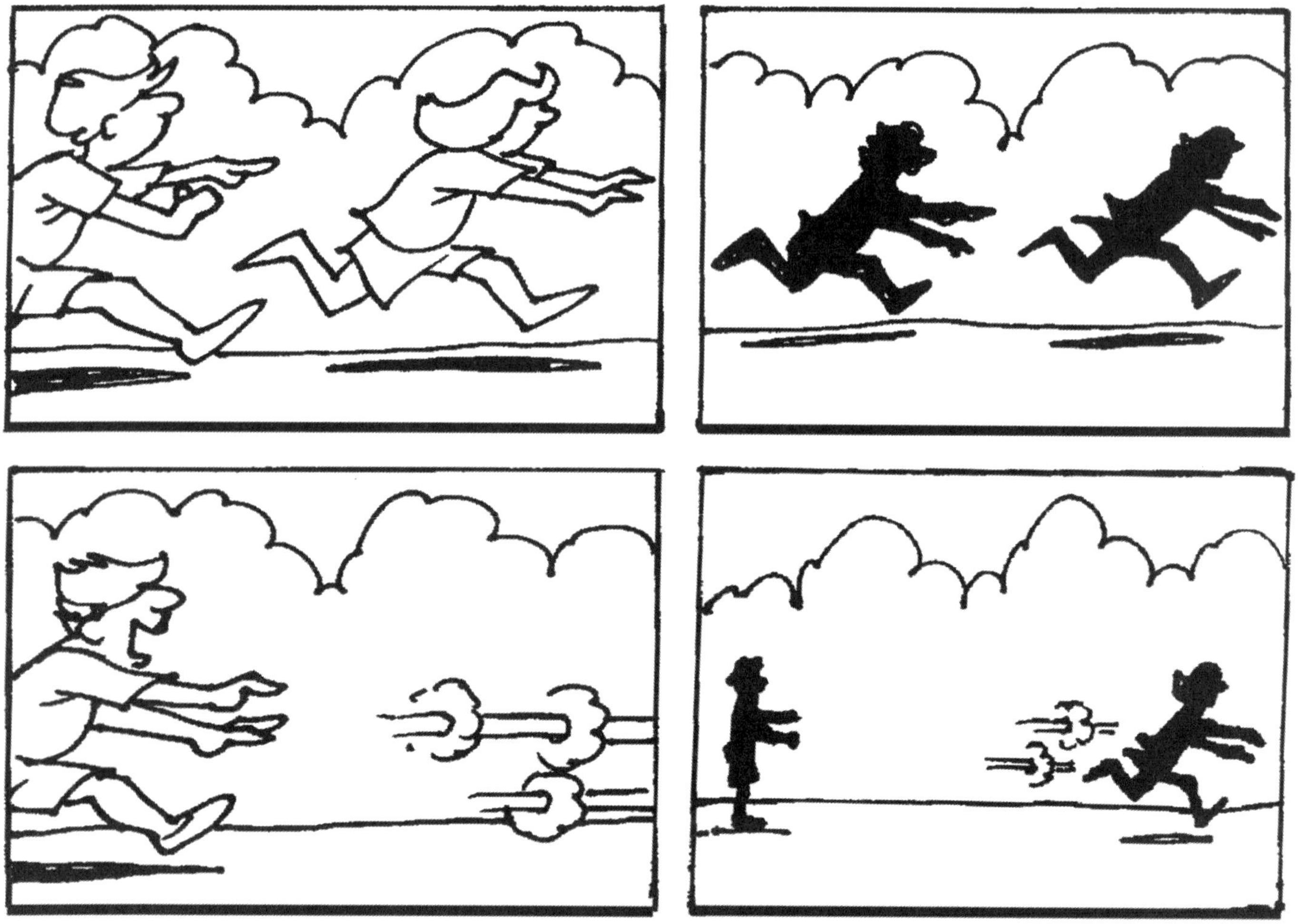

DO's & DON'T's

Here is some helpful advice on lettering your dialogue inside your cartoon balloon:

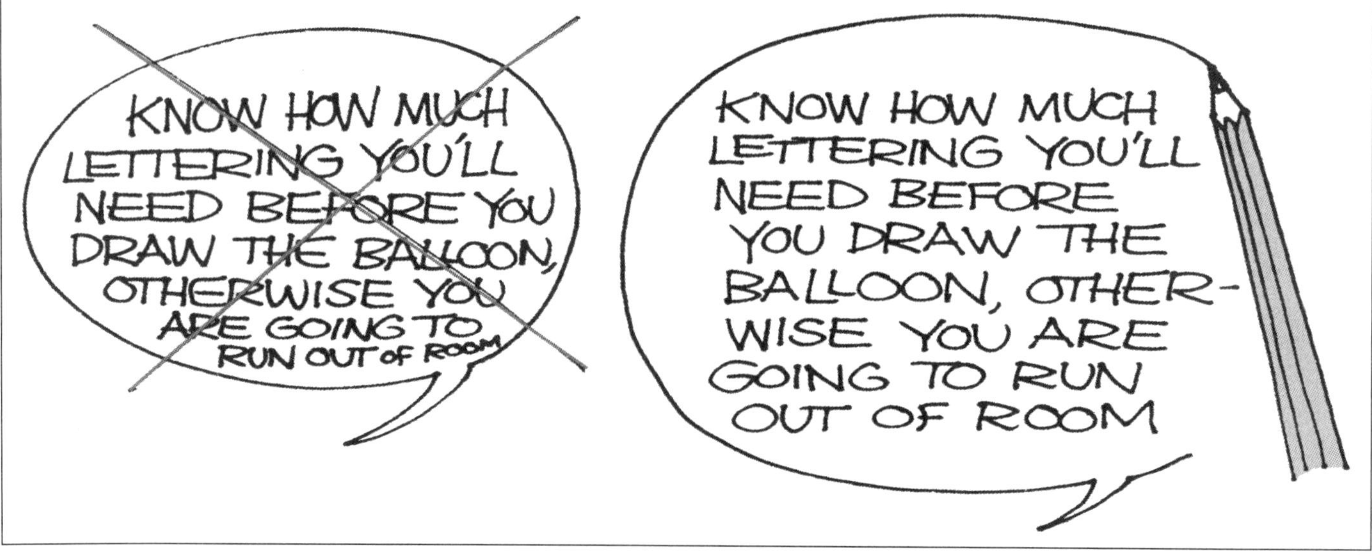

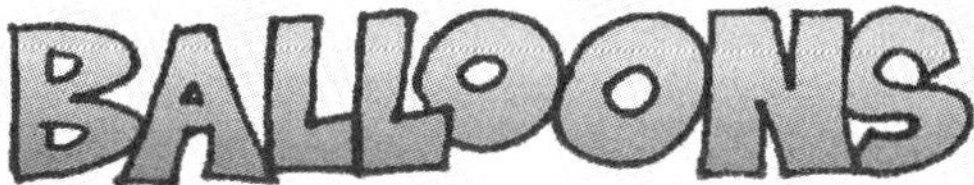

Dialogue and thought balloons come in all shapes and sizes. Use your imagination to create dozens of balloon types matching the sound or feeling with an appropriate shape.

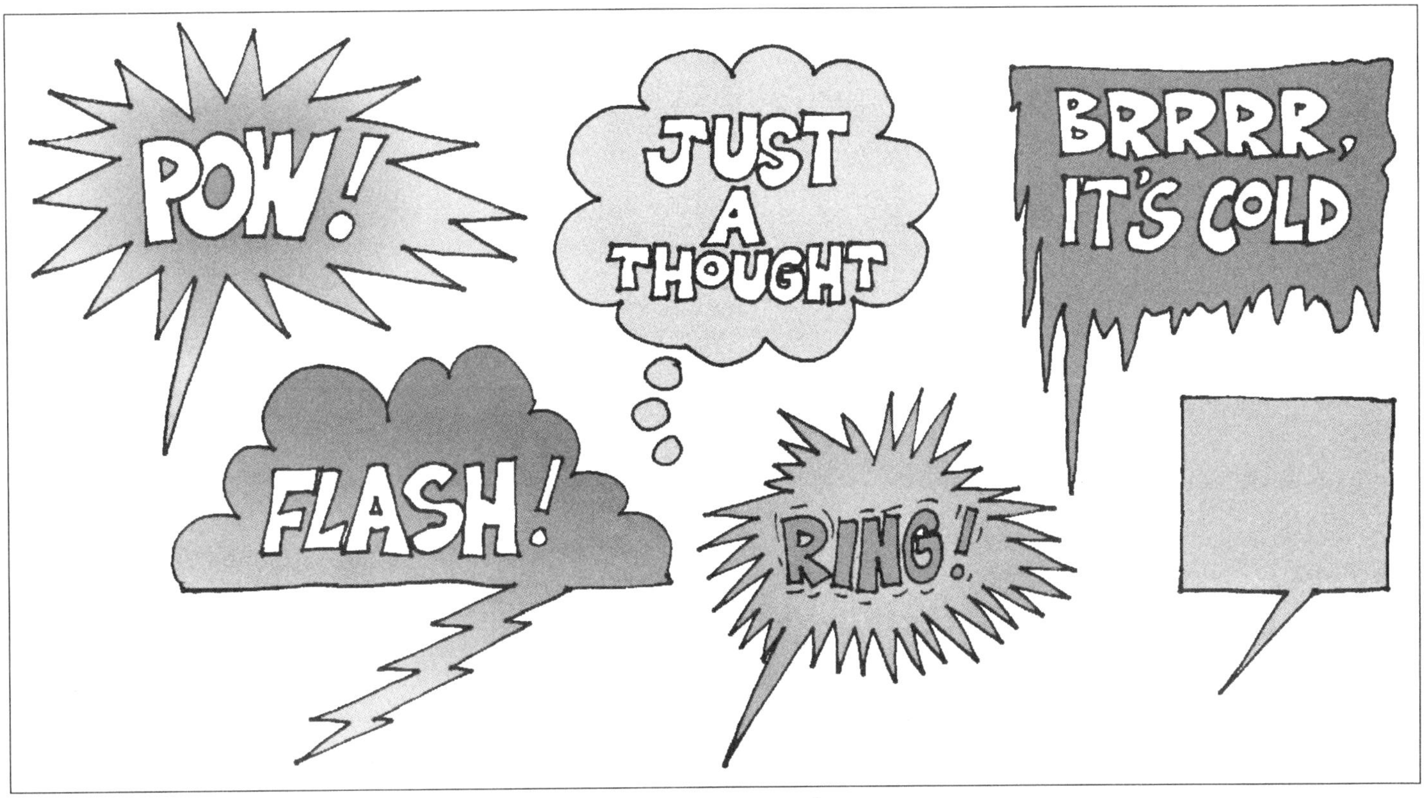

In the space below draw more balloon shapes that reflect action, sound, color and feelings you might use in a cartoon strip:

SPECIAL EFFECTS

Here are a few tricks you can use to make your cartoon come to life. Like in the movies, cartoons have special effects too! Here's how to make a car look like it's moving fast!!

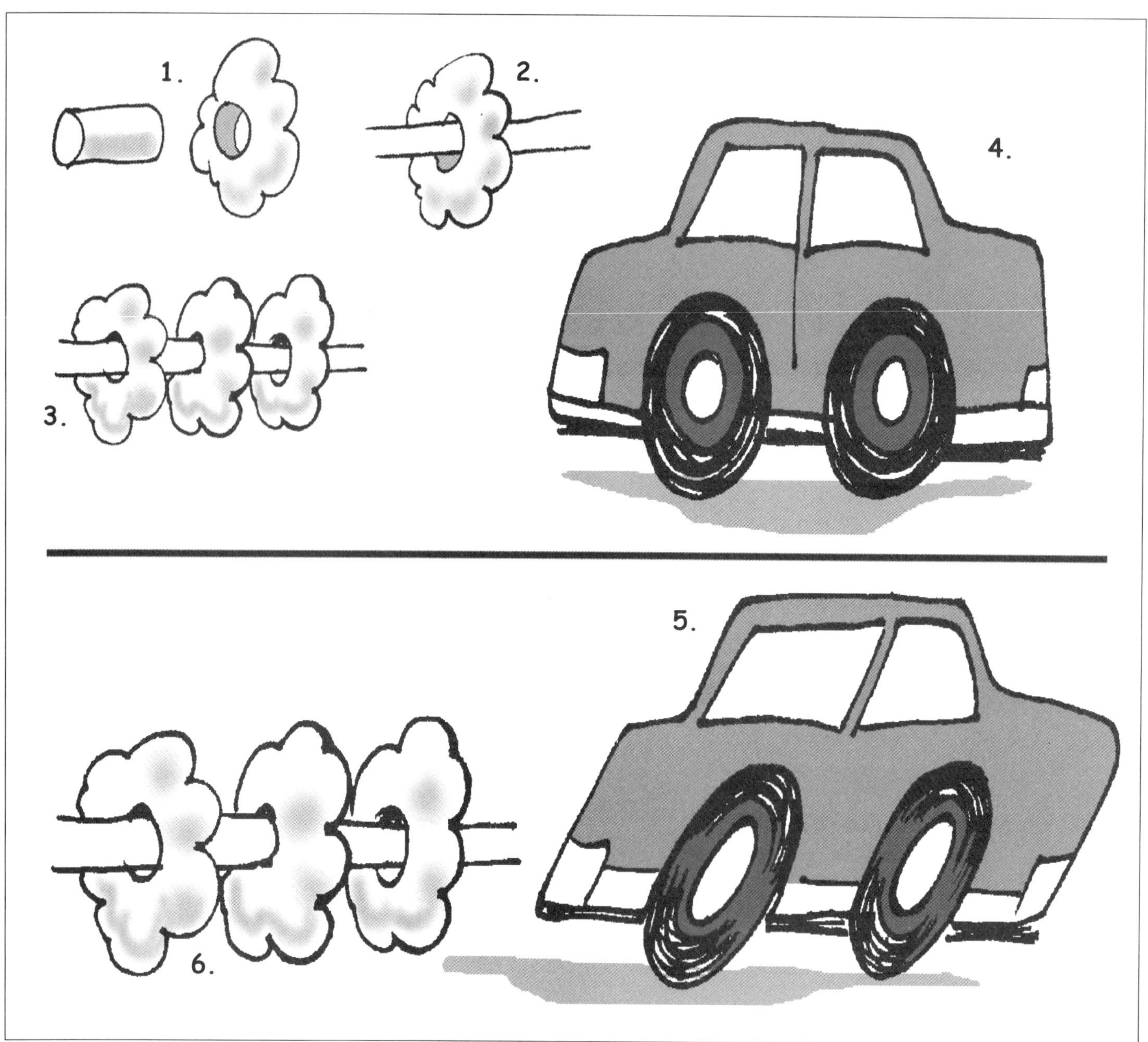

1. Start by drawing a tube and a cloud with a hole in it. **2.** Draw the two again, but this time place the tube through the cloud. **3.** Repeat the same drawing a few times. **4.** Draw a car standing still. **5.** Draw the same car, but this time stretch the wheels and angle the car forward. **6.** By placing the clouds behind the car it will look like it's going fast!

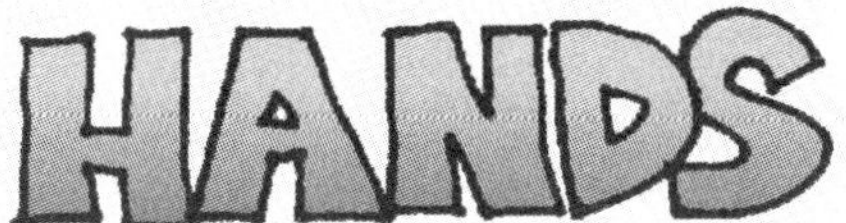

Use the hand you don't draw with to model hand gestures. Cartoon characters usually have four fingers. Create a model sheet of hand positions so you can refer to it when drawing your character.

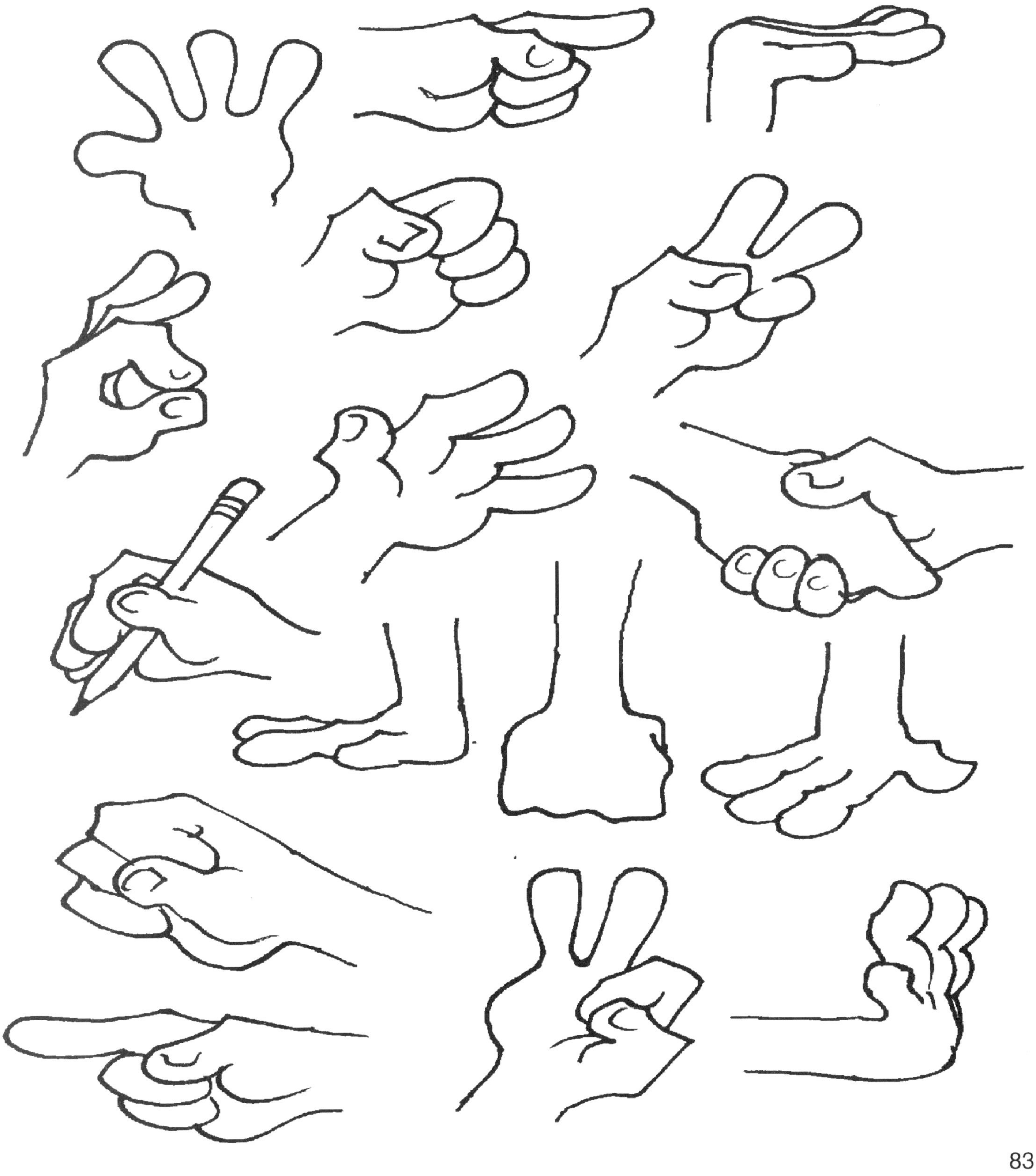

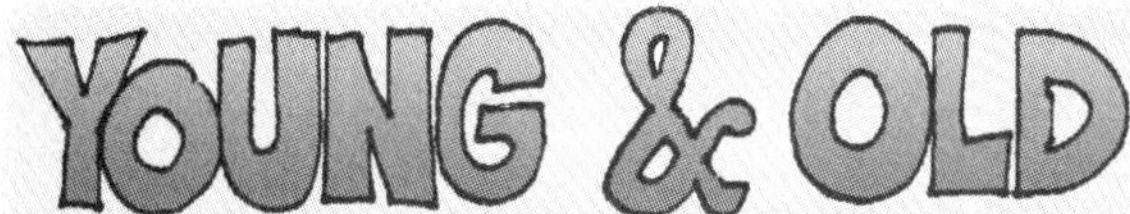

The shape of the face changes depending on the character's age:

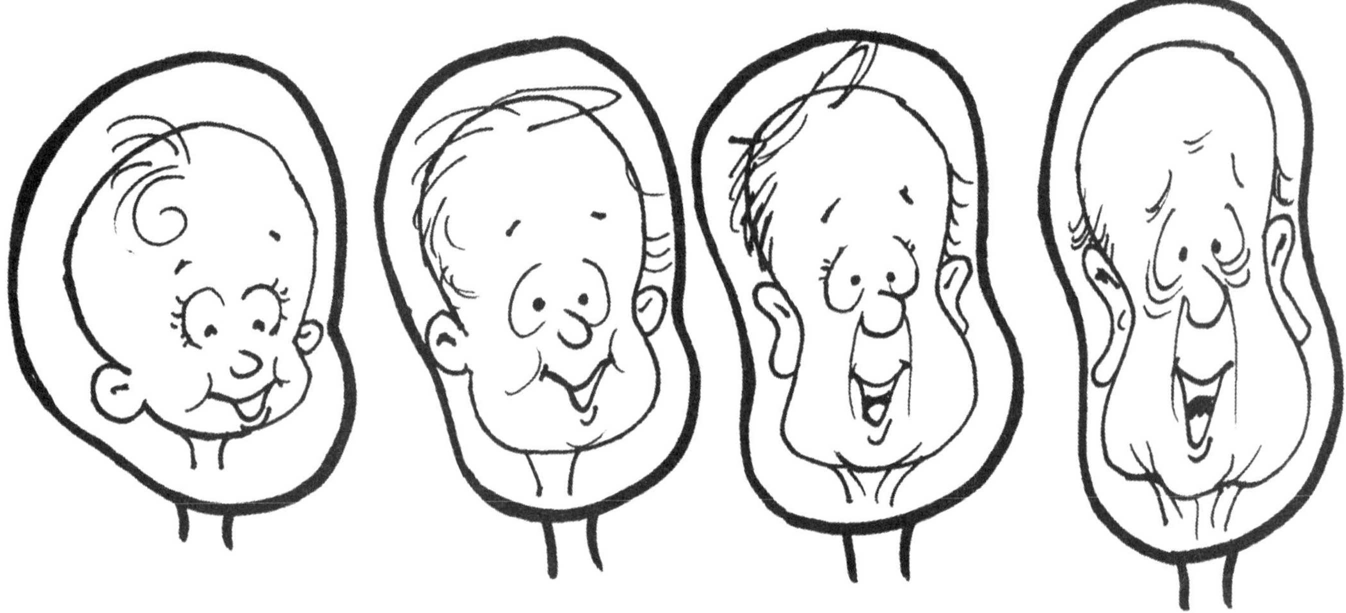

1. A baby's face is pear-shaped with a large forehead, small nose and tiny ears.

2. A youngster's face is still pear-shaped but is stretched more than a baby's face. The nose is slightly larger and the ears are higher on the head.

3. An adults face is more peanut-shaped with a larger nose and longer ears.

4. An older adult's face is peanut-shaped and stretched. The ears and nose are larger.

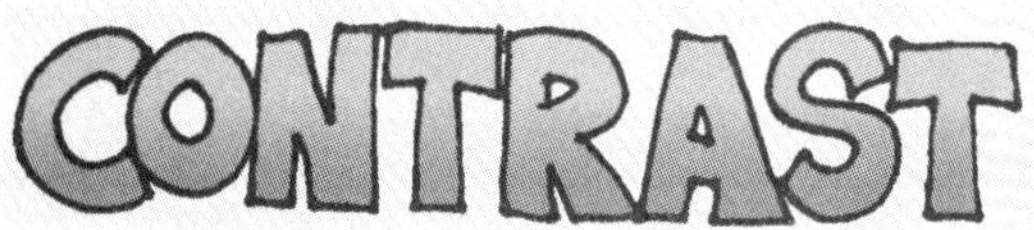

Adding black areas to the background, as well as, foreground panels will help your character to stand out.

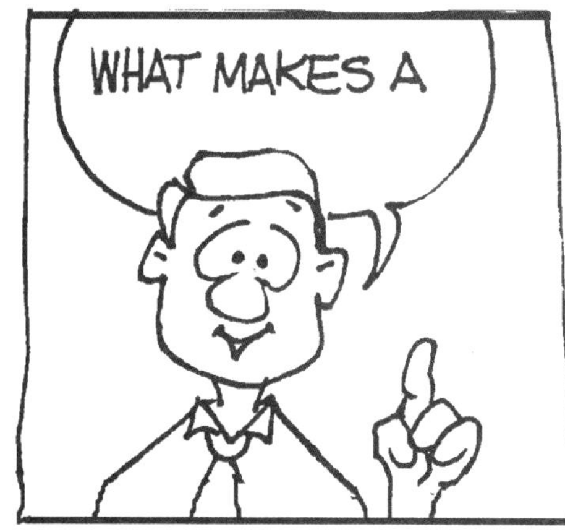

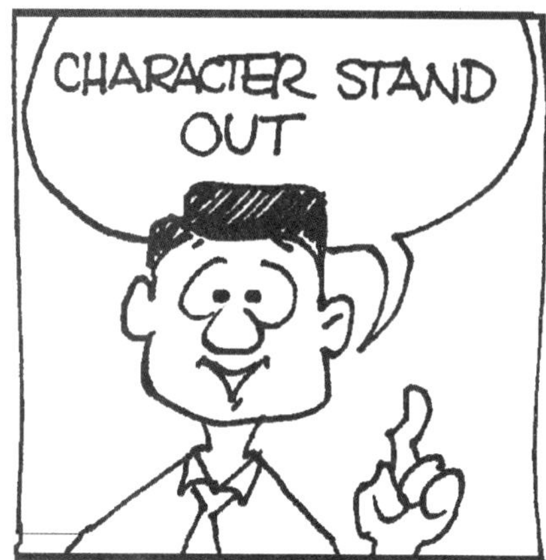

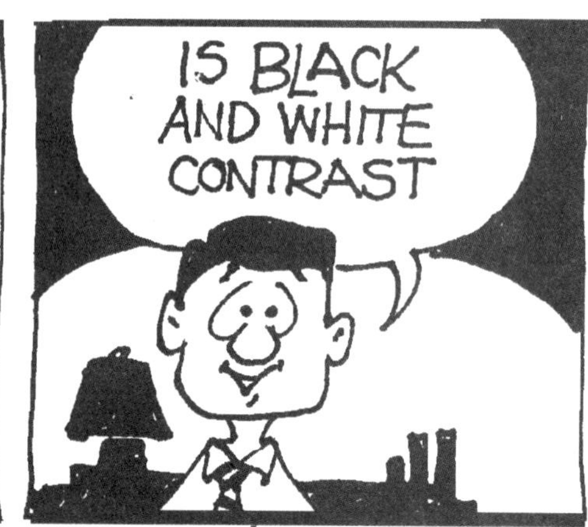

ANIMALS

Create a dog or a cat using the following step-by-step approach:

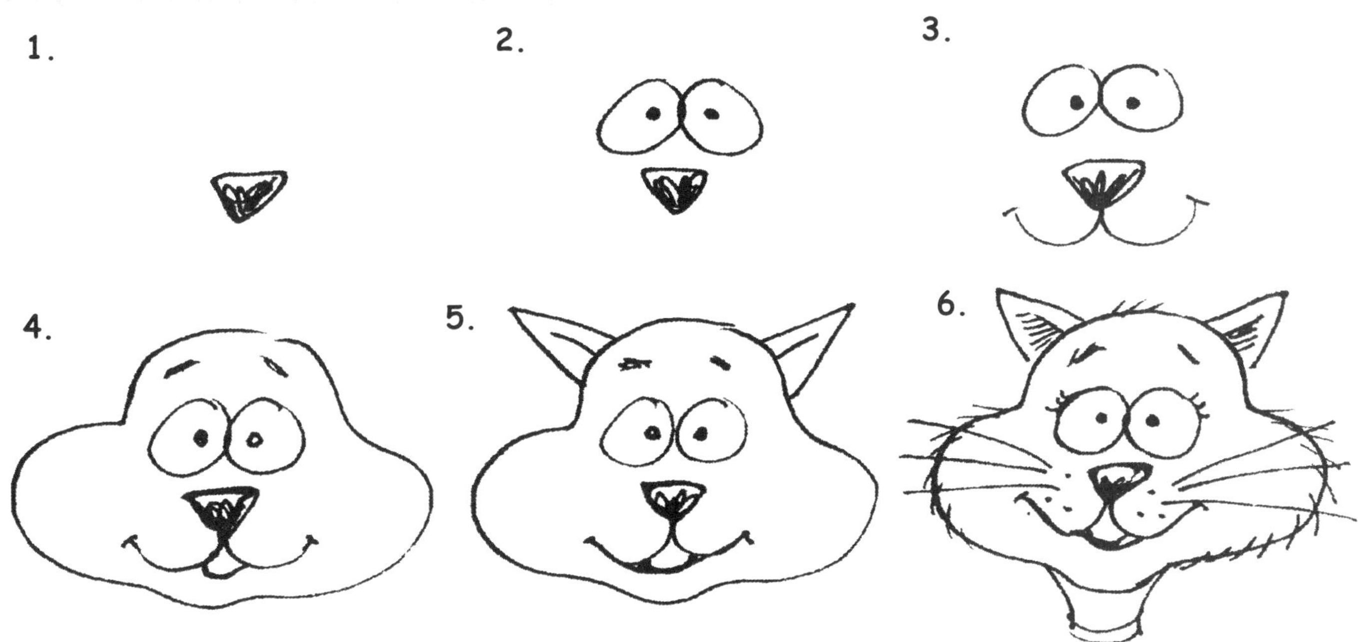

1. Start by drawing a triangle-shaped nose **2.** Draw two egg-shaped eyes and two eyeballs. **3.** Add a smile **4.** Give some shape to the cat's face. **5.** Add some ears. **6.** Put in detail like whiskers, freckles and eyebrows.

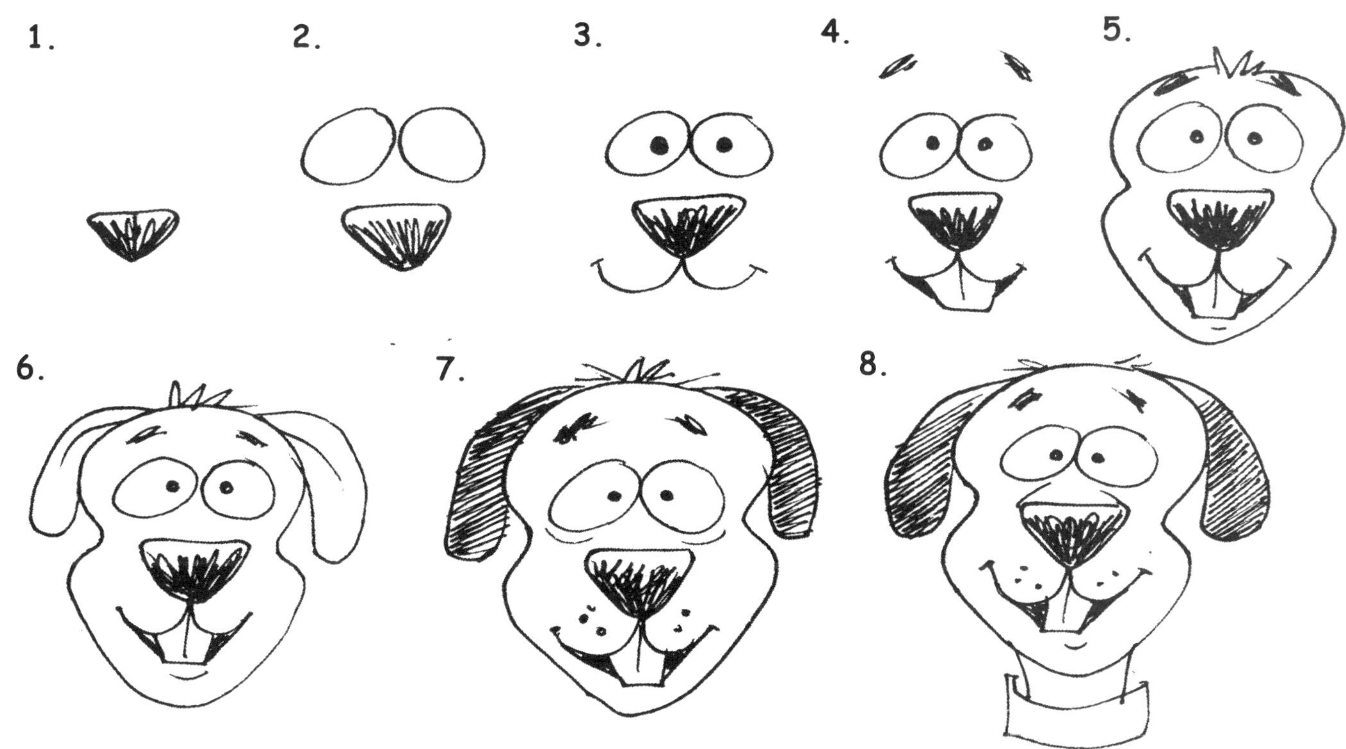

1. Start by drawing a triangle-shaped nose **2.** Draw two egg-shaped eyes. **3.** Add two eyeballs and a smile **4.** Add eyebrows and teeth. **5.** Give shape to dog's face. **6.** Add two ears. **7.** Shade in ears. **8.** Add a neck and a collar

Hair Styling For The Birds...

Cartoon exercise: Design a fowl hairdo

Dress this egret up with a cool hairstyle. He is having a bad hair day. You add the hair. You design the look. Then give the style a name. Three egrets have hairdos so far. Make six more...

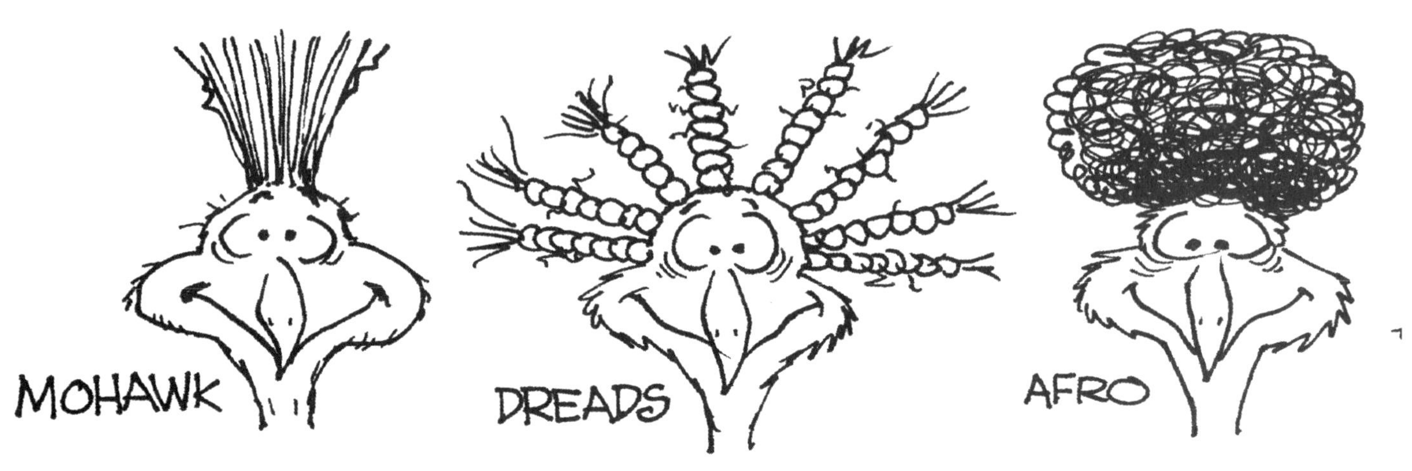

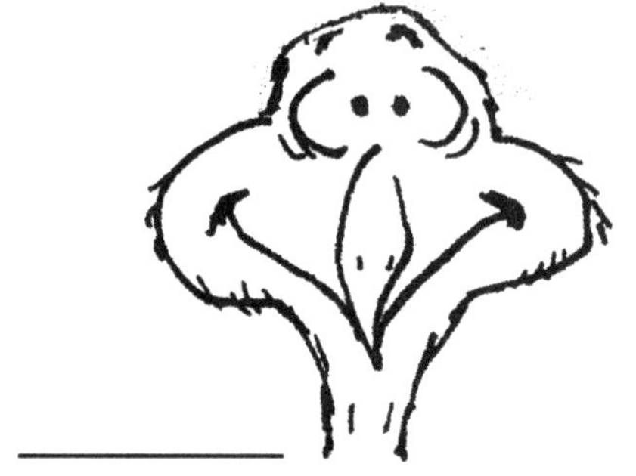

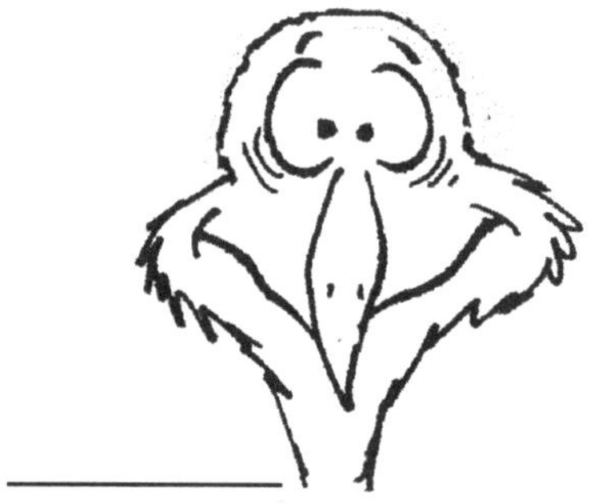

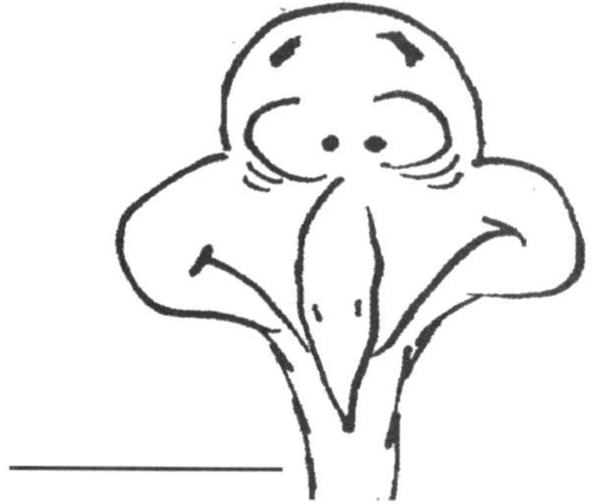

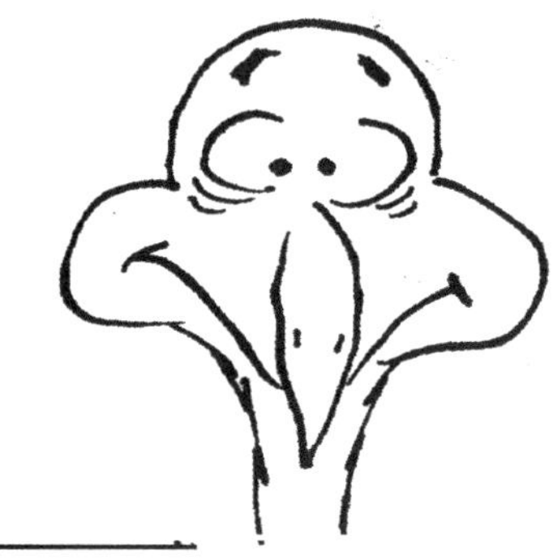

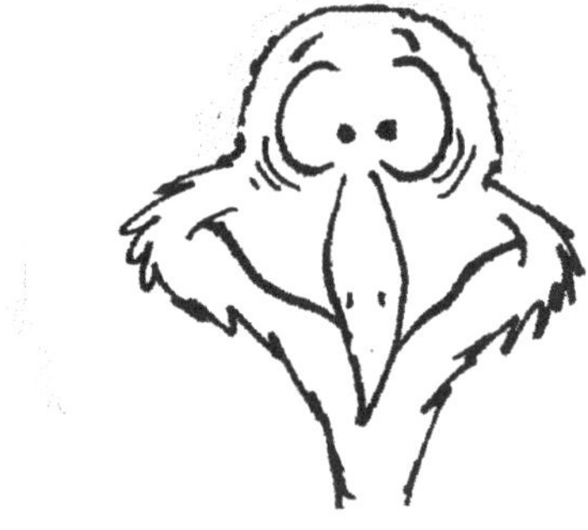

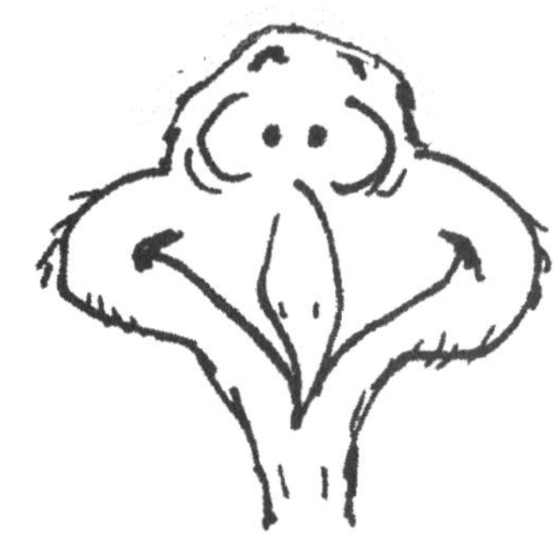

...What A Hair-brained Idea!

Keep the creativity flowing. Don't give up. Are you stuck for new ideas? Think of styles you've never seen. Then think of some famous shapes - shapes in nature, shapes made by man and shapes in space. You can "do" it.

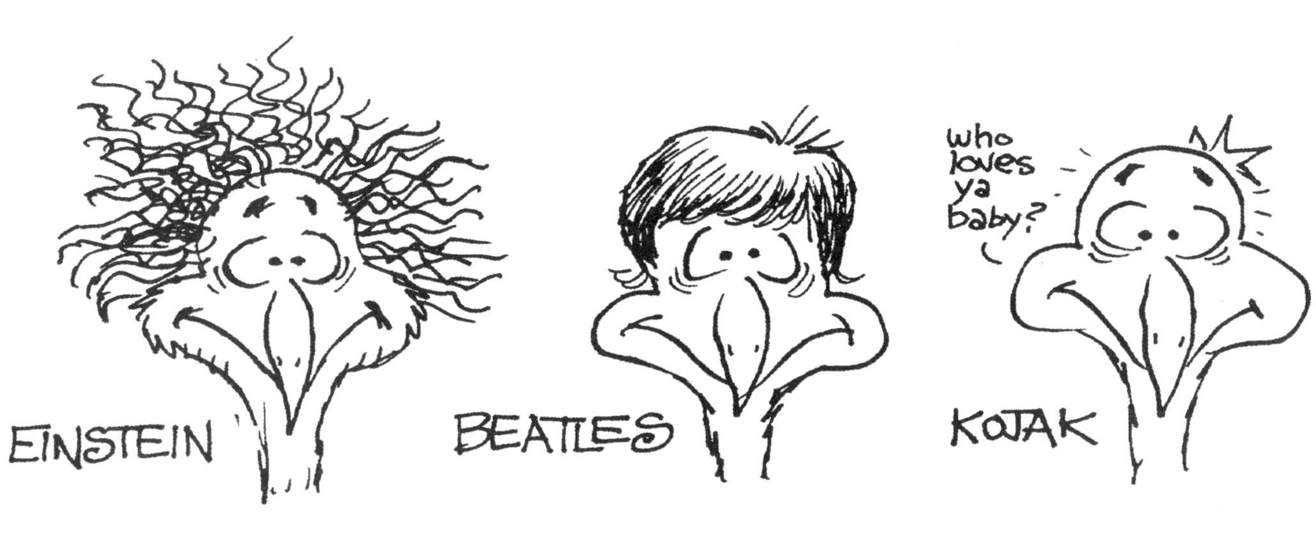

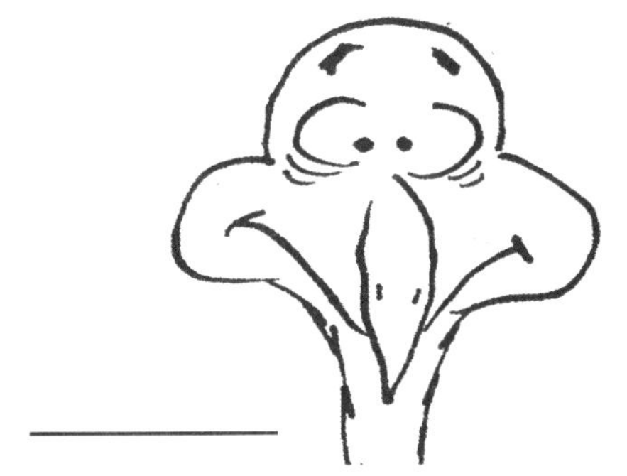

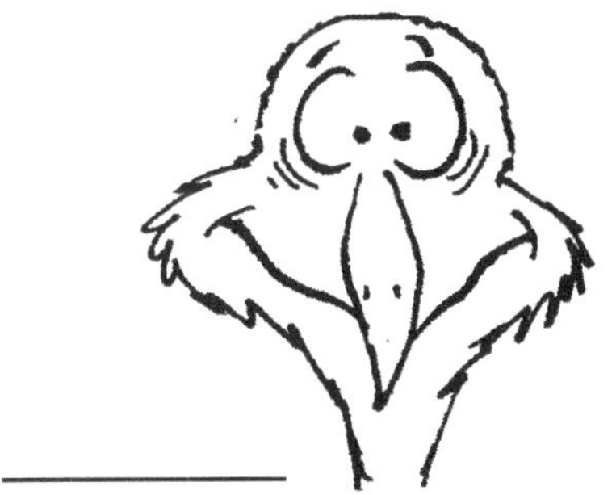

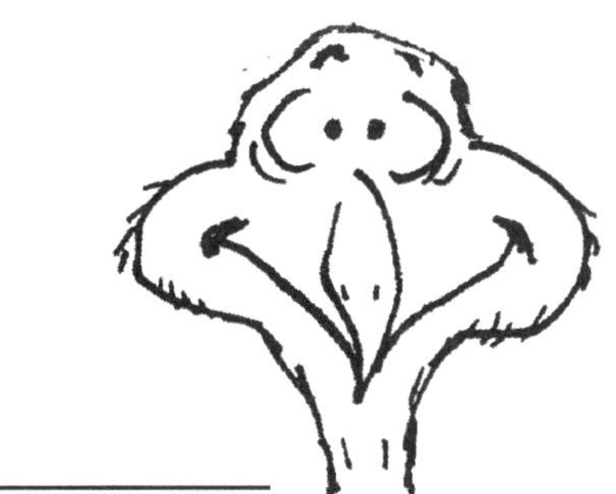

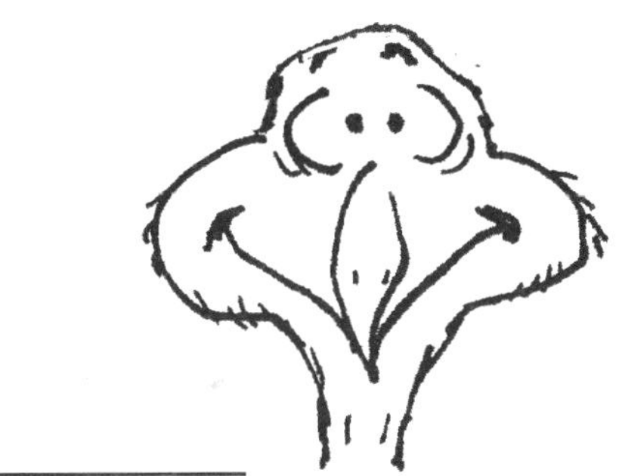

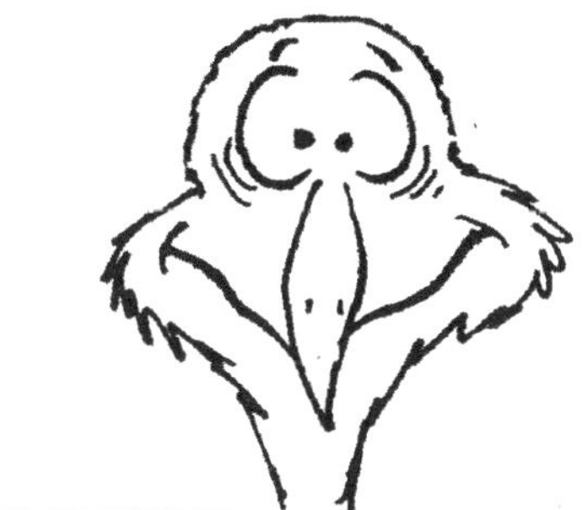

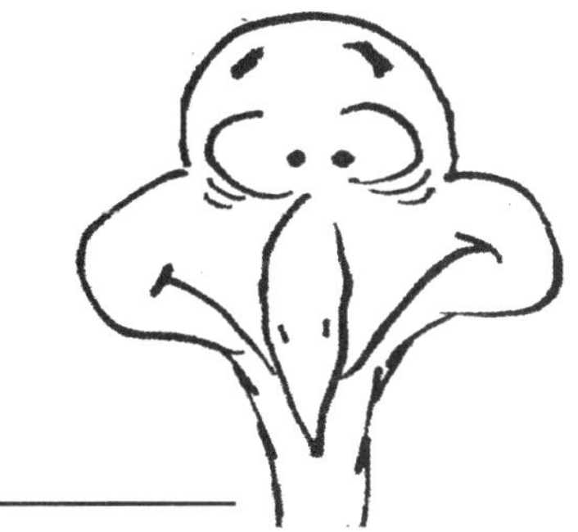

Cartoon Exercises

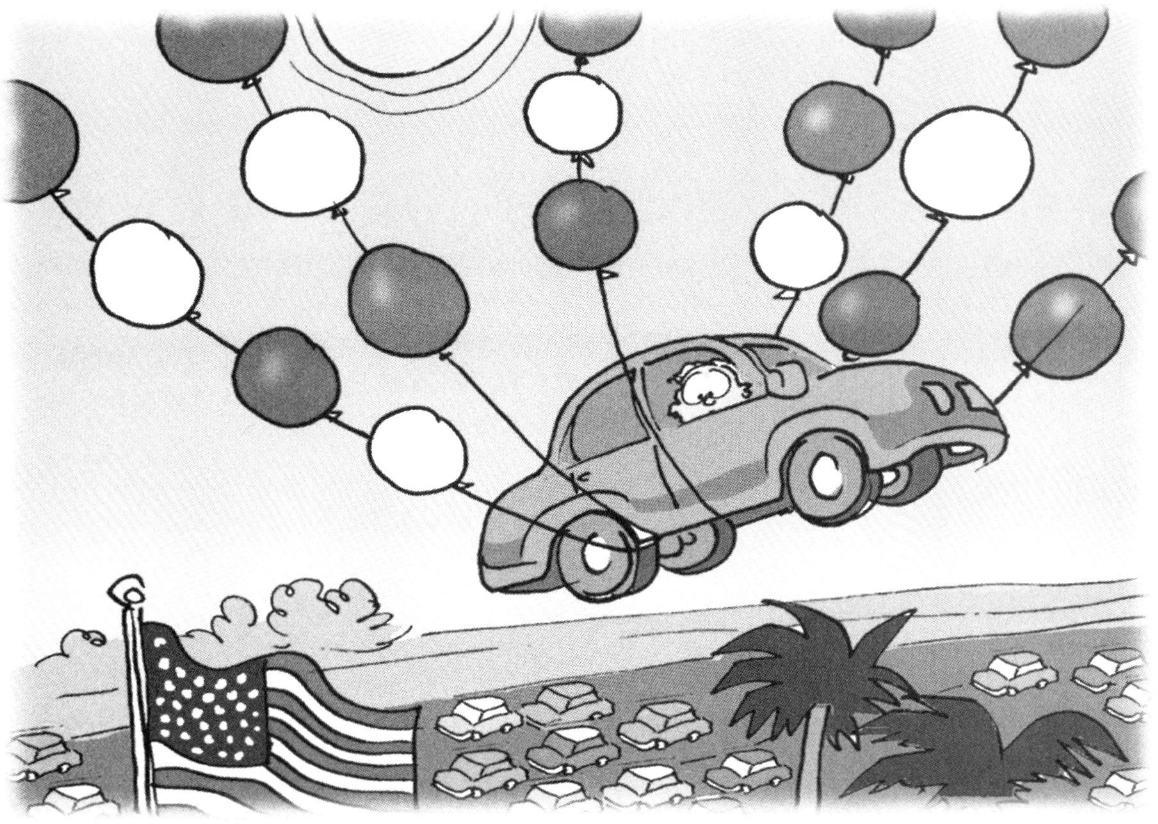

"You cannot use up creativity.
The more you use the more you have."

- Maya Angelou

Fishing For Prime Numbers

Prime numbers: is a natural number which is only divisible by 1 and itself

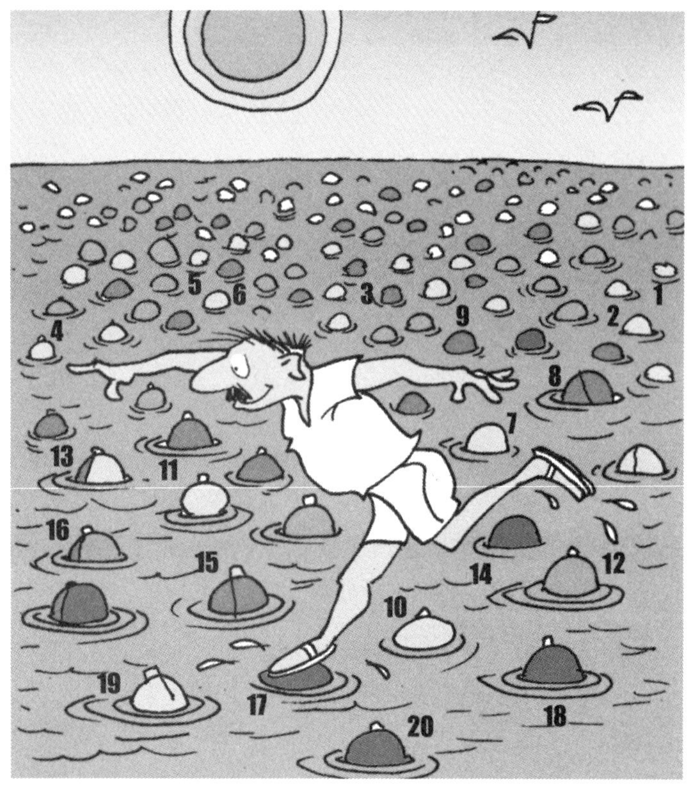

Cartoon Exercise:
Bobbin' Hoppin'

If the fisherman to the left is jumping on prime-numbered bobbers only, which numbers will he touch?

Cartoon Exercise:
If there are 10,000 Islands many are prime numbered islands.

Write down some prime numbered islands from 1 to 10,000 a fisherman might pass on his travels...

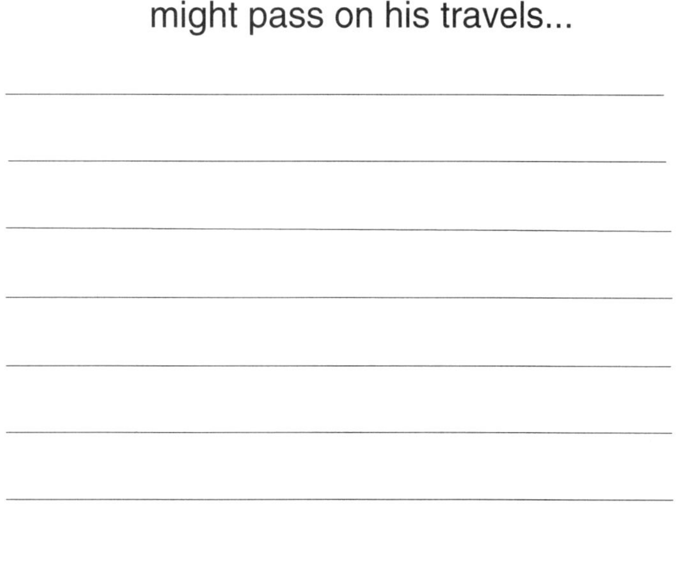

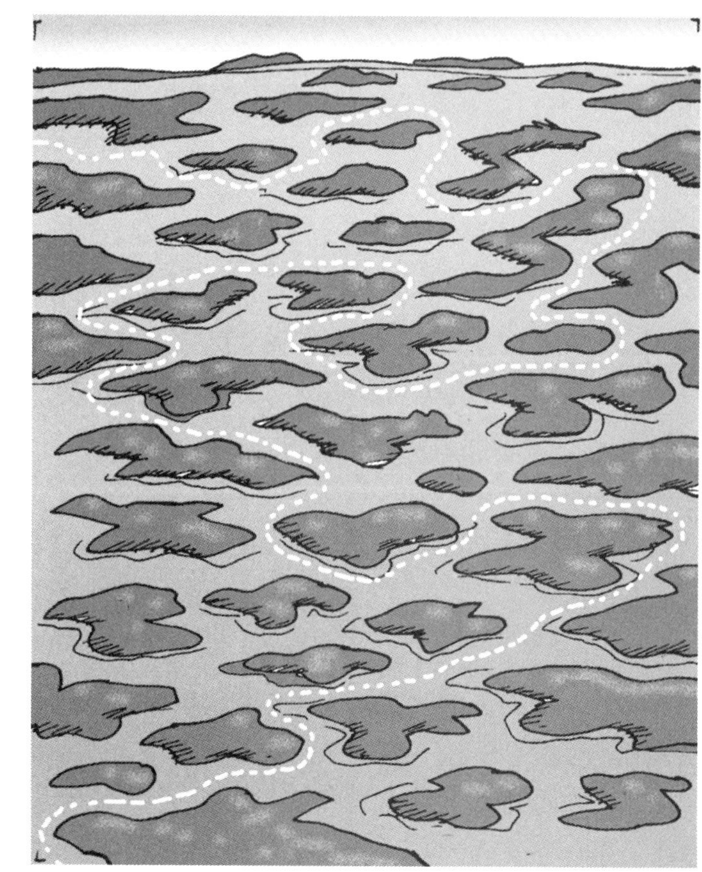

Hey, Look Out Below!

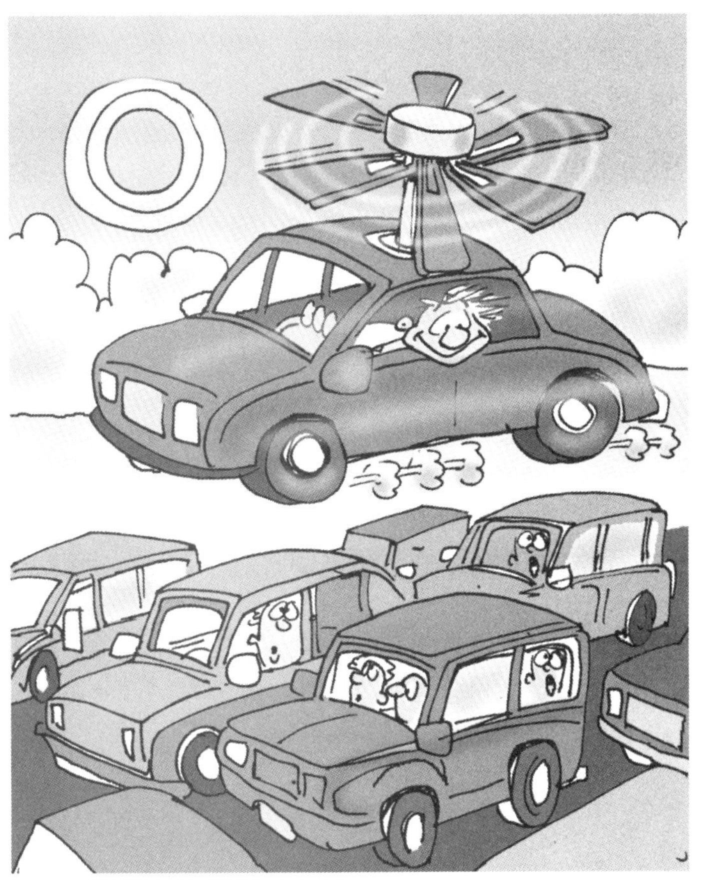

Cartoon Exercise:
Get in your Coptorcar

Fly this coptorcar and you'll get where you want to go with ease. There's only one problem. The driver doesn't see the signal light hanging up ahead. What else might this driver need to watch out for, flying 20 feet off the ground?

____

____

____

____

____

____

____

Cartoon Exercise:
Dive, dive, dive!

Look out below! Incoming!!

How fast can a pelican dive?
How fast can a penguin dive?
How fast can a osprey dive?
How fast can a peregrine falcon dive?
Don't just lay there, find out!

A pelican can dive at _____ mph.

A penguin can dive at _____ mph.

An osprey can dive at ______mph.

A peregrine falcon can dive at ______mph.

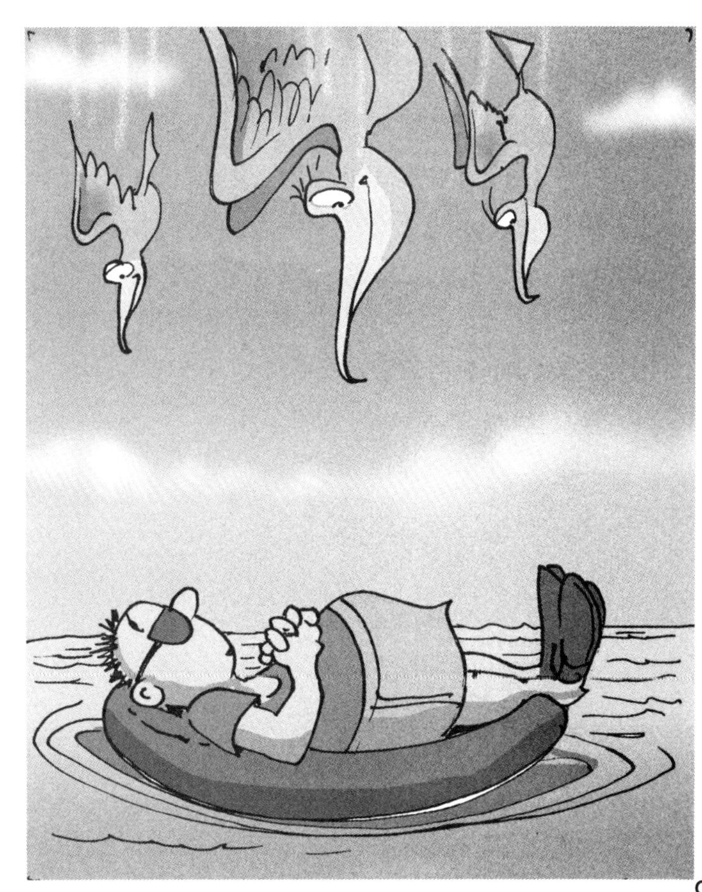

Hey, What Do You Hear?

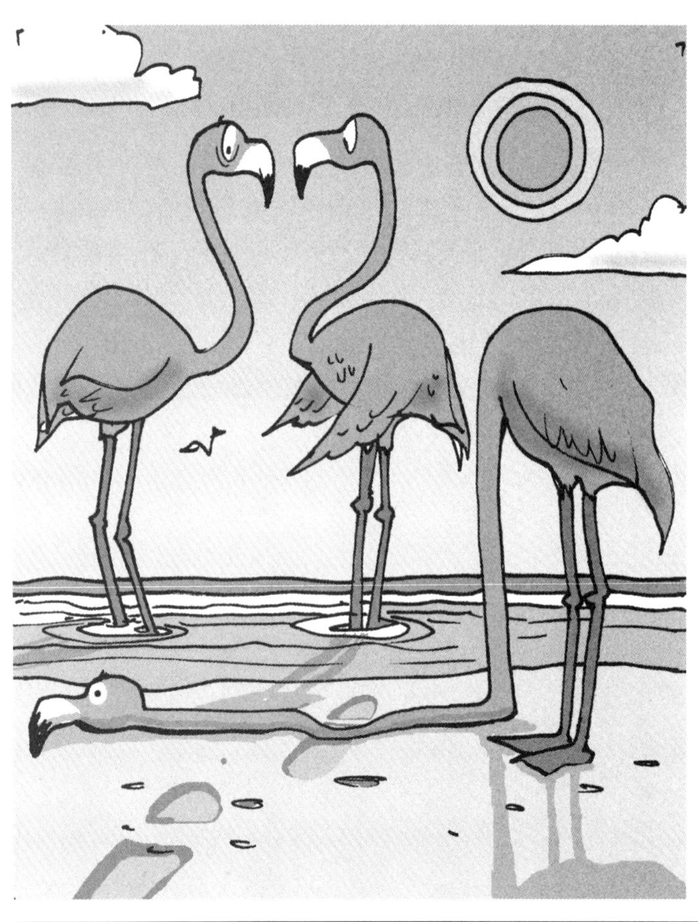

Cartoon Exercise:

Write a few captions for the cartoon to the left. What would the two flamingos in the water be saying to each other?

Flamingo 1:

Flamingo 2:

What about Flamingo 3?

Cartoon Exercise:
Sounds of the Surf

Have you ever held a shell up to your ear and listened to the sounds of the sea? What other sounds would you hear at the beach? Write a short paragraph and tell us what you hear.

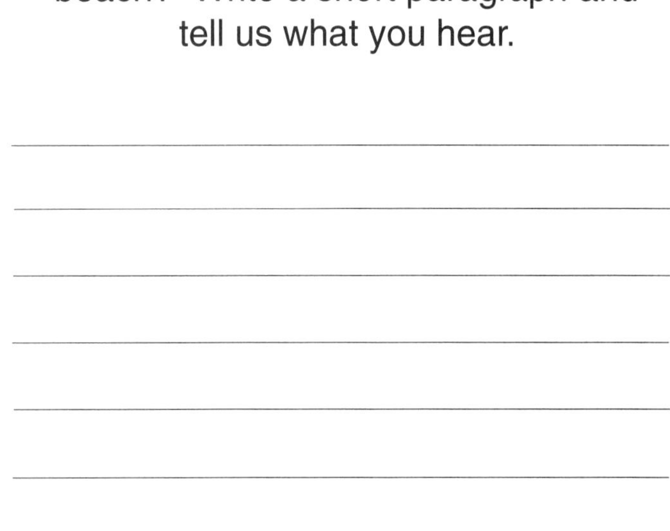

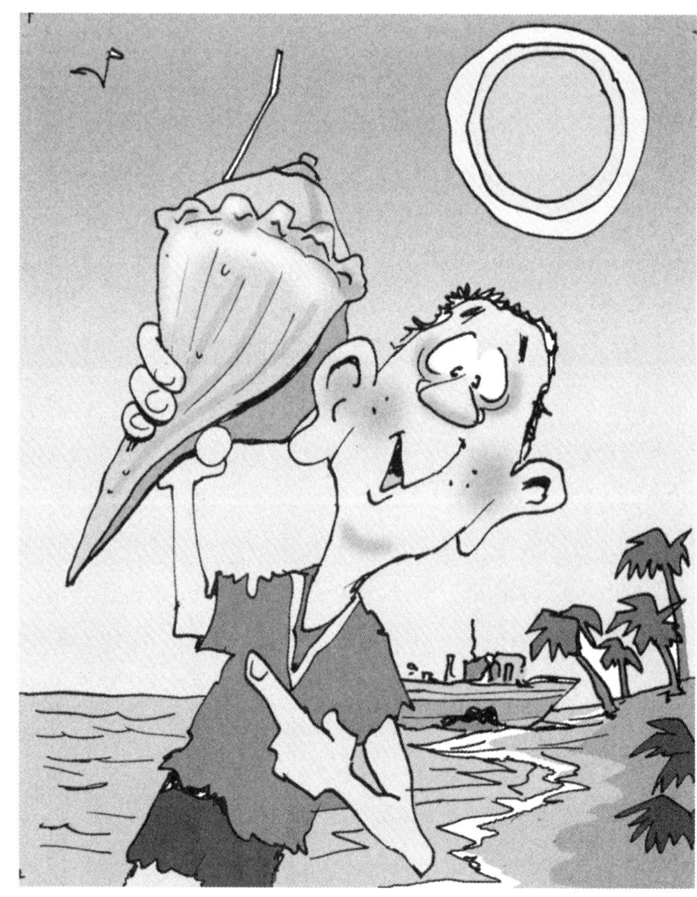

Food Service

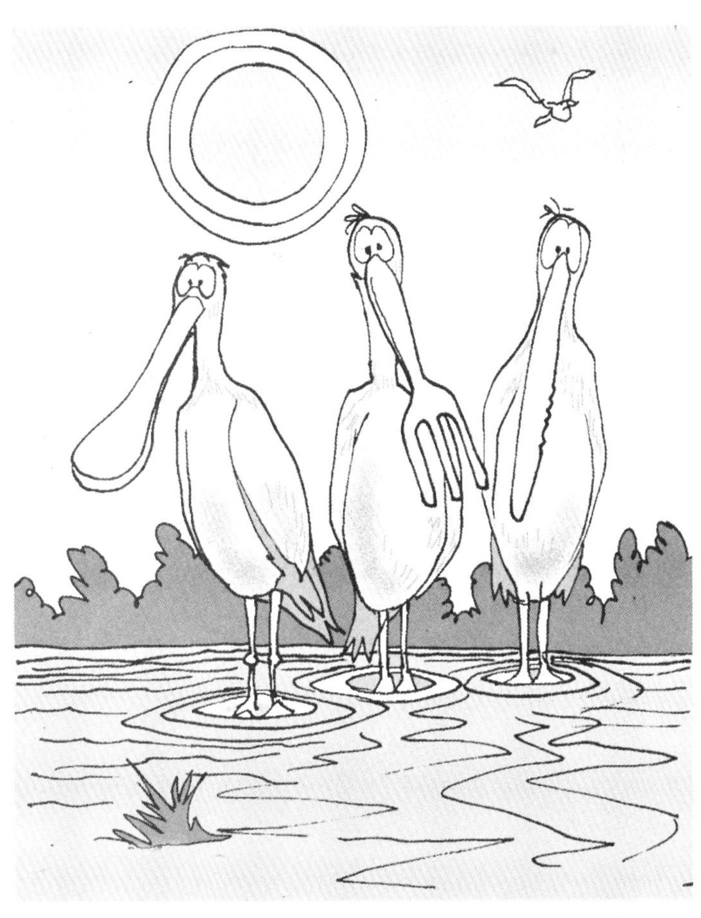

Cartoon Exercise: Getting a Bill for the Meal

We've heard of a roseate spoonbill. But, did you ever think there could also be a roseate forkbill and a roseate butter knifebill? What other roseate bills can you imagine?

Cartoon Exercise: Now That's Service!

Can you imagine going to the fruit tree of your choice and pouring yourself a fresh glass of juice? What is your favorite fruit drink? What healthy fruit trees would you plant in your yard? What flavors would you mix?

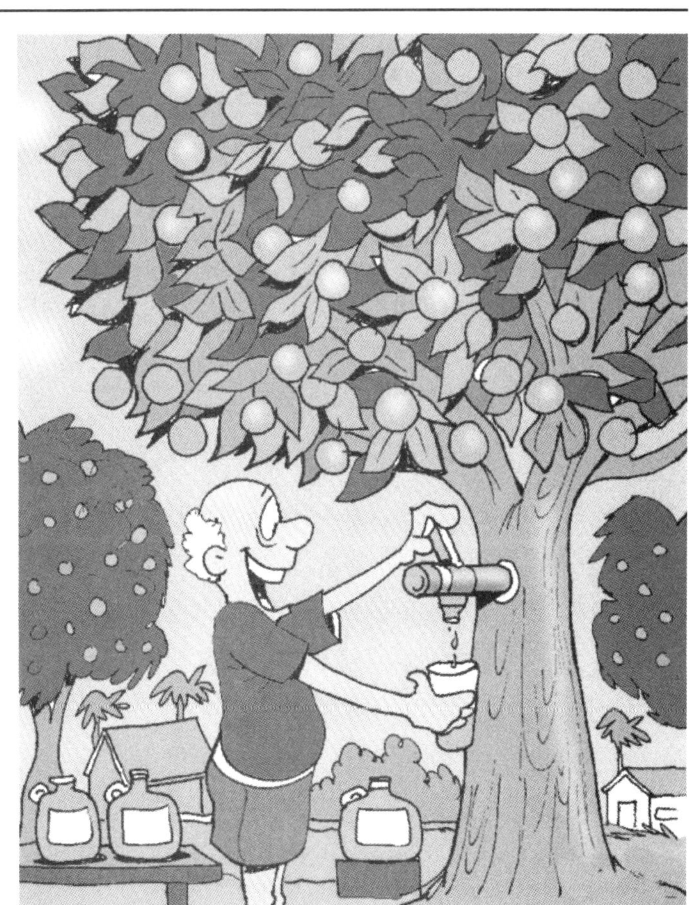

Gone Fishing

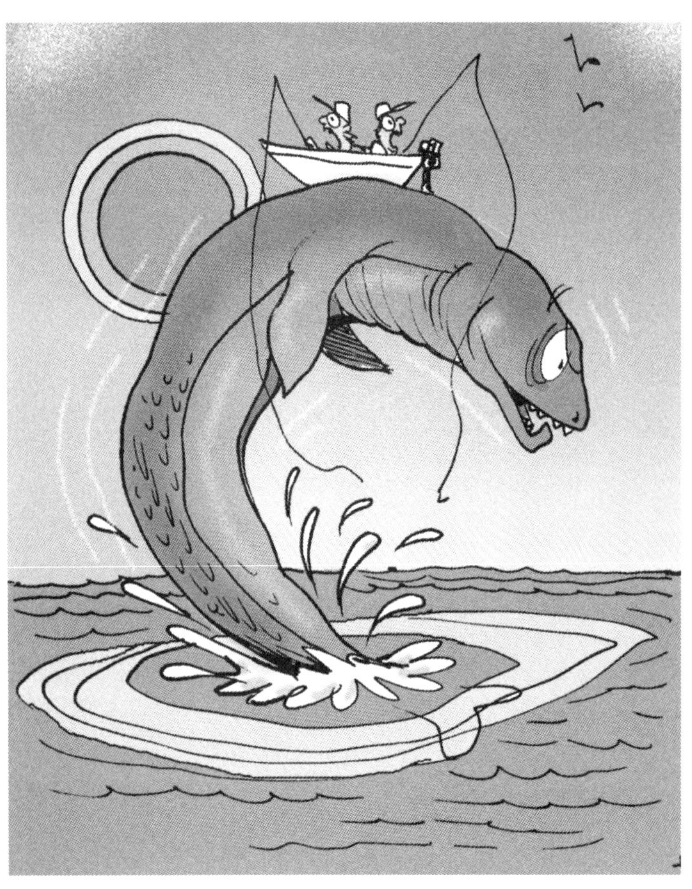

Cartoon Exercise:
A Gigantic Fish Tale

The fish to the left is the last remaining prehistoric creature from the sea. Give it a nickname. What would its dinosaur fish name be? Can you write a fish tale telling us what it was like trying to catch this monster?

Cartoon Exercise:
Florida "Fly" Fishing

What do you think this "fly" fisherman will catch in his nets today? Only fish?

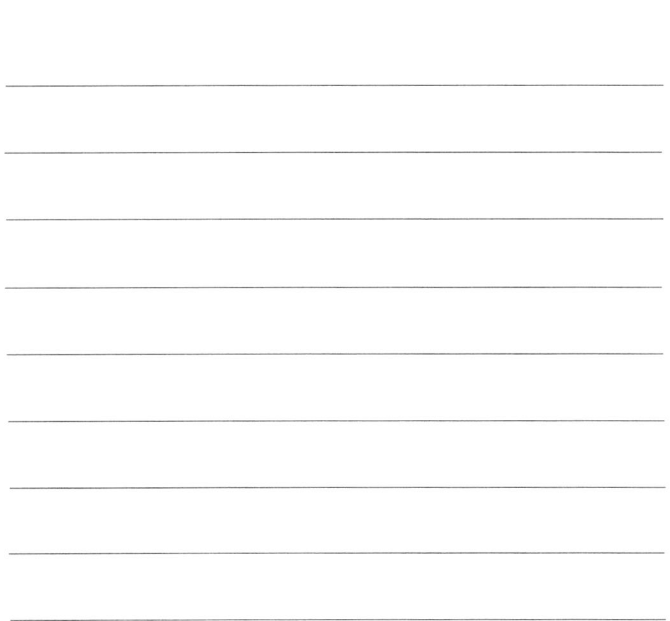

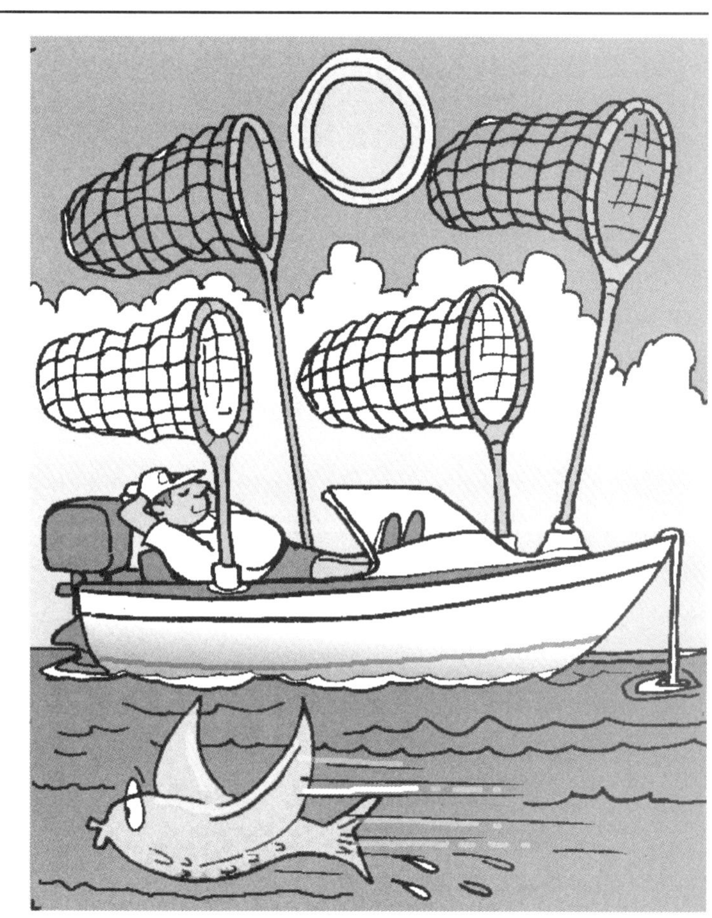

Something's Fishy

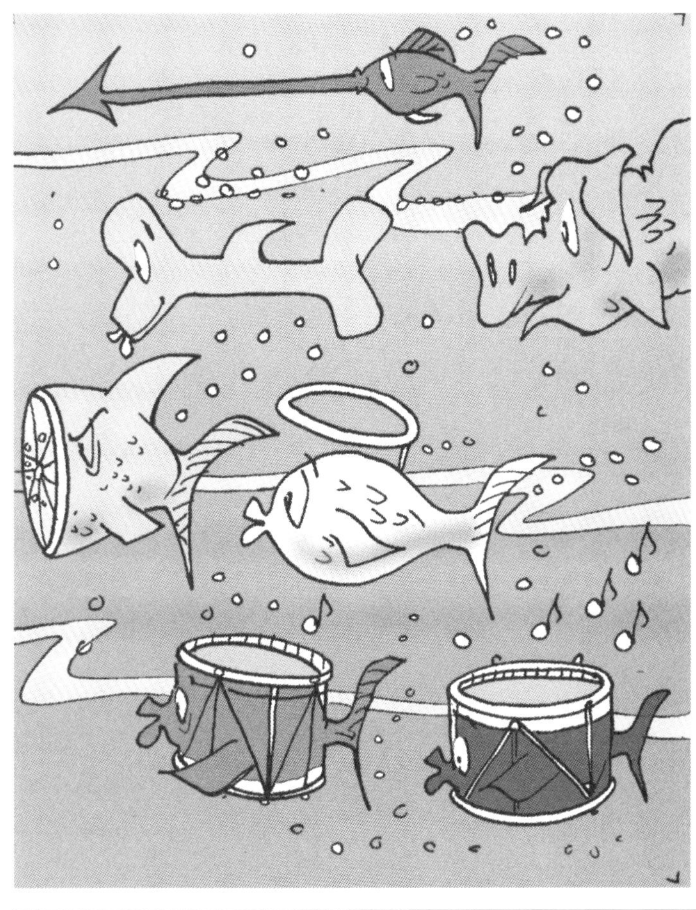

Cartoon Exercise:
Funny named fish

Can you name the different kinds of fish in the cartoon to the left? Answers are below. How many funny named fish can you think of yourself?

spearfish, bonefish, hogfish, lemon shark, angelfish, and two drumfish

Cartoon Exercise:
Let's swim to the hardware store

The fish to the right are real fish. They're just drawn in cartoon form. Can you guess their real names? Answers are below.

From left to right:
hammerhead shark, fantail fish, sawfish, shovelfish and an electric eel

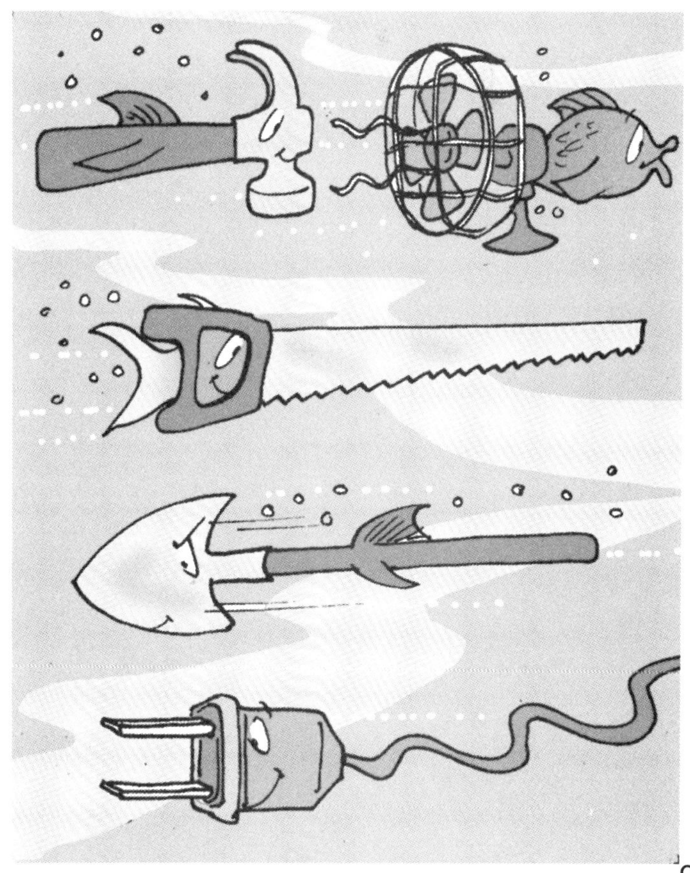

Are You Safe?

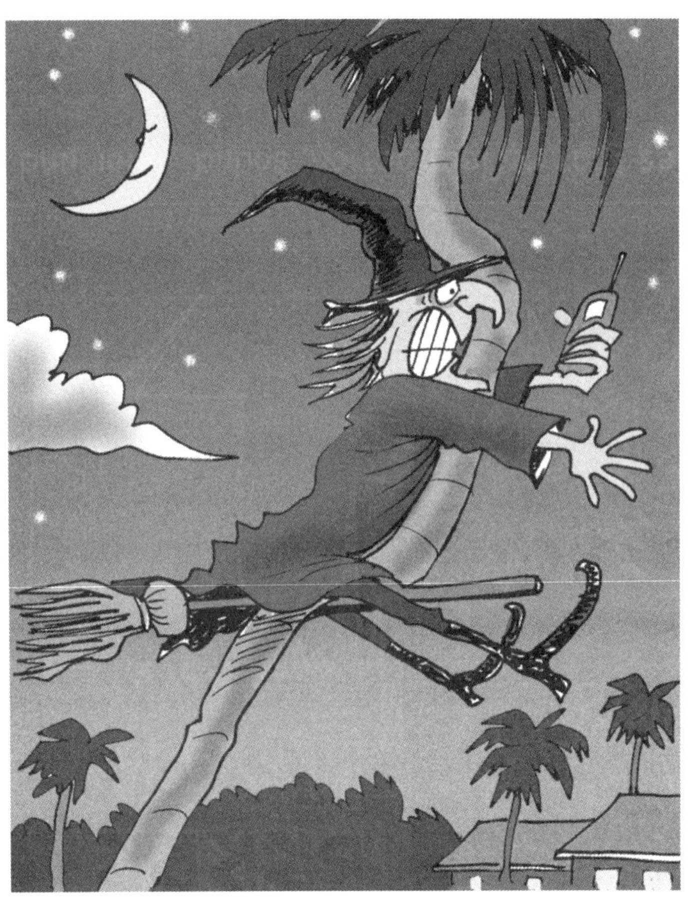

Cartoon Exercise:
Two hands on the broomstick

This witch was texting while flying. How many different ways can you be distracted while driving? Make a list below.

Cartoon Exercise:
Creepy crypt

Do you like to write scary stories? How about creating a Halloween story by describing what might happen in the cartoon to the right. Write the opening paragraph below.

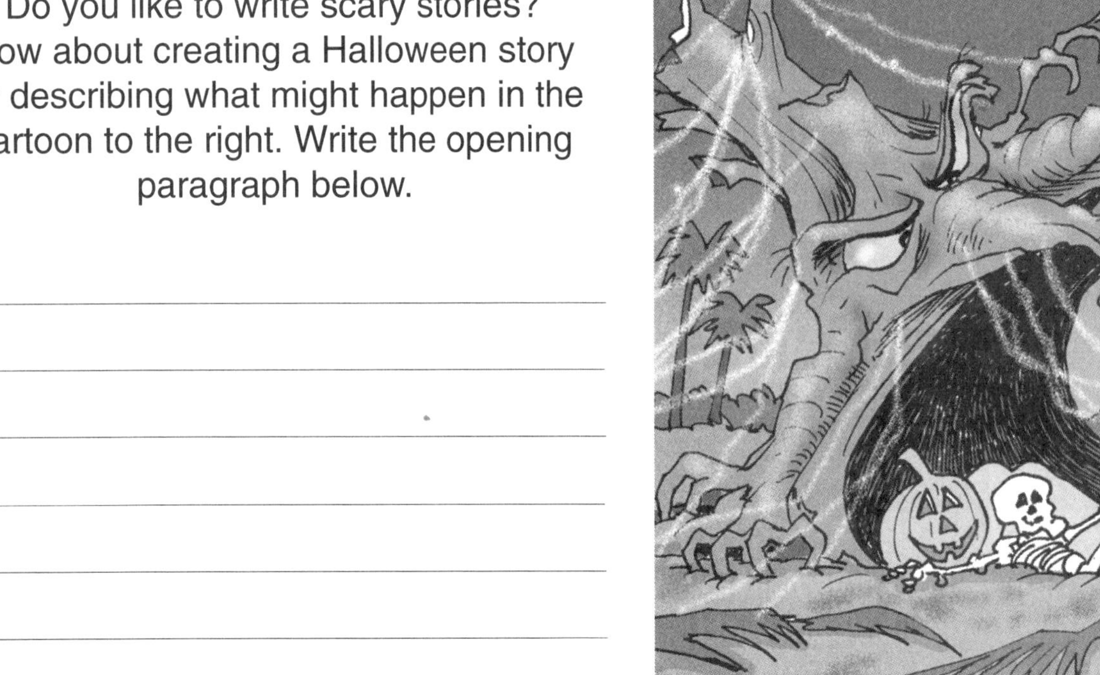

Ideas That Change Lives

Cartoon Exercise:

Thomas Edison's light bulb has changed the way people see. The shape of the light bulb has also changed. What other inventions have changed shape over the years?

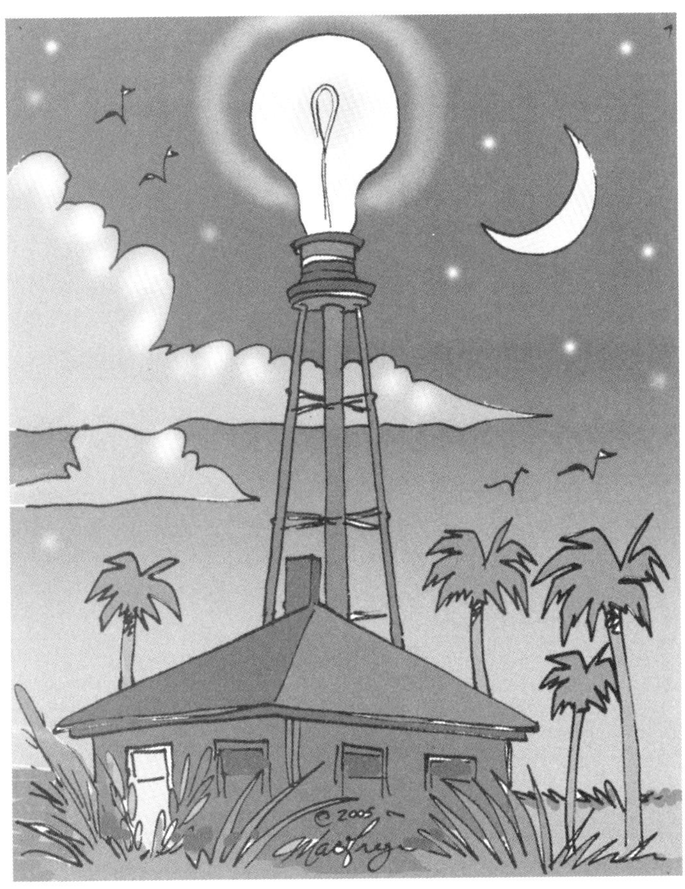

The old design

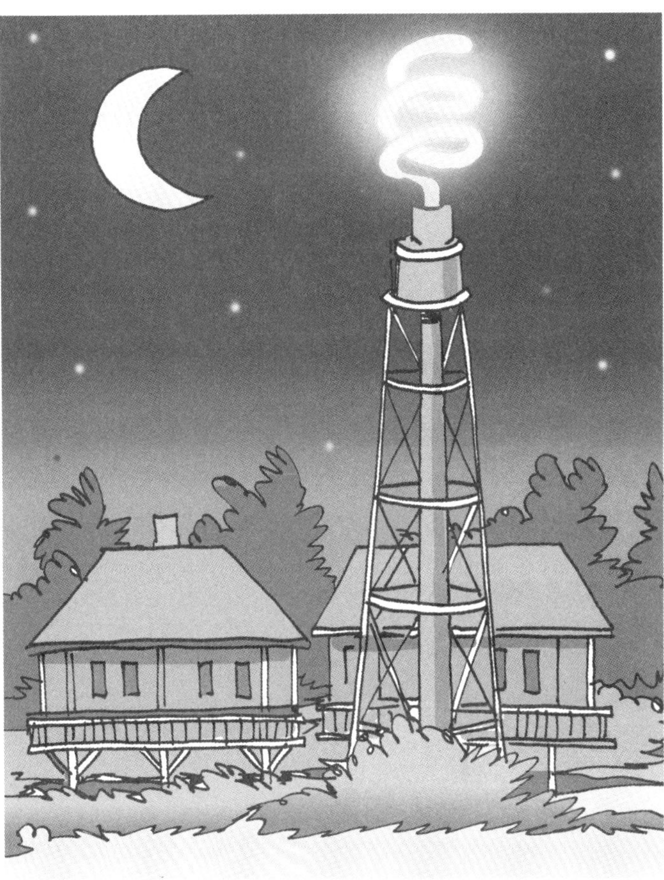

The new design

What's On The Horizon?

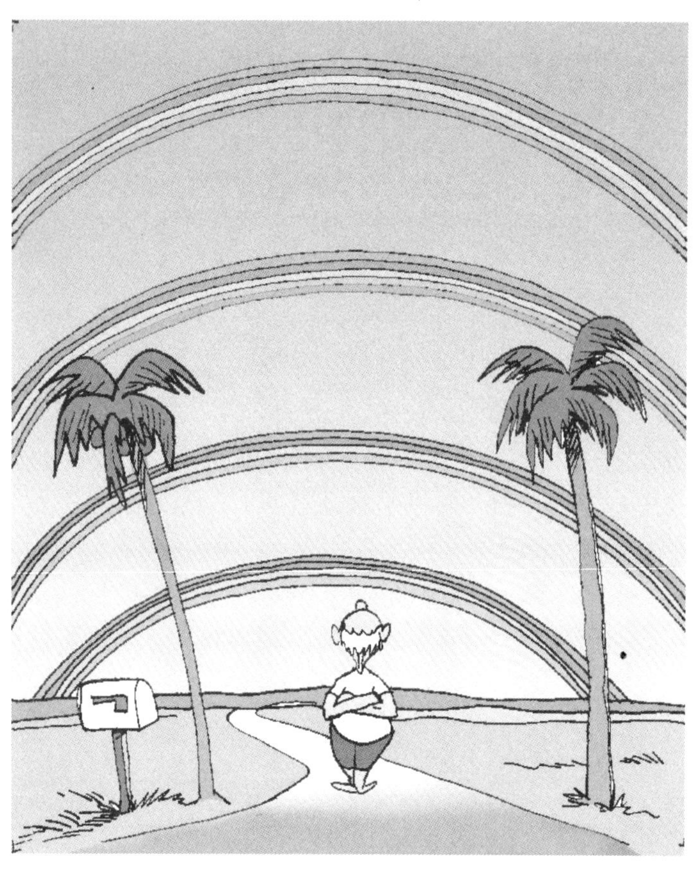

Cartoon Exercise:
Somewhere Over Four Rainbows

Have you ever wished upon a rainbow? Have you ever seen a double rainbow? Ever see a triple rainbow? Now, if you saw a quadruple rainbow what four wishes would you make?

1 ______________________

2 ______________________

3 ______________________

4 ______________________

Cartoon Exercise:
Hitching a Ride

This fisherman is being taken for a ride on his floating pontoon recliner by a large fish. Where do you think the big fish might take him?

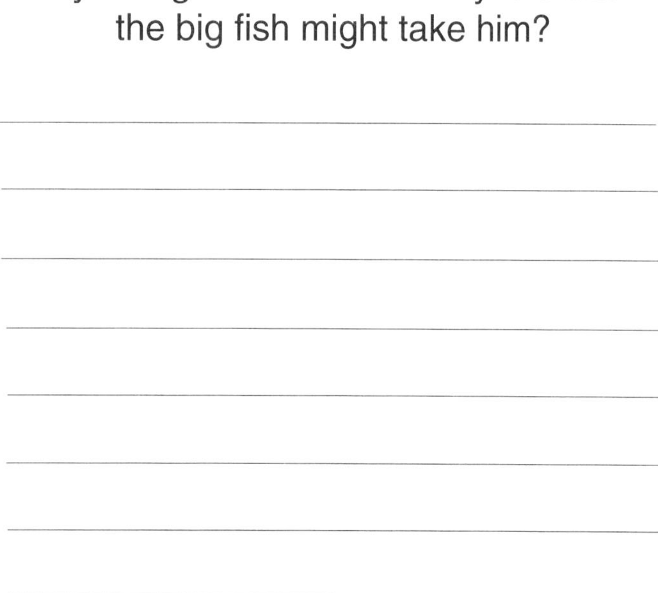

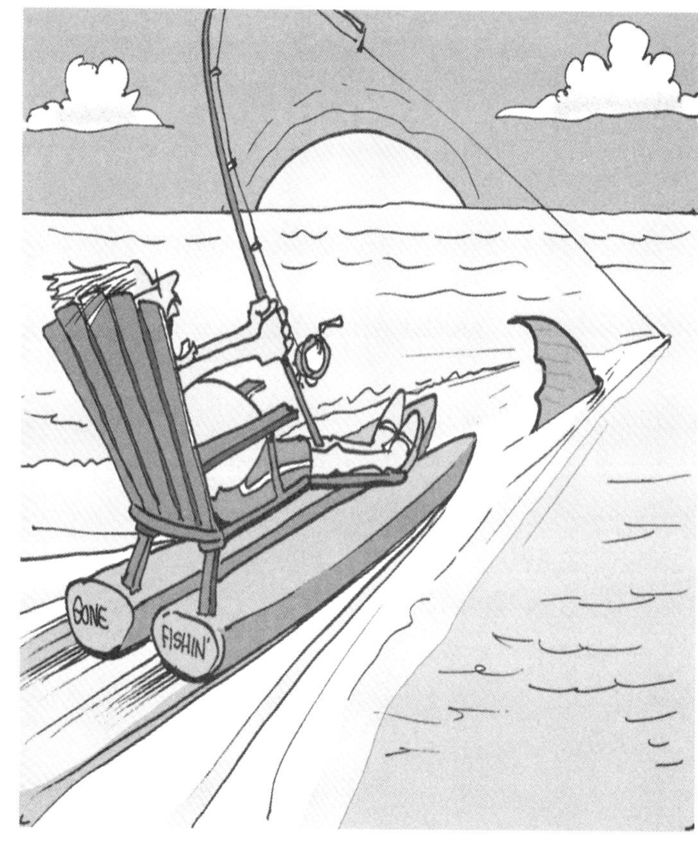

You Do The Math

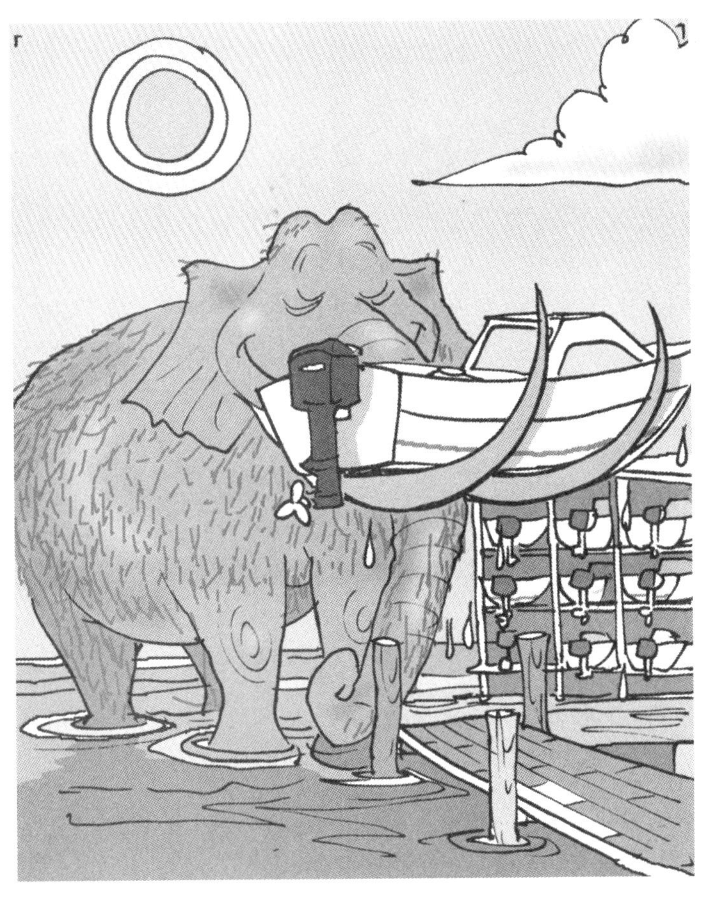

Cartoon Exercise: Mammoth Service

Who needs a forklift or a boat lift when you have a trained woolly mammoth to get your boat in and out of the water? How many tons do you think a woolly mammouth can lift?

____

(Remember 1 short ton = 2,000 lbs)

Cartoon Exercise: Backyard Tidal Wave!

See what happens. You've got to go out and cut the grass, but you can't because it's too wet. You let it go with more excuses the next week. Finally, you go out there and try to cut it - *fat chance.*

Now, figure out how many times the lawn gets cut a year? ___________

How many gallons of gas would you use in a year? _____________________

How many miles do you walk a year cutting your grass? _______________

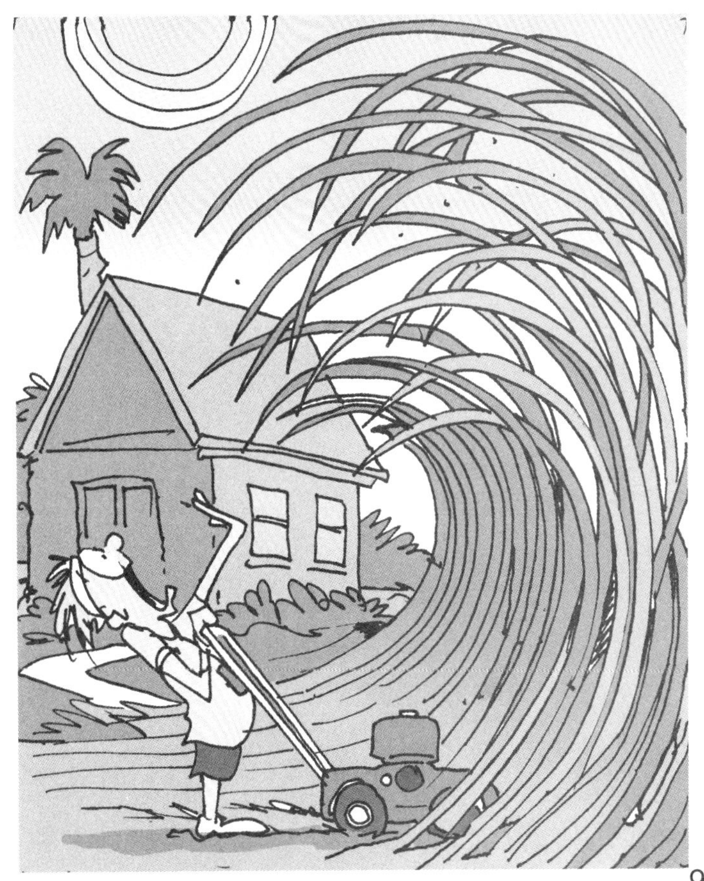

What-cha-ma-call-it?

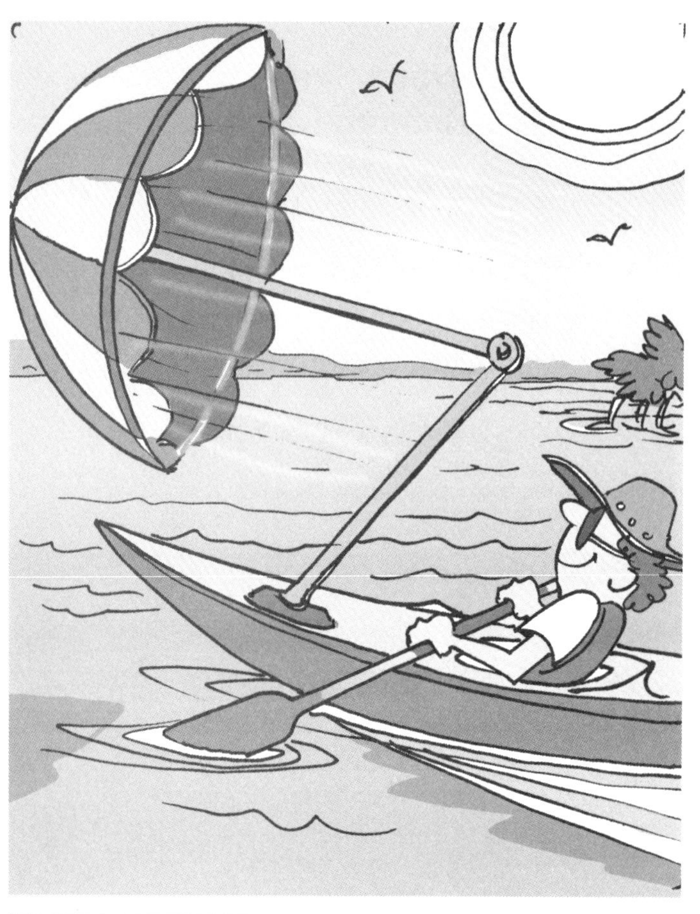

Cartoon Exercise:
How many different ways can the man on the left use his umbrella to go on his kayak trip?

Cartoon Exercise:
It flies without a sound and without a motor. It has everything but a name. What would you call this thing? Help this inventor find a name for his creation. List your ideas below...

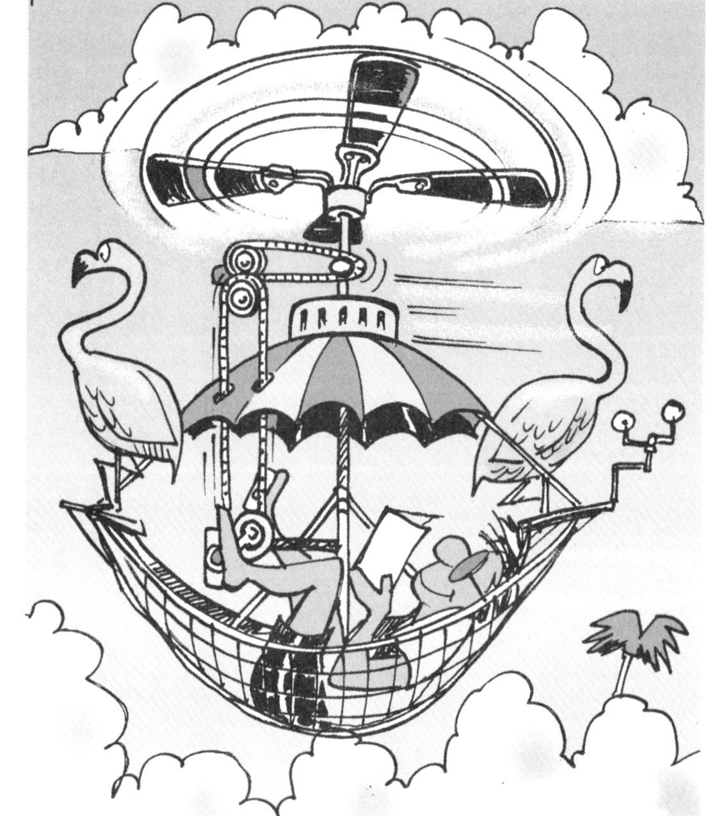

A Rube Goldberg Contraption

Cartoon Exercise:

Look at what is happening near each letter and describe how this Rube Goldberg contraption works. Can you think up your own contraption?

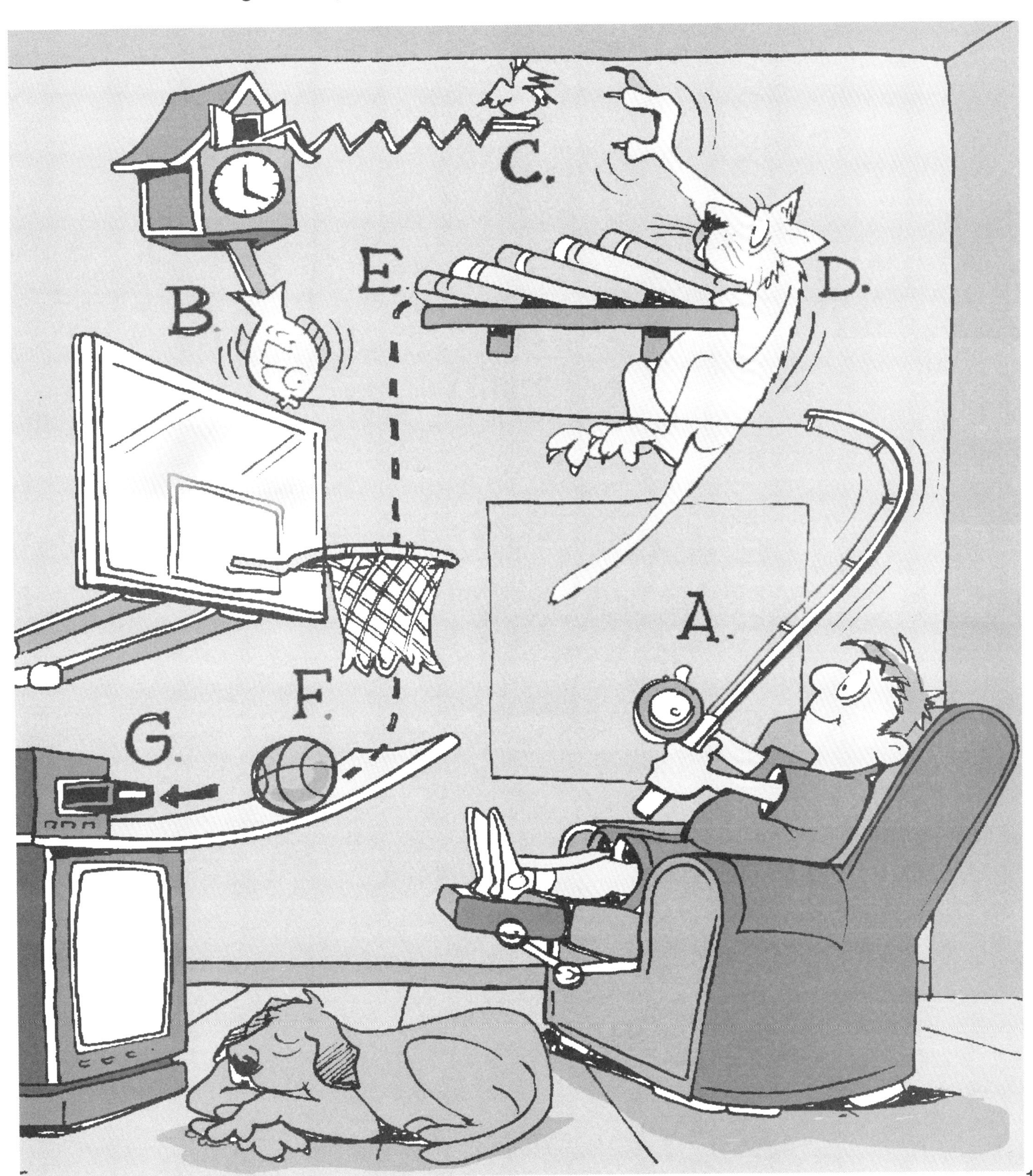

Build Your Own Castle

Cartoon exercise: Design a sand castle on the beach

Hit the beach. Bring some buckets and some pails, an assortment of shovels, plastic spoons, a plastic spray bottle and your imagination. It's time you built your own castle.

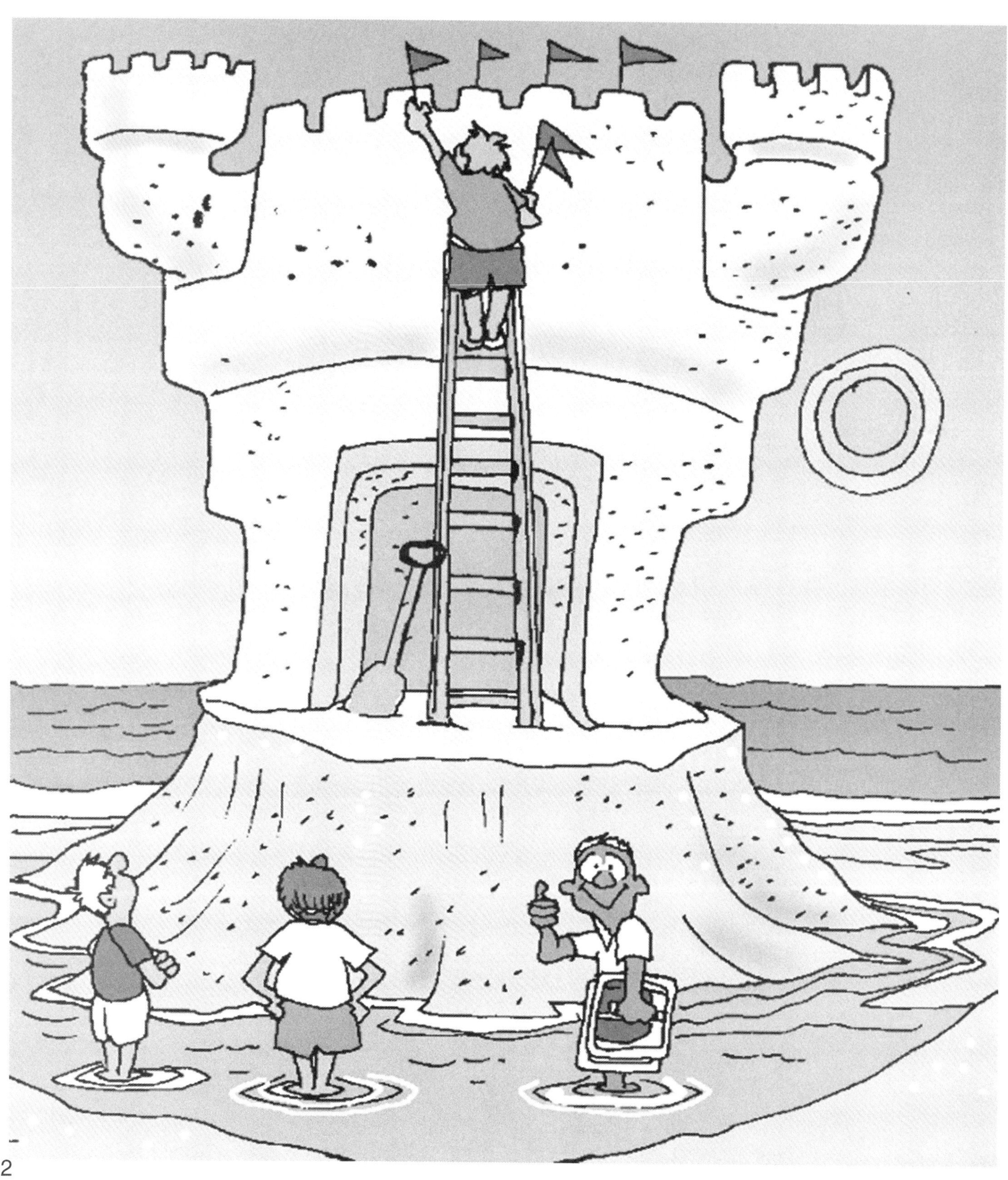

What If You Are Lost?

Cartoon Exercise:

What are you told to do when you get lost? Can you retrace your steps?
Where do you ask for help? Who do you ask for help?
How do you find your way back? Where is your central meeting place?

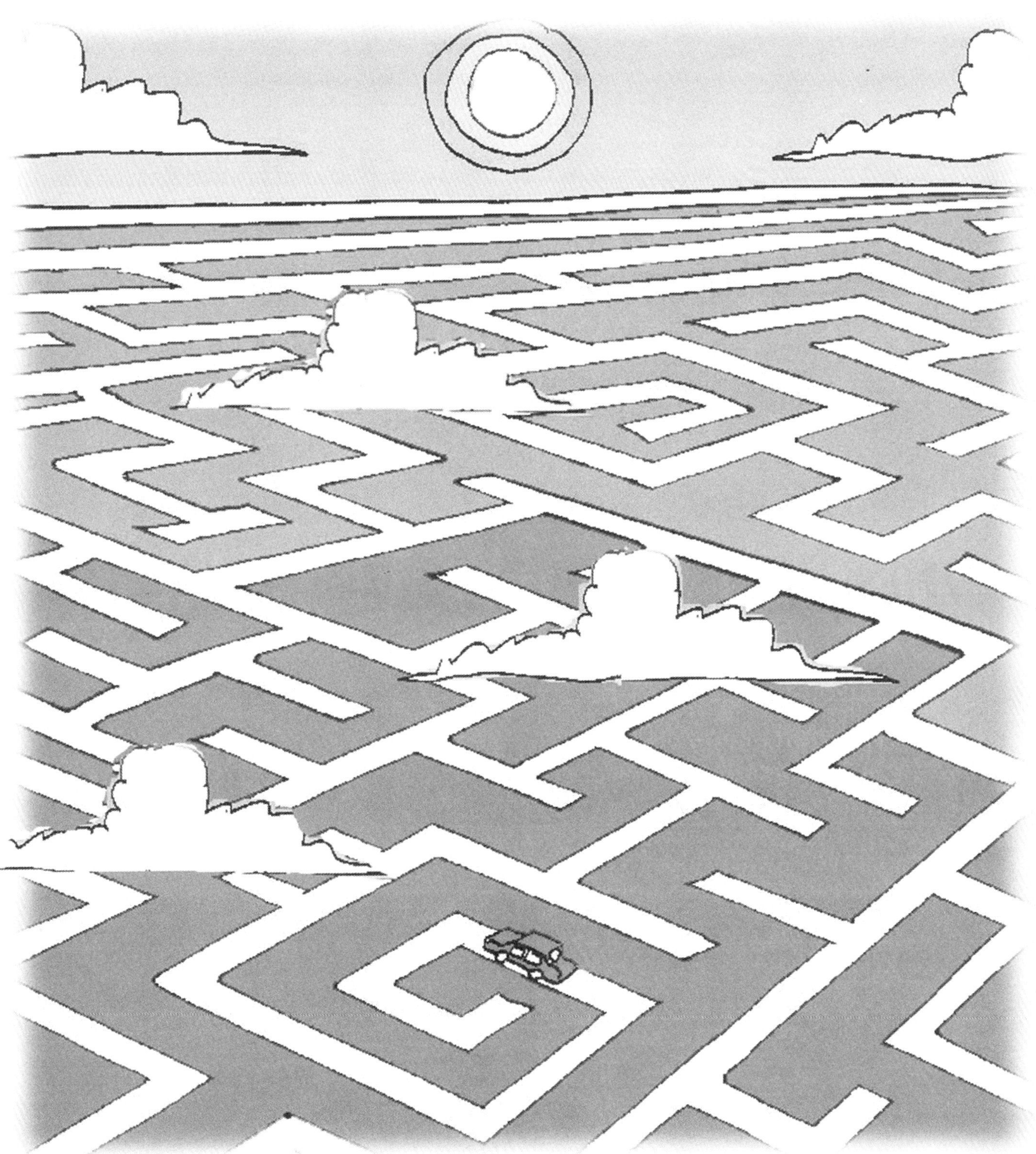

Color Your World

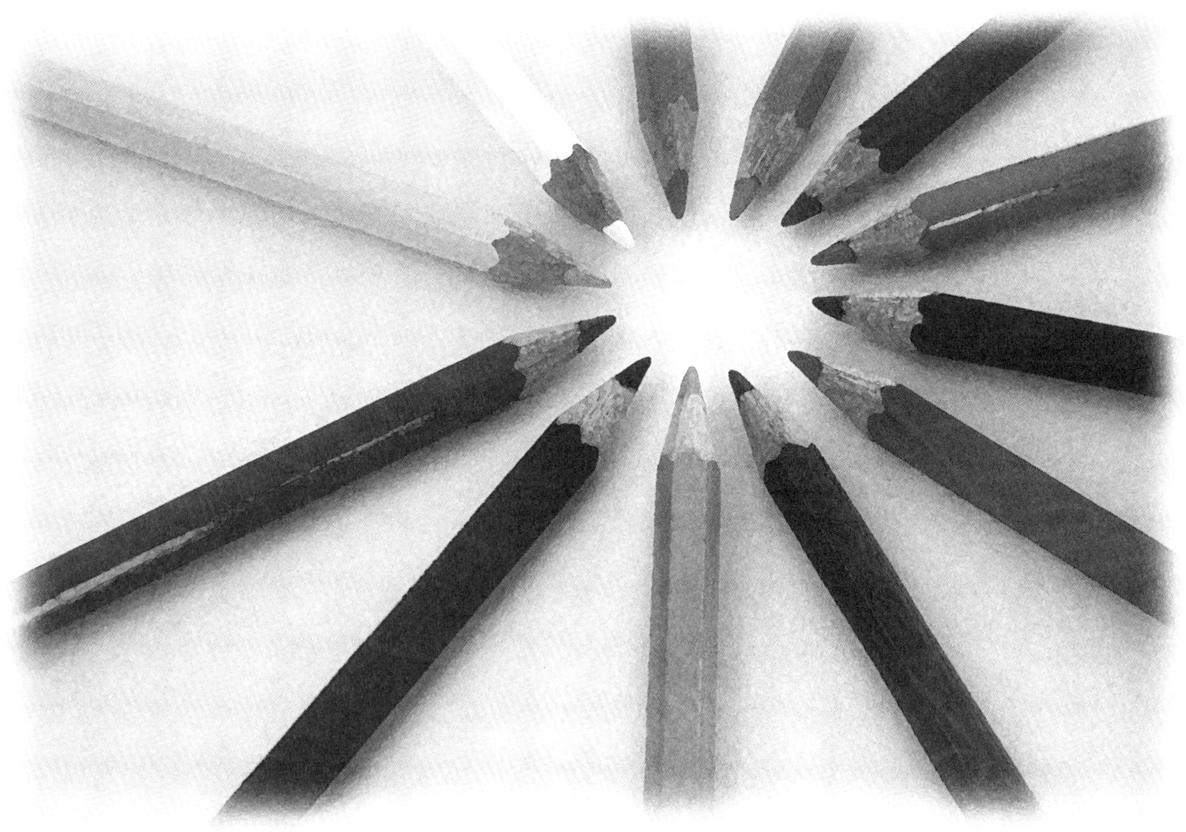

"The whole world, as we experience it visually, comes to us through the mystic realm of color."

- Hans Hofmann

Oh, The Wildlife You'll See...

Coloring Exercise:

Color this cartoon. This couple is about to go on a nature walk. You will guide them. What birds and animals will you see? Draw a map on the sign below to guide our tourists.

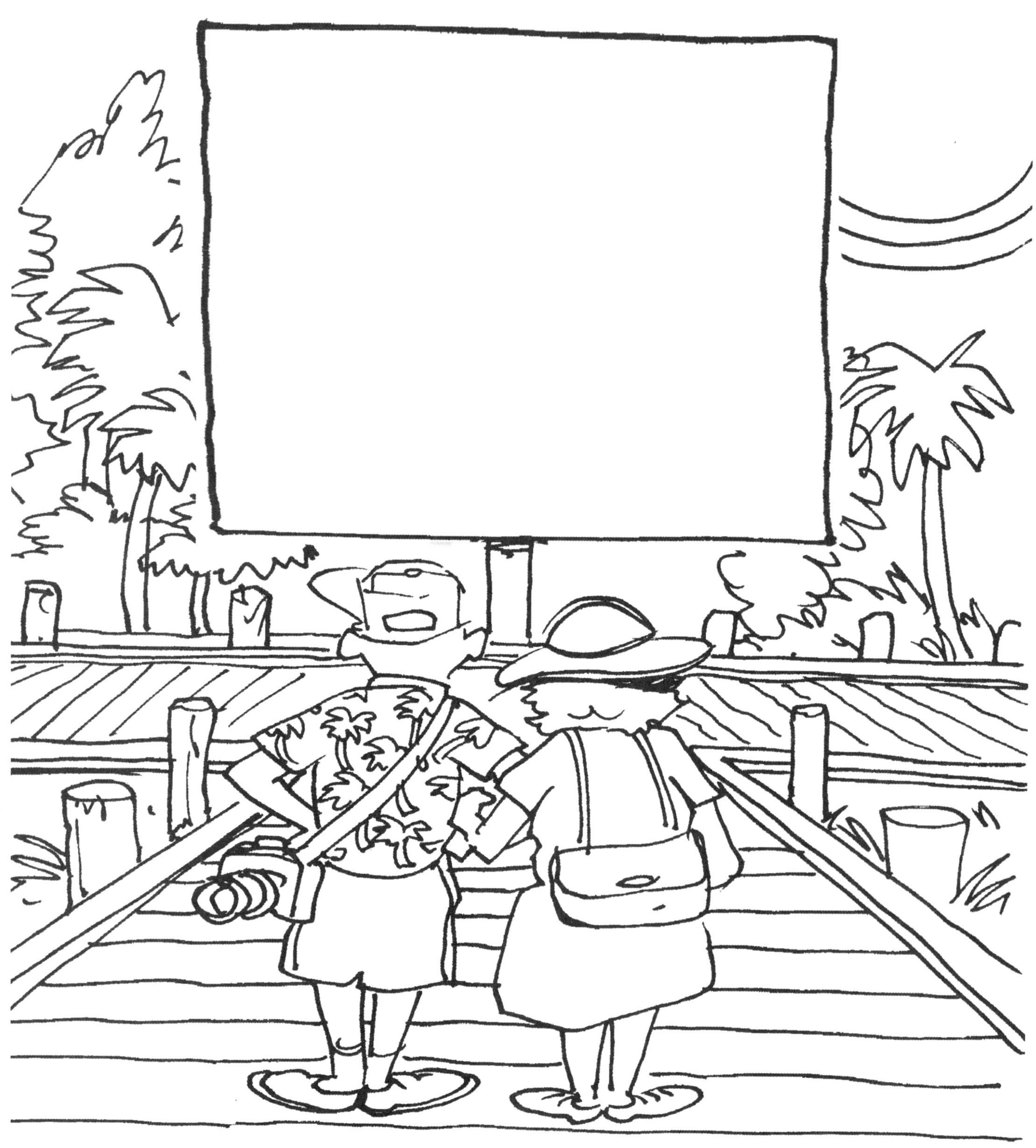

...Or Won't See

Coloring Exercise:

Color this cartoon. Can you find the Florida panther? The photographer can't. The Florida panther is endangered. Make a list of endangered animals in your state. How many are there?

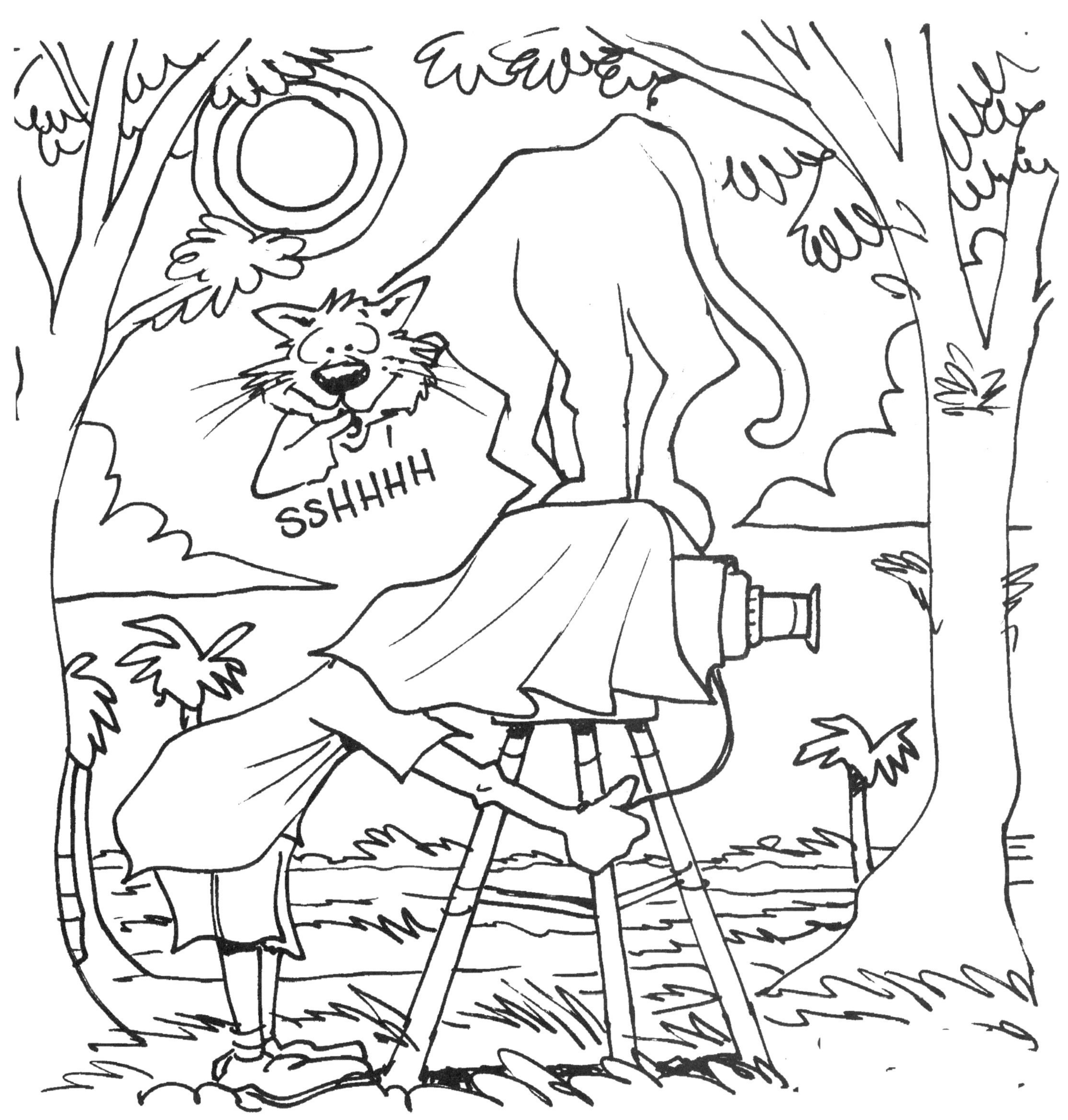

Take On A New Sport

Coloring Exercise:

Color this cartoon. Ever play jet ski polo? Probably not, it doesn't exist - at least not yet. Can you invent five new games or sports? What would they be?

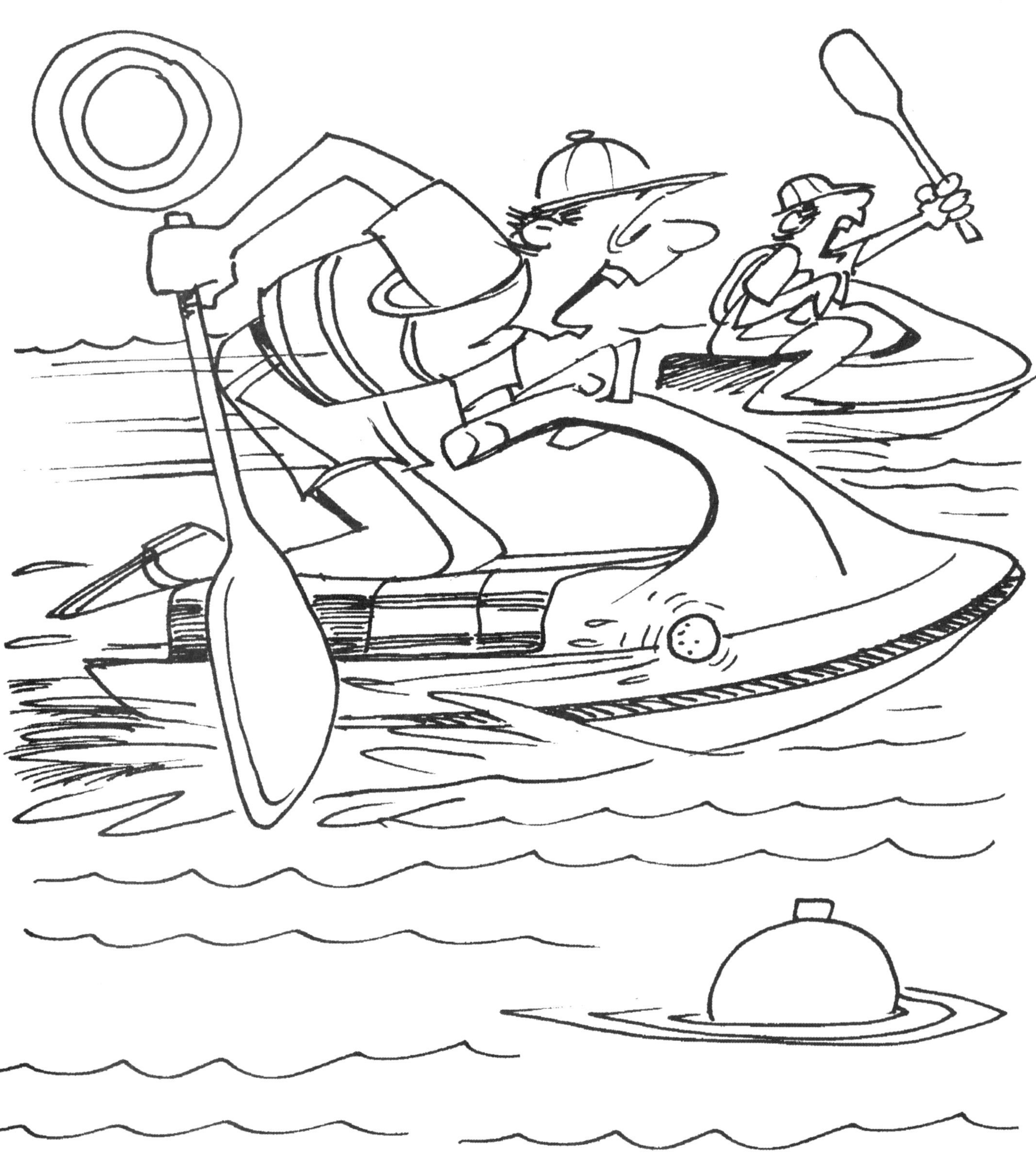

Pedal Power

Coloring Exercise:

Color this cartoon. Hey, that's not fair. Three people are doing all the pedaling and three are getting a free ride. When you are on your bike remember to hold on with both hands, put your feet on the pedals and wear your helmet!

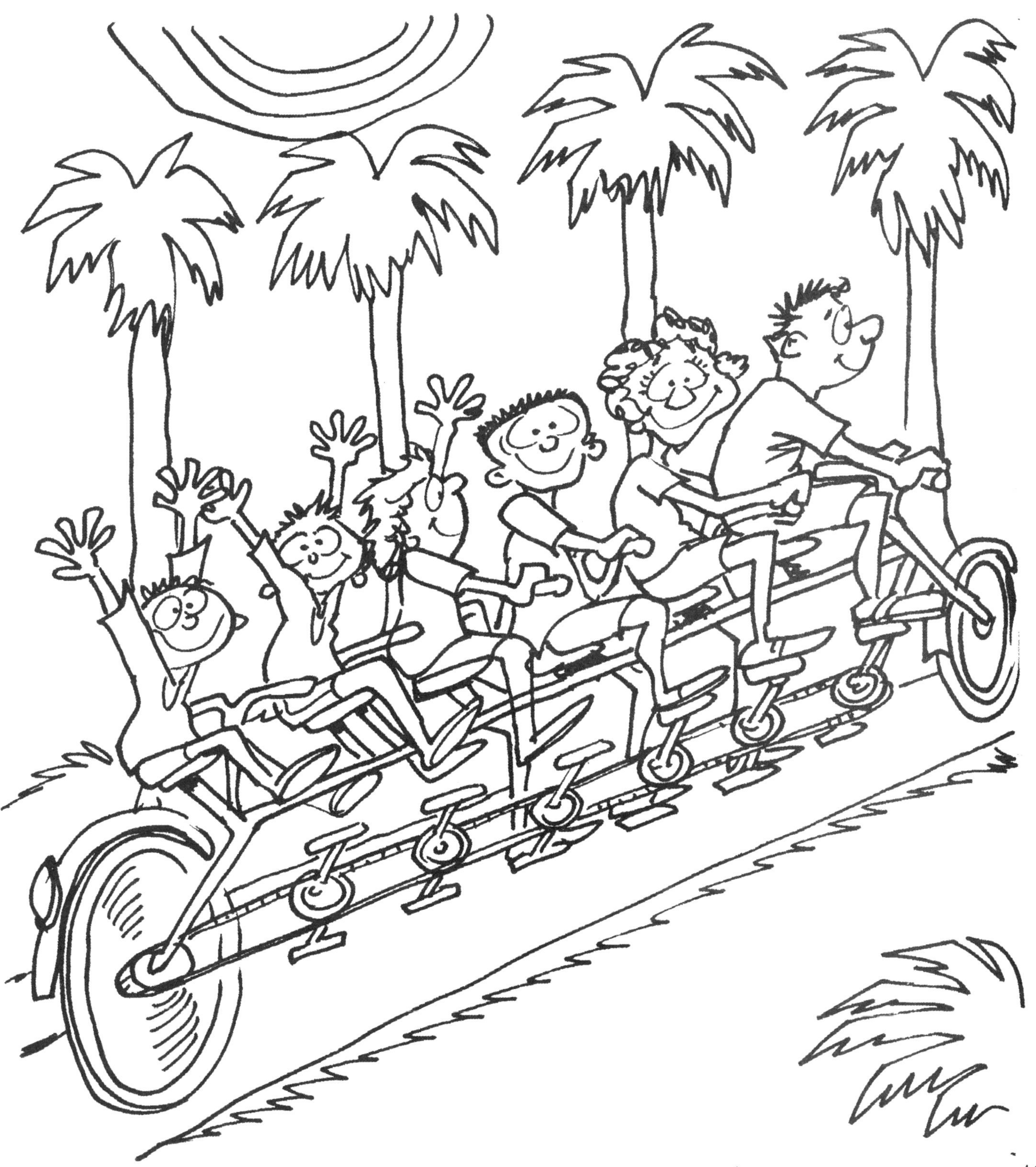

The Sky Is Full of Flavors

Coloring Exercise:

What is your favorite flavor? What if all the clouds in the sky could be a different fruit? Which one would you reach for? Now, color this cartoon. You can taste the flavors of the clouds by eating different flavored candies while you draw. Try it!

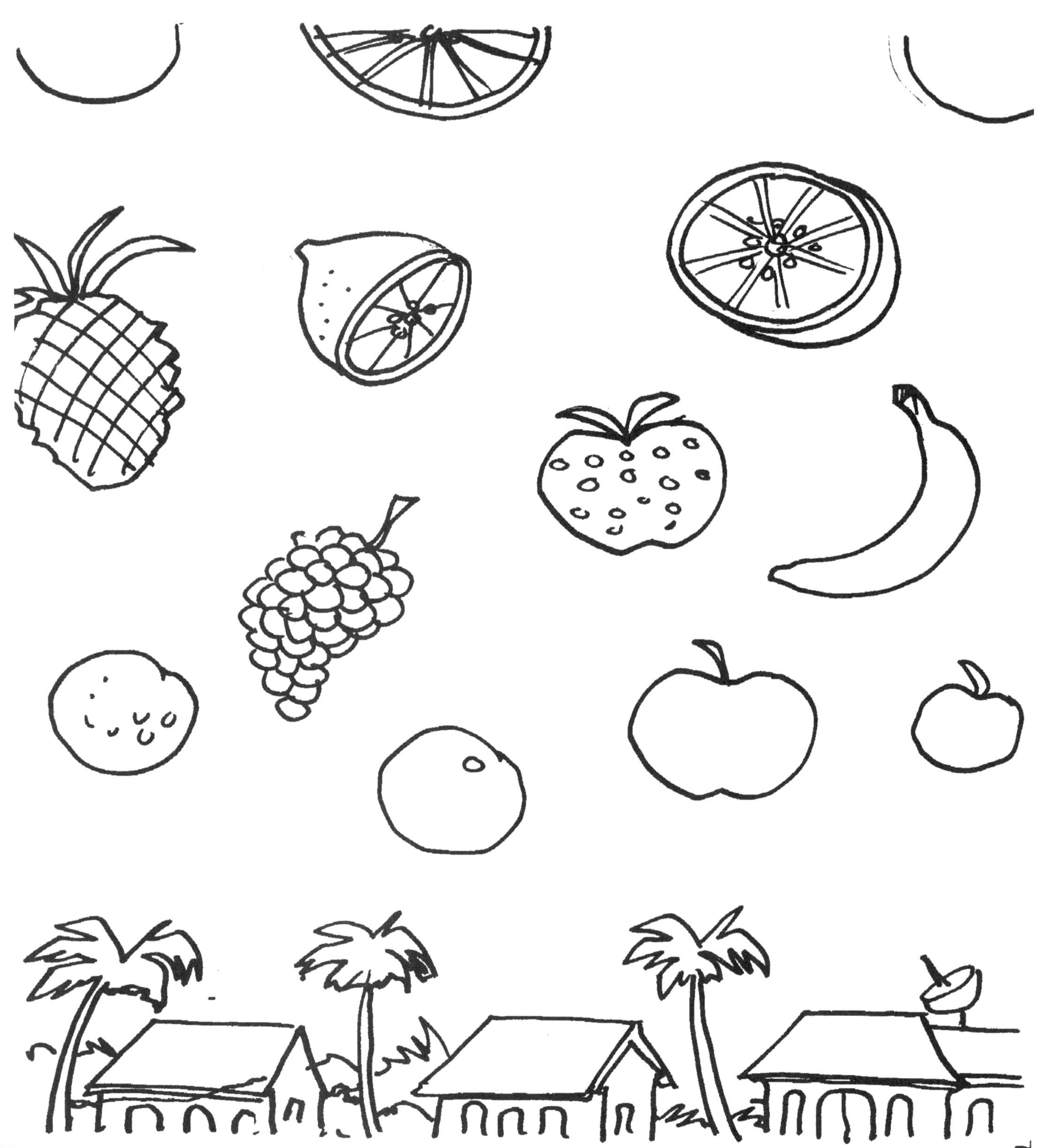

Magic Pumpkin Palms

Coloring Exercise:

Color these pumpkin palms. What grows on trees? Ever see a magic pumpkin palm? So what grows on your make-believe trees? Make a list.

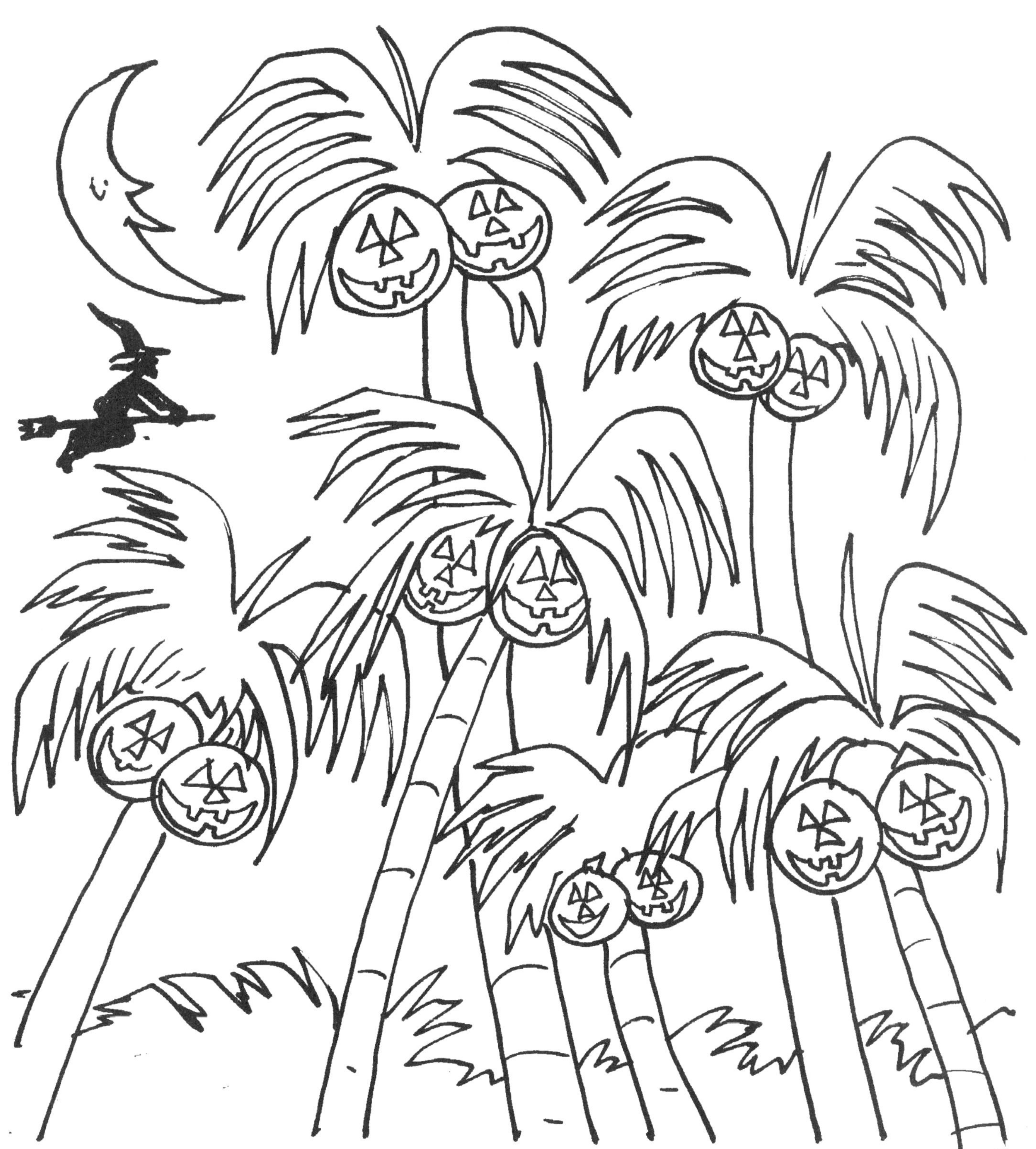

Let's Ride The Waterslide!

Coloring Exercise:

Color this cartoon. Can you imagine having your own waterslide in the backyard of your house? How fun would that be?

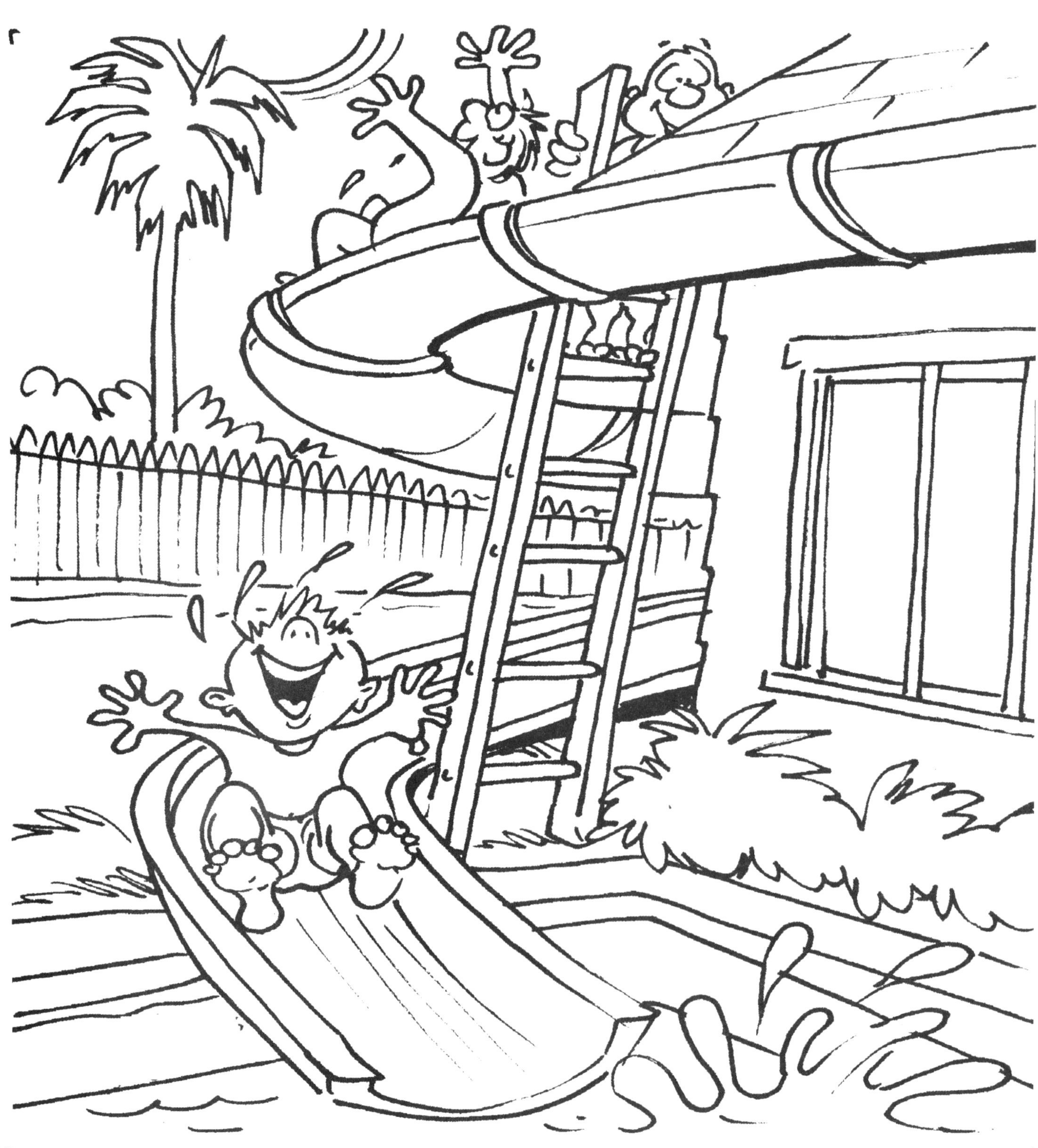

Raining Cats and Dogs!

Coloring Exercise:

Wow! It's pouring rain! It's raining so hard, it's raining cats and dogs! Hey, do you have a dog or cat at home? What is its name? As you color the cartoon below think of as many names as you can for all the dogs and cats in the rainstorm.

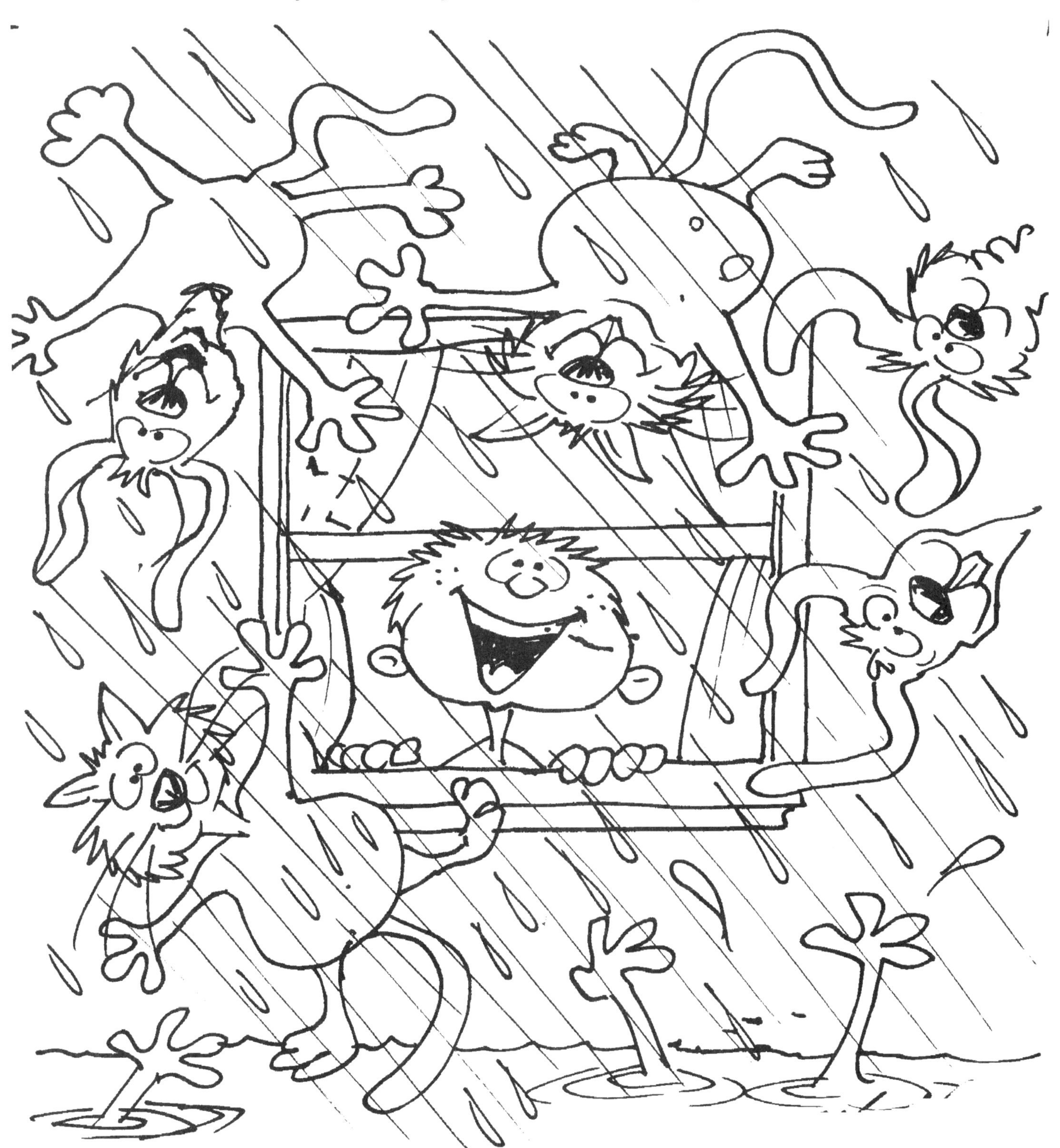

Wow! That's Huge! What Is It?

Coloring Exercise:

Color this cartoon. Dad has a lot of unused duct tape lying around the house, so you decide to make the biggest duct tape ball in the world. How tall would it be? What is it's circumference? How many miles of tape did you use? Wow!

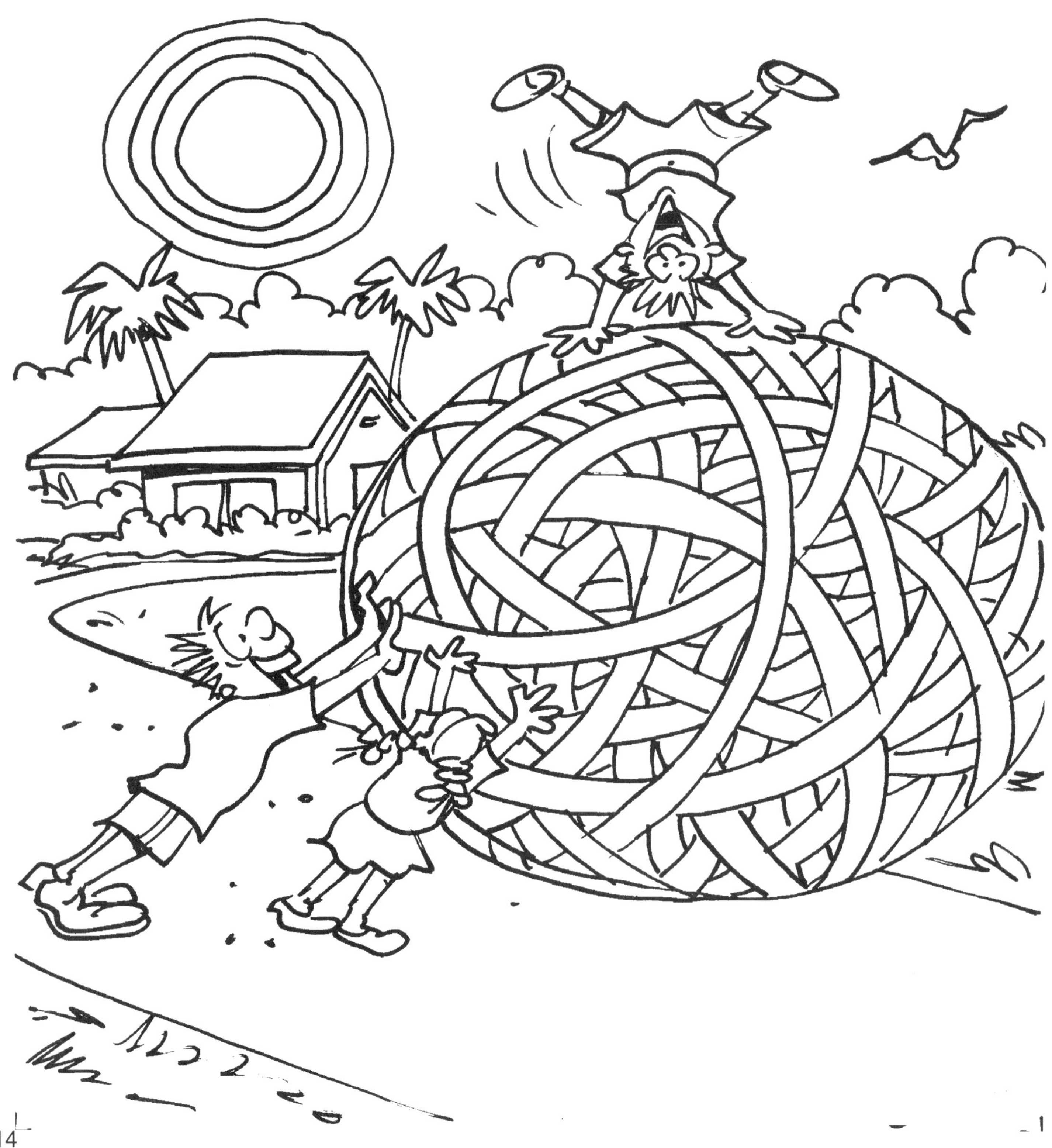

Off To The Turtle Races!

Coloring Exercise:

Color this cartoon. Give each turtle a racing name and try and figure out which one will cross the finish line first. What other slow animals might go faster if they could race with wheels attached to them?

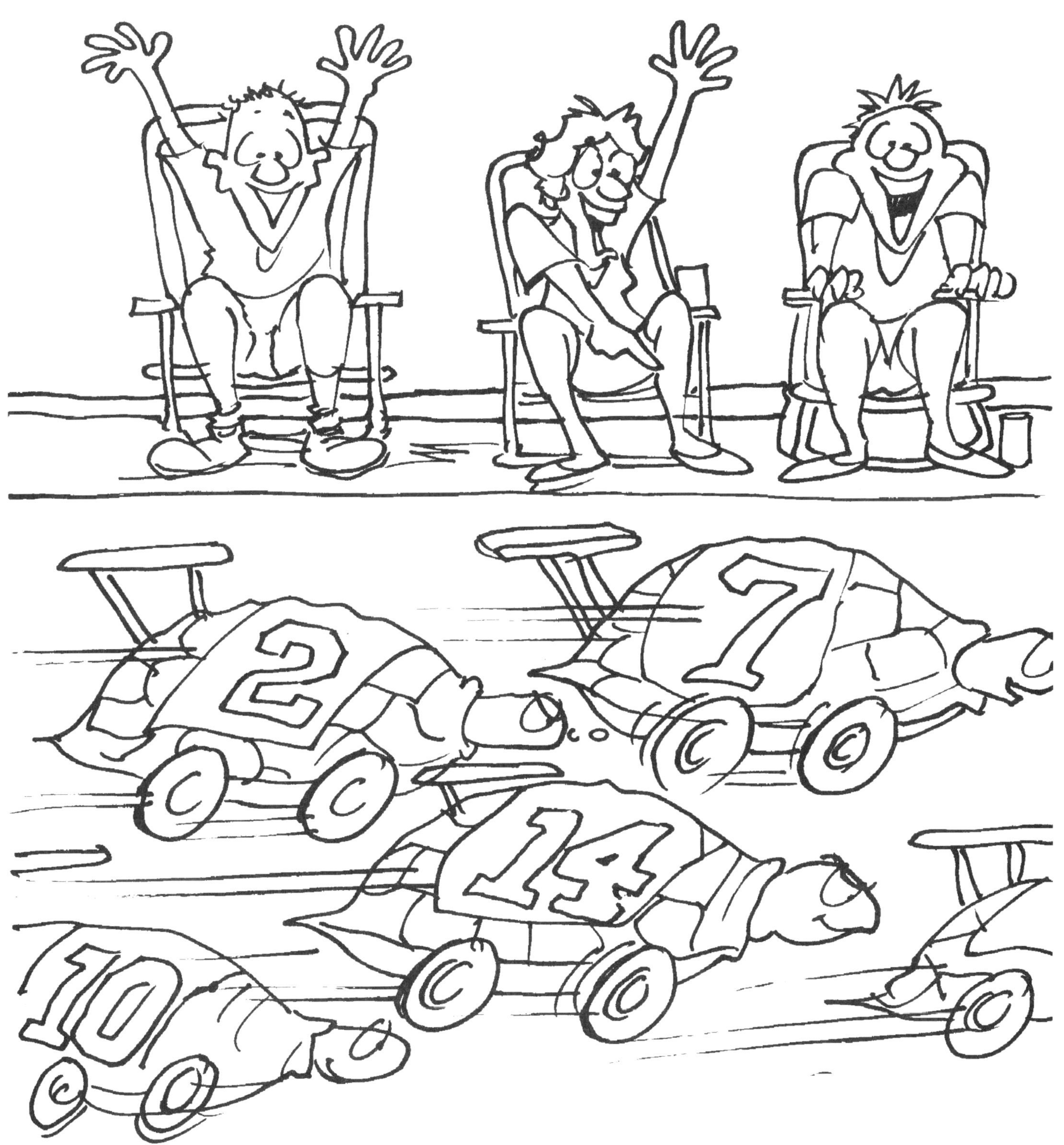

Pirate Treasure

Coloring Exercise:

Color this cartoon. This pirate is finding treasures on the beach with a metal detector. What do you think he might find? Have you ever found treasure on the beach?

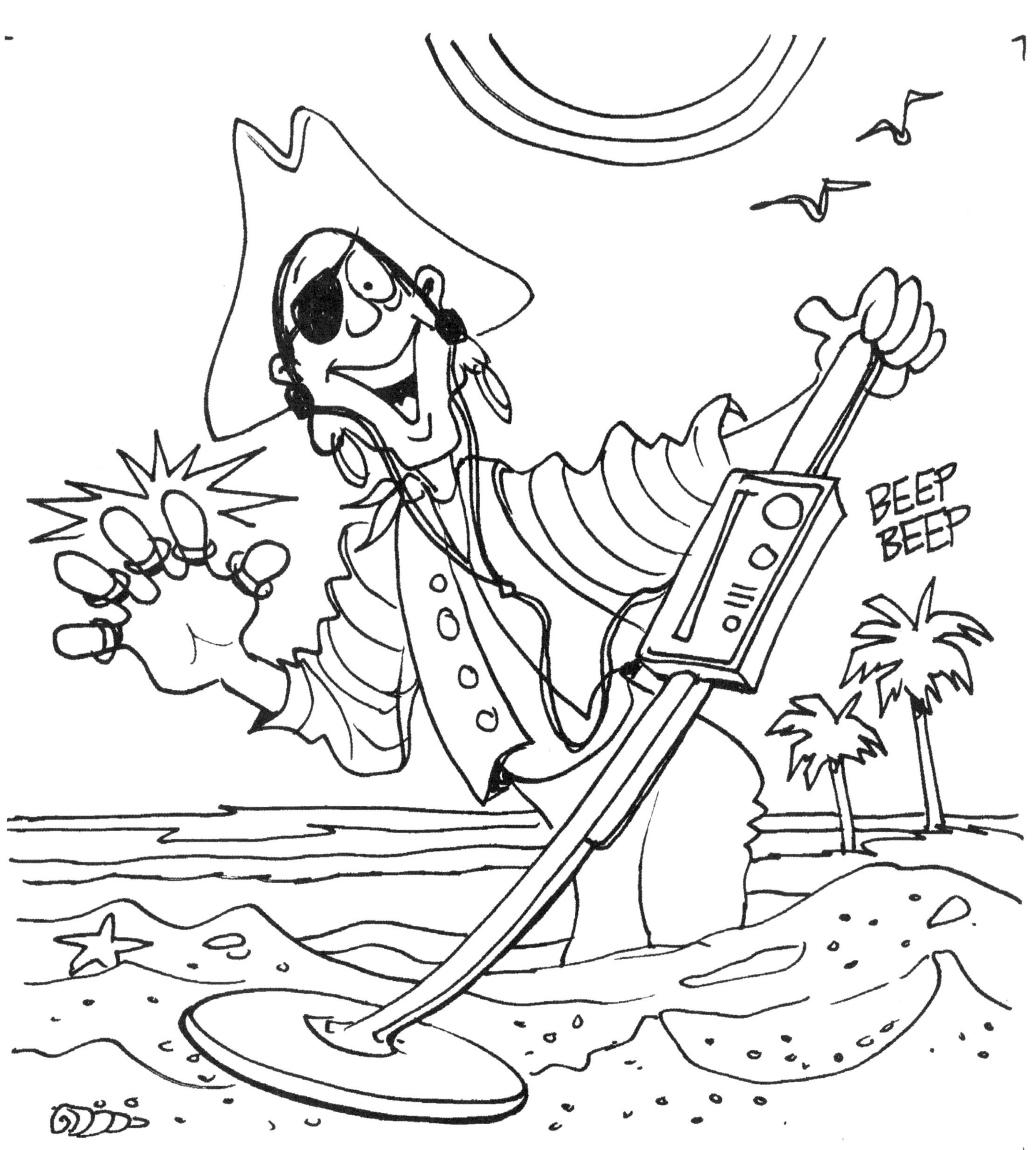

Walk The Plank, Matey

Coloring Exercise:

Color this cartoon. What color would you use for the ship?
The inner tube? The pirate flag? The cannons?
Speaking of cannons, have you ever done a cannonball, jumping off a pirate ship?
What other kinds of jumps might you do off a pirate ship diving board?

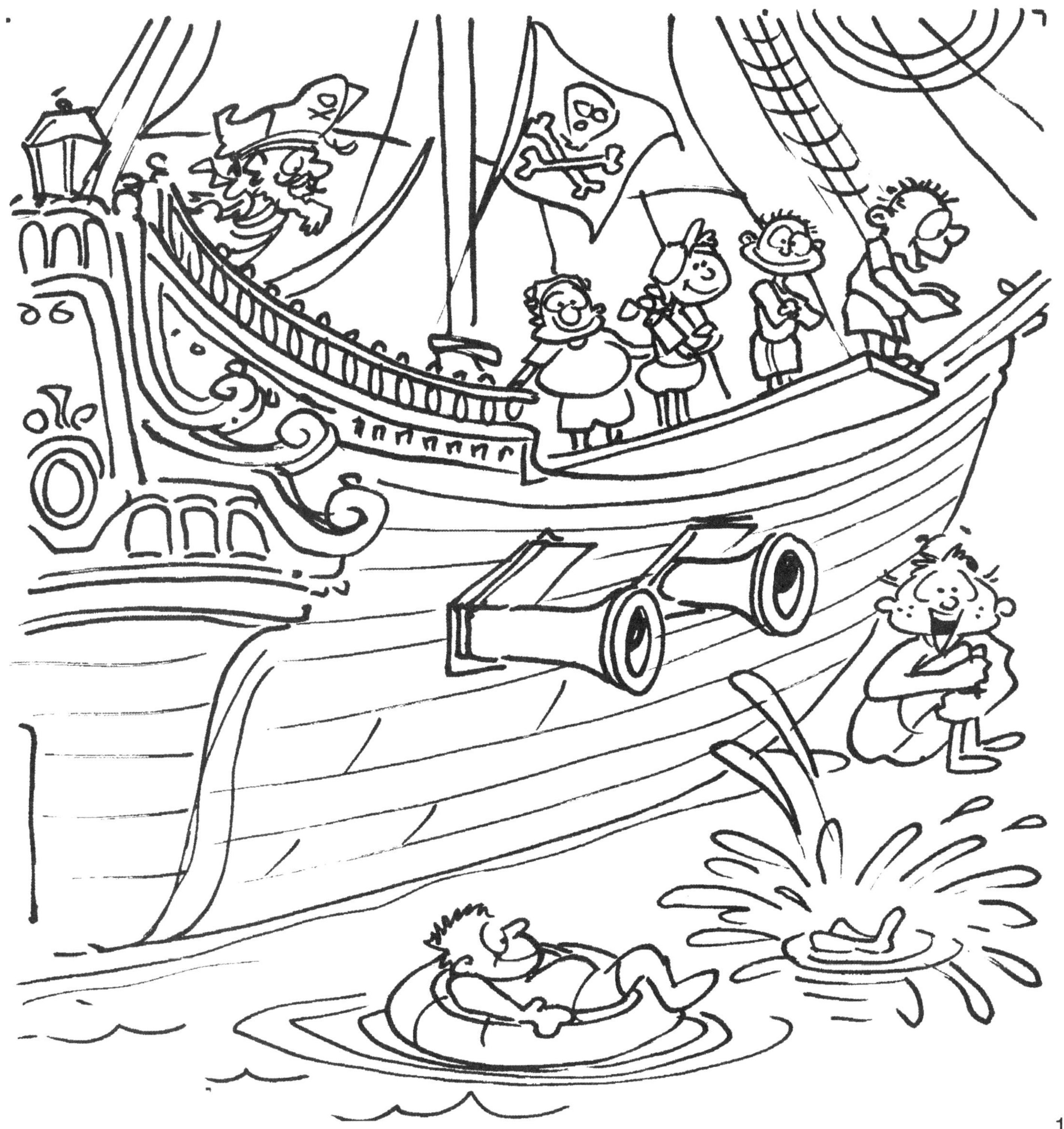

Aye Eye Mate!

Coloring Exercise:

Color this cartoon. It looks like this pirate has spotted something in the distance. What do you think he sees? Come up with five things that he might spot out in the water.

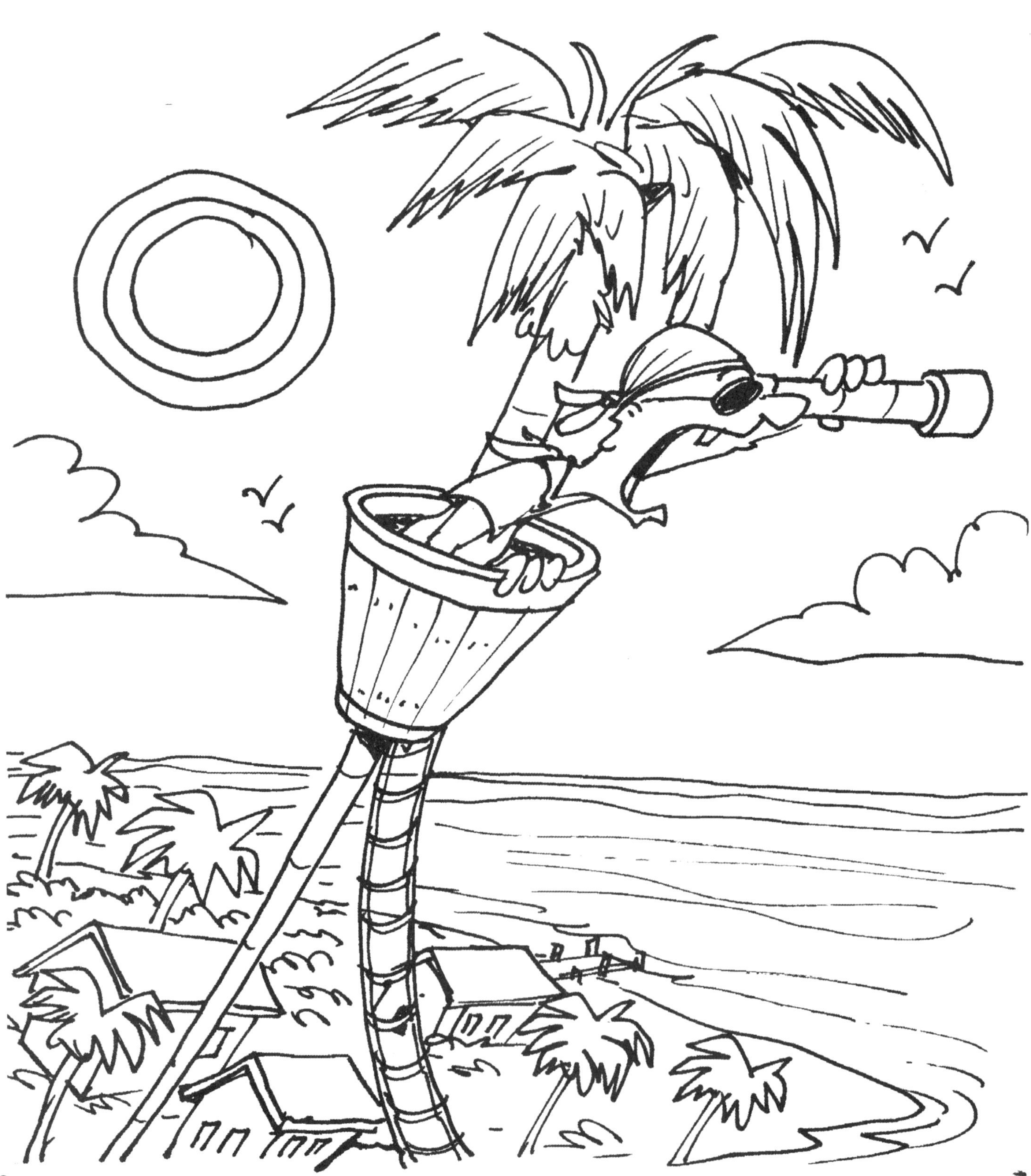

A Parade Of Pirate Ships

Coloring Exercise:

Color this cartoon. Is it possible the pirate to the left saw all these ships coming through the drawbridge? There are nine ships. Can you give each ship a name?

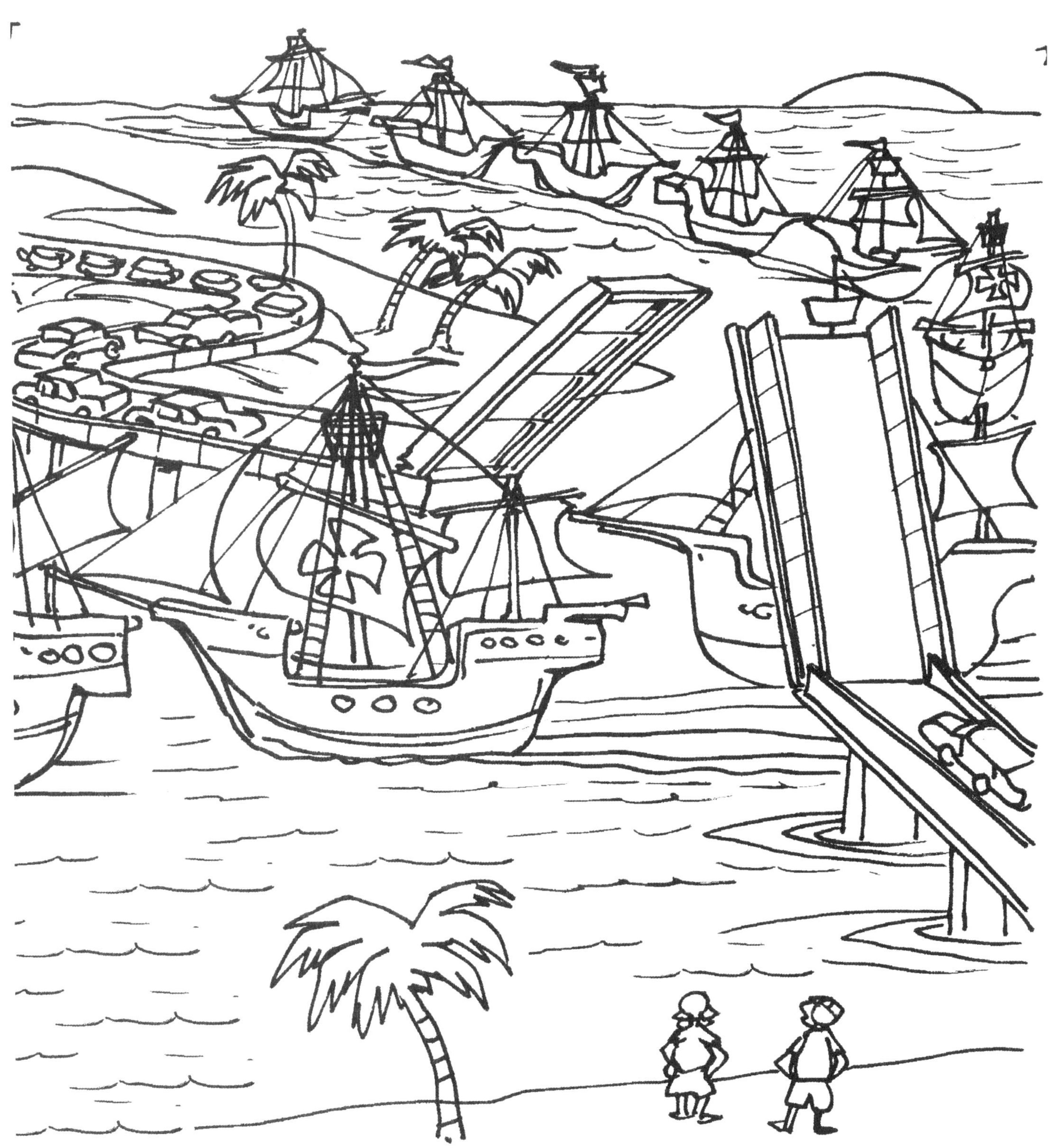

Taking A Dip In A Cool Pool

Coloring Exercise:

Color this cartoon. This guy is having a hard time getting into the pool.
How cold do you think the water is?
What temperature do you think is too cold to go in the pool?

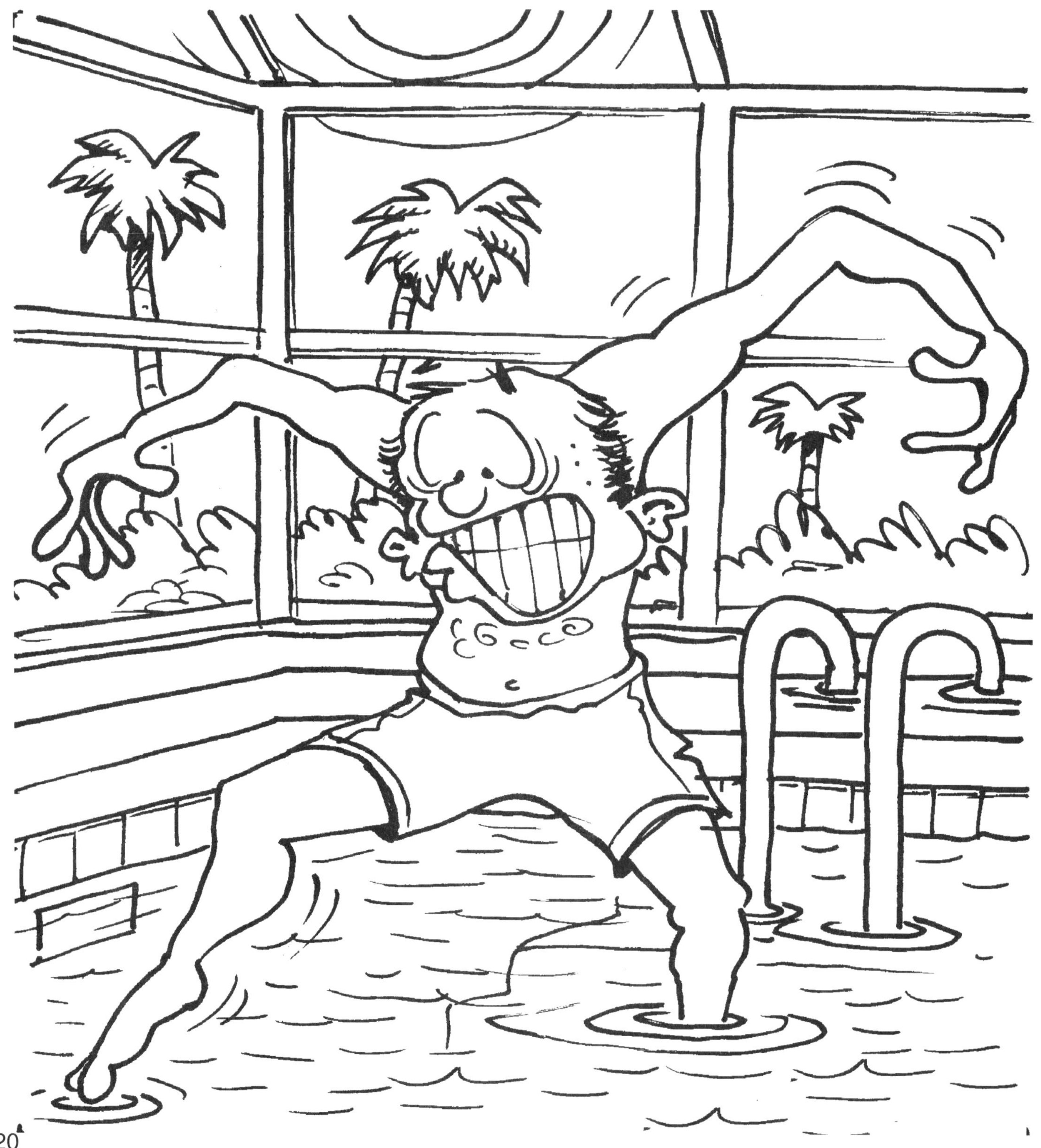

What's Your Favorite Team?

Coloring Exercise:

What is your favorite team? What are your team colors? Have this guy root for your team. Color his clothes, hat and pennant with home team colors.

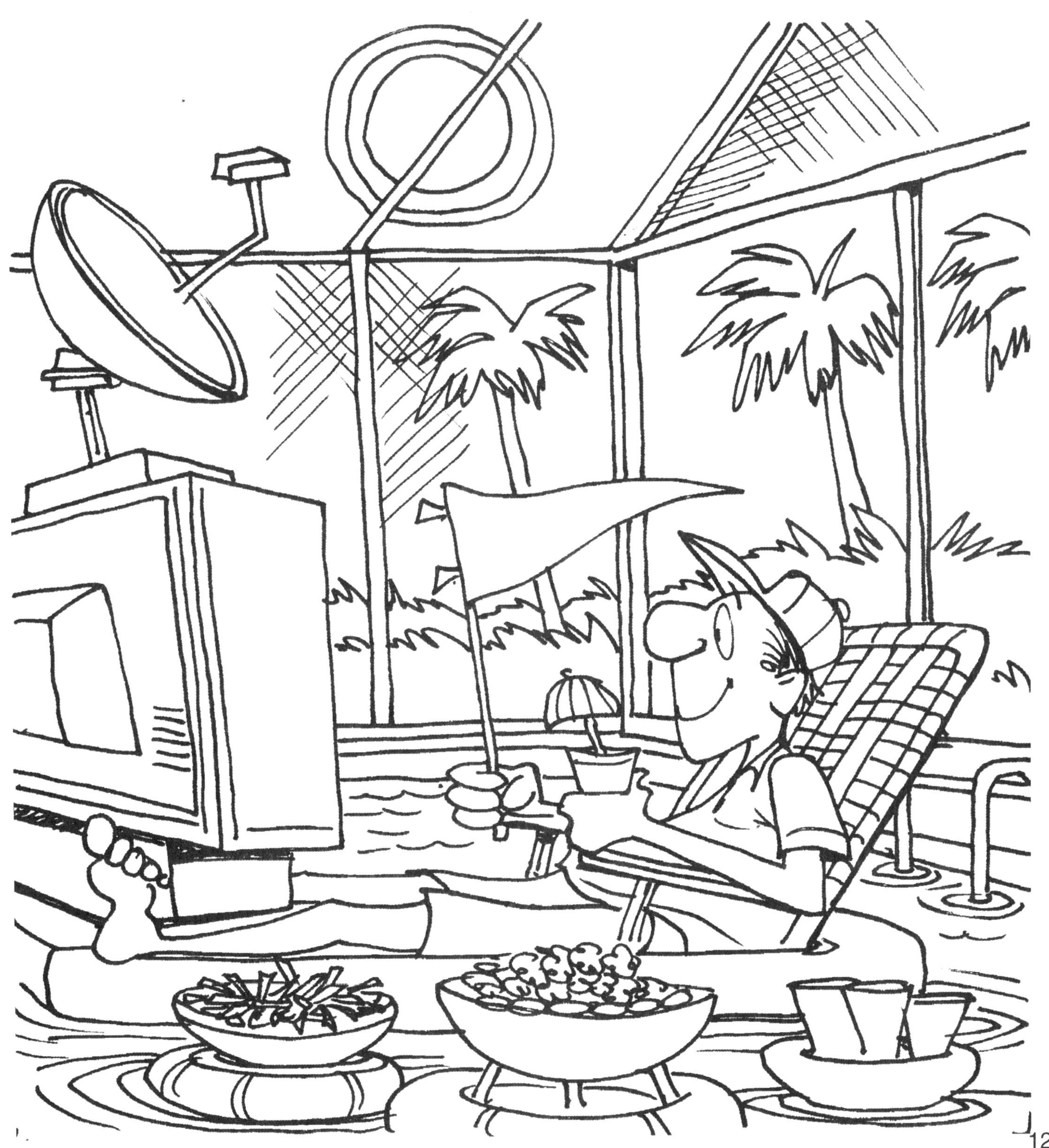

You Can't Fool Me

Coloring Exercise:

What's wrong with this picture? While you are coloring, ask yourself which kayak you really want to get into.

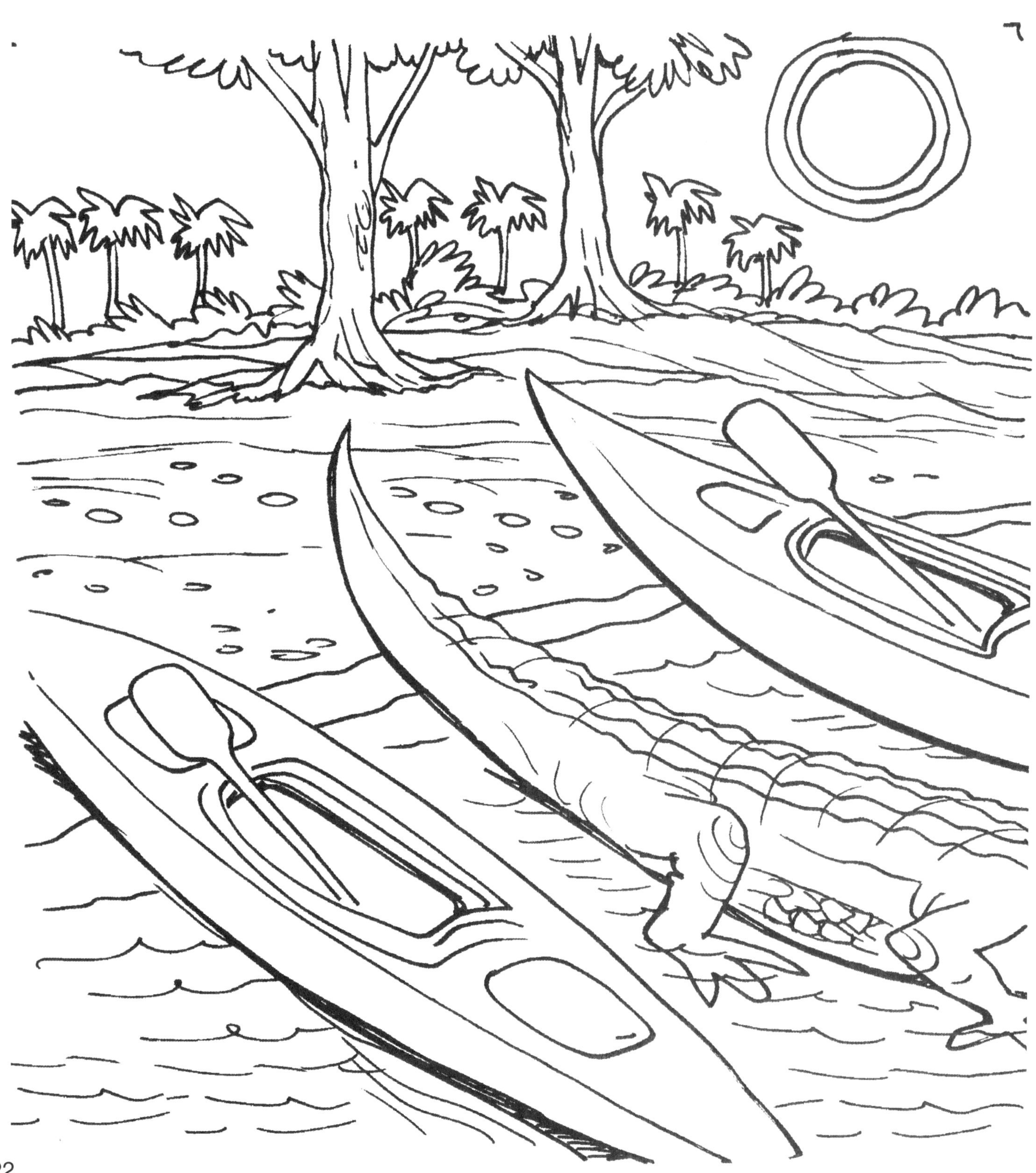

Hey, Look Over Your Shoulder!

Coloring Exercise:

Color this cartoon. How fast can you paddle a kayak? These folks have no idea what is following them. But, when they do, look out, they will break all water speed records for kayak paddling! How fast might they paddle to escape the gator?

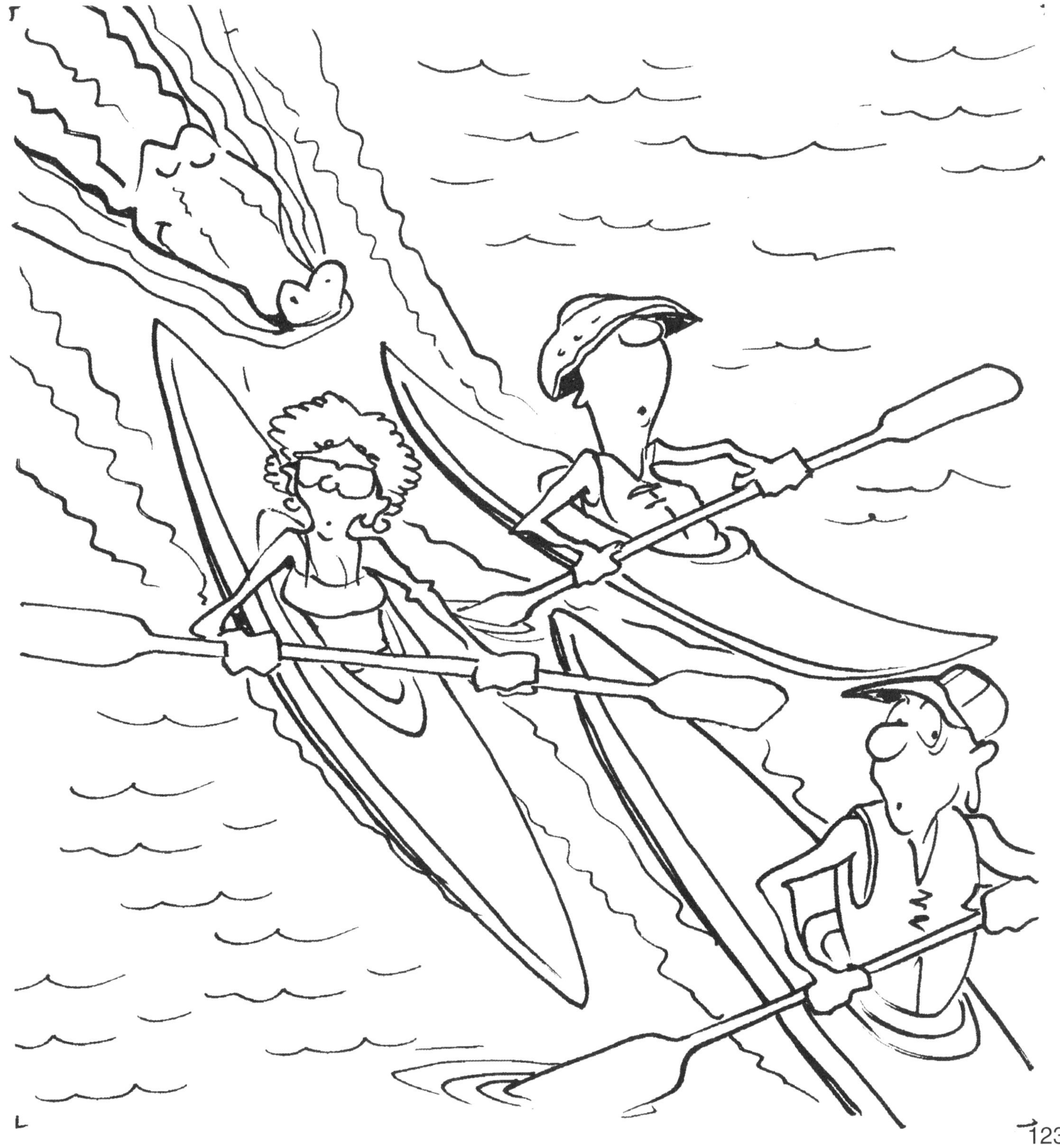

Up, Up and Away!

Coloring Exercise:

Color this cartoon. This windsurfer not only jumped a huge wave, it looks like he's going to jump over the causeway in one leap. Or is he? On the next page you'll find out.

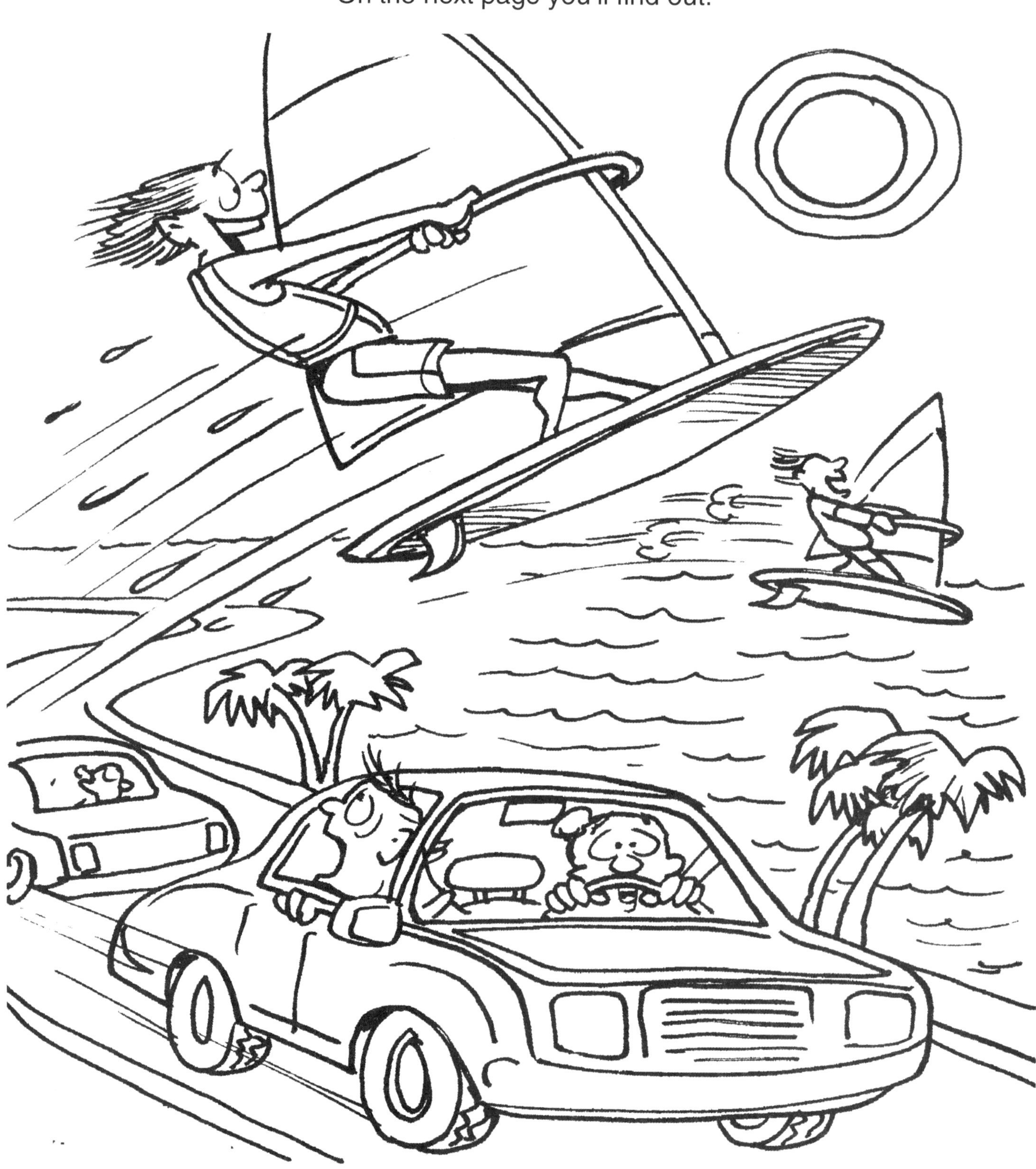

Oops... Now What?

Coloring Exercise:

Color this cartoon.The windsurfer jumped so high he got stuck in a palm tree. Now how in the world is he going to get down?

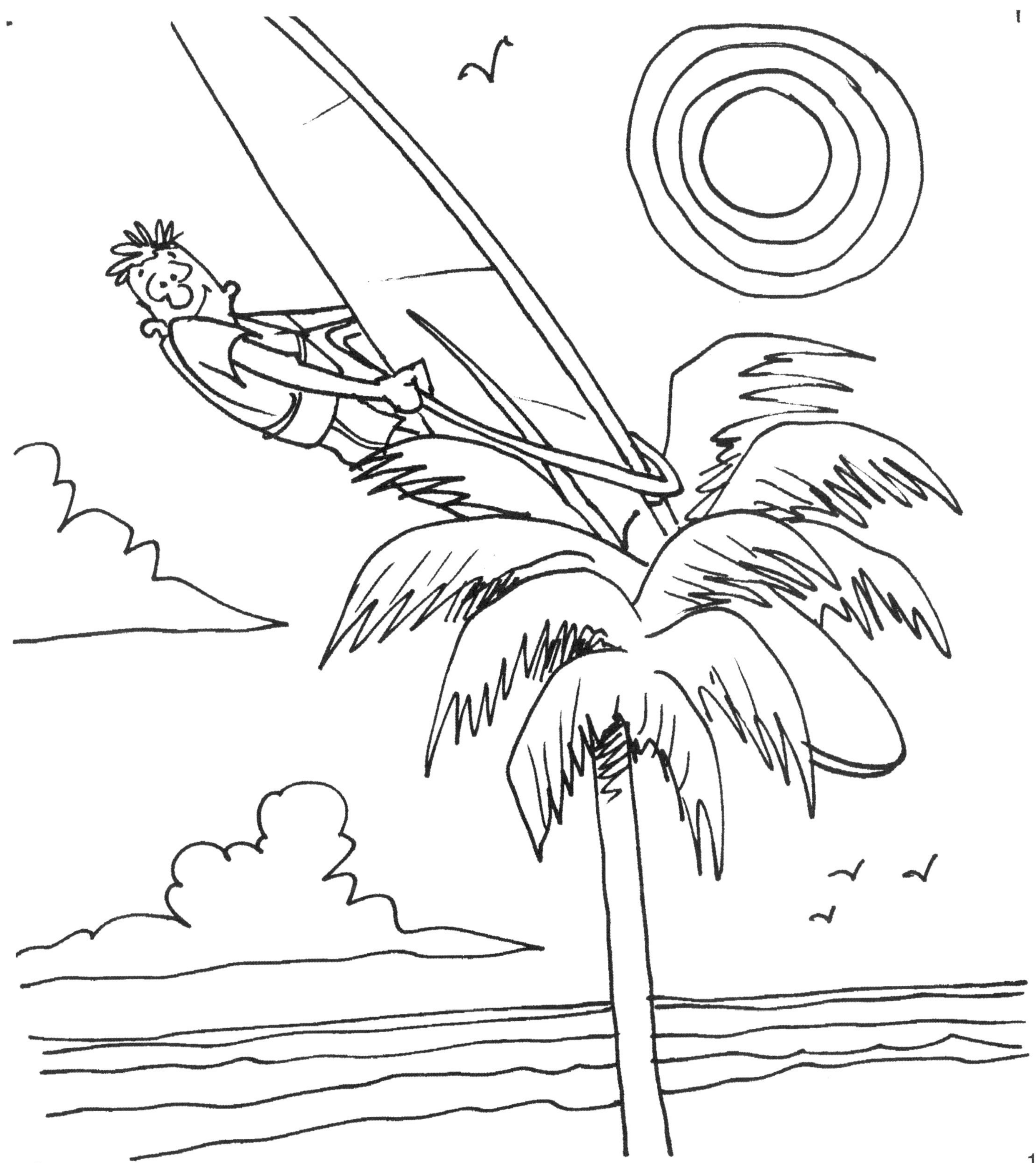

Surf's Up!

Coloring Exercise:

Color this cartoon. This surfer dude is riding the wake of a tourist boat much to the delight of the passengers and some dolphins. Do you like to go boogie boarding? Have you ever gone surfing?

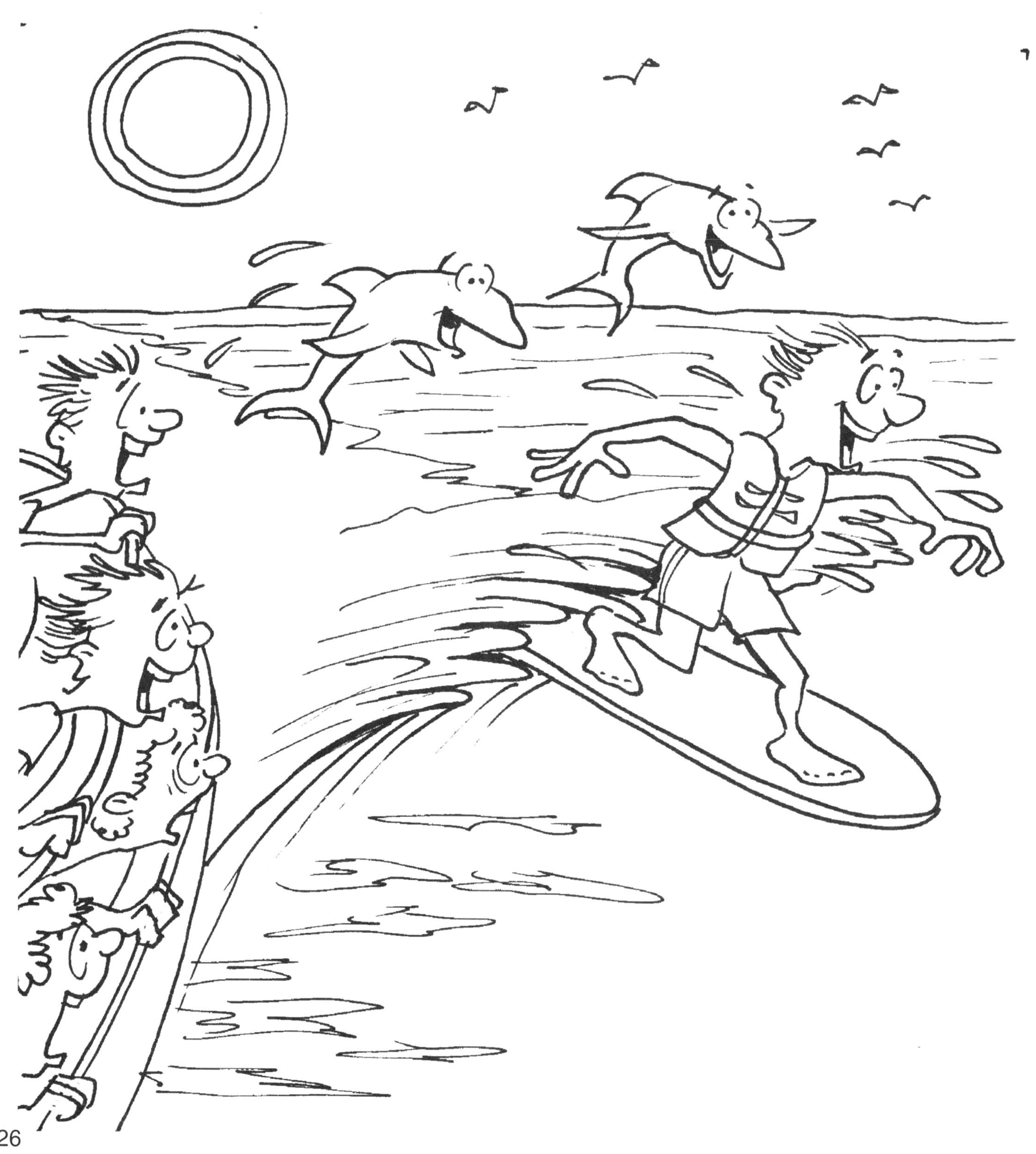

Hey, Don't Look Now, But...

Coloring Exercise:

Color this cartoon. Don't look now, but there's a fin between your legs. Is it a playful dolphin or is it a shark? How can you tell? What advice do you have for our waterskier?

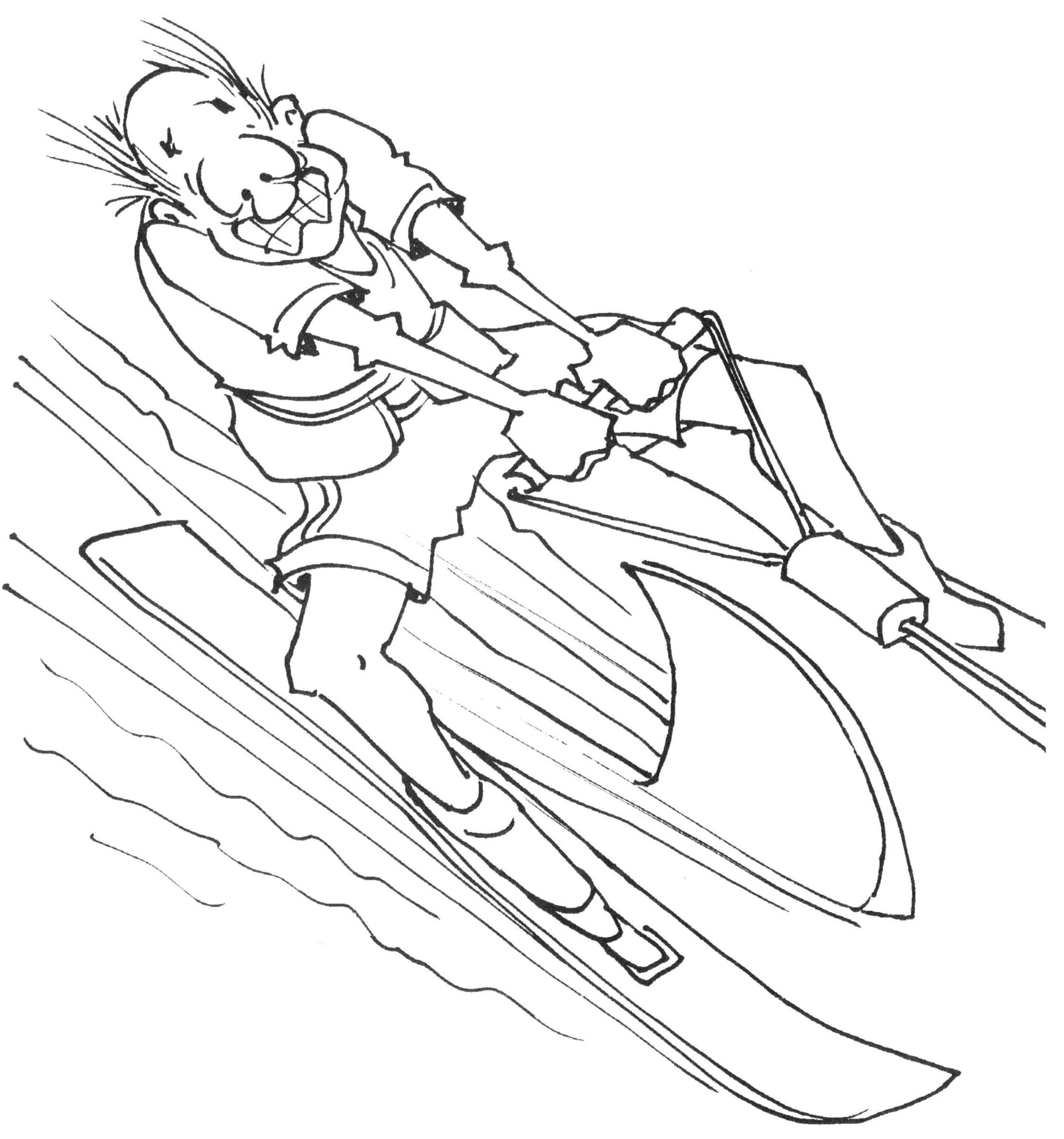

Anywhere In Your Chair...

Coloring Exercise:

Color this cartoon. Do your Mom and Dad have a favorite chair?
Do you have a favorite chair in your house?
If you could go anywhere in your chair, where would you go?

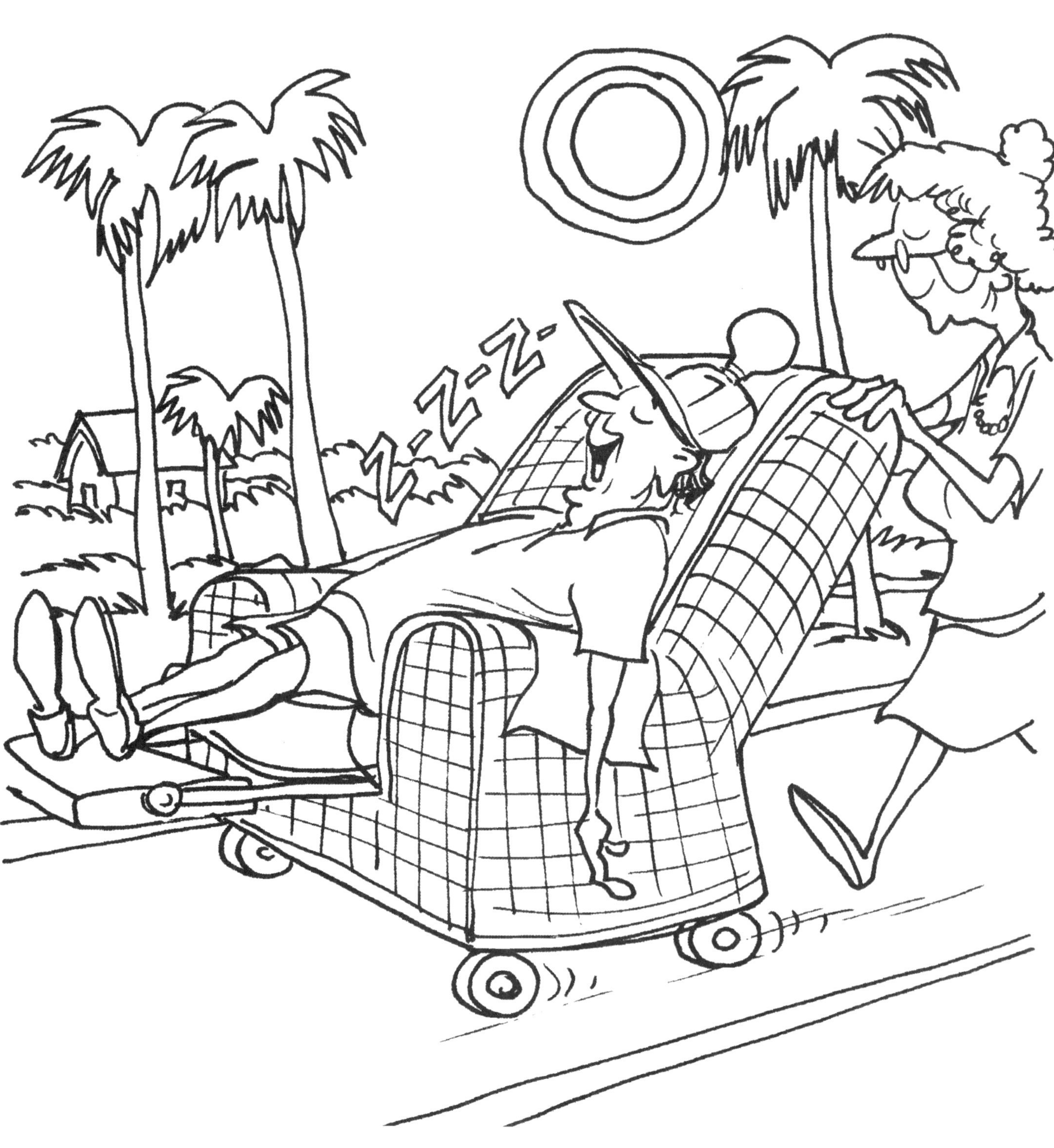

Go Grandma, GO!

Coloring Exercise:

Color this cartoon. How fast is 12 miles per hour? How far will grandma travel at 12 mph in 15 minutes? _____ In 30 minutes? _____ In 2 hours? _____ In 3 hours? _____ Go granny, Go!

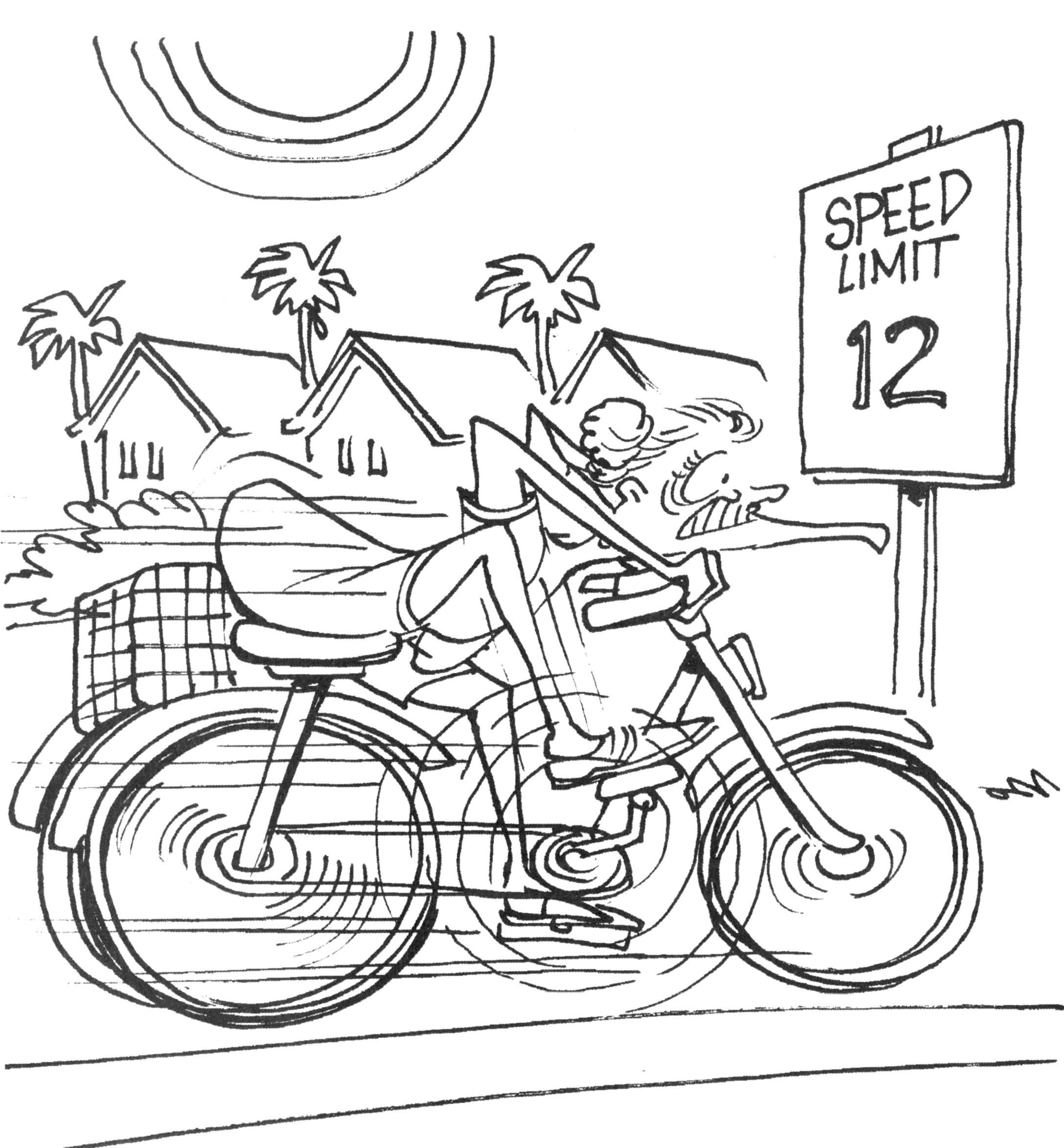

A Real Tree Topper

Coloring Exercise:

Color this cartoon. Instead of a partridge in a pear tree, there's an anhinga in a palm tree. Anhingas like to dry themselves by spreading their wings. But this anhinga is a real holiday tree top decorator. What's on top of your holiday tree?

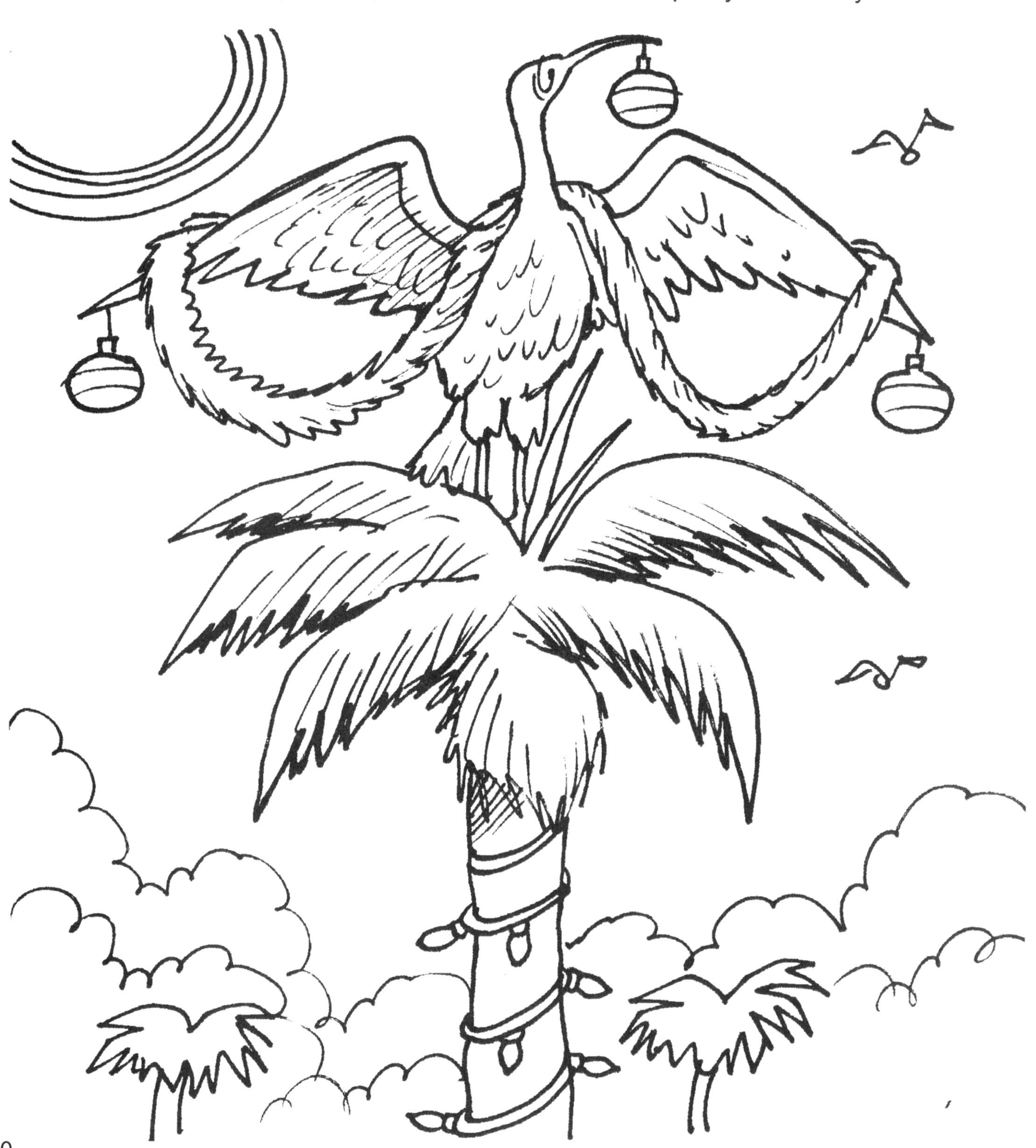

Giddyup Little Flamingos

Coloring Exercise:

Color this cartoon. Since there are no reindeer in Florida you have to use nine flamingos to pull your sled. Can you come up with names for these nine flamingos?

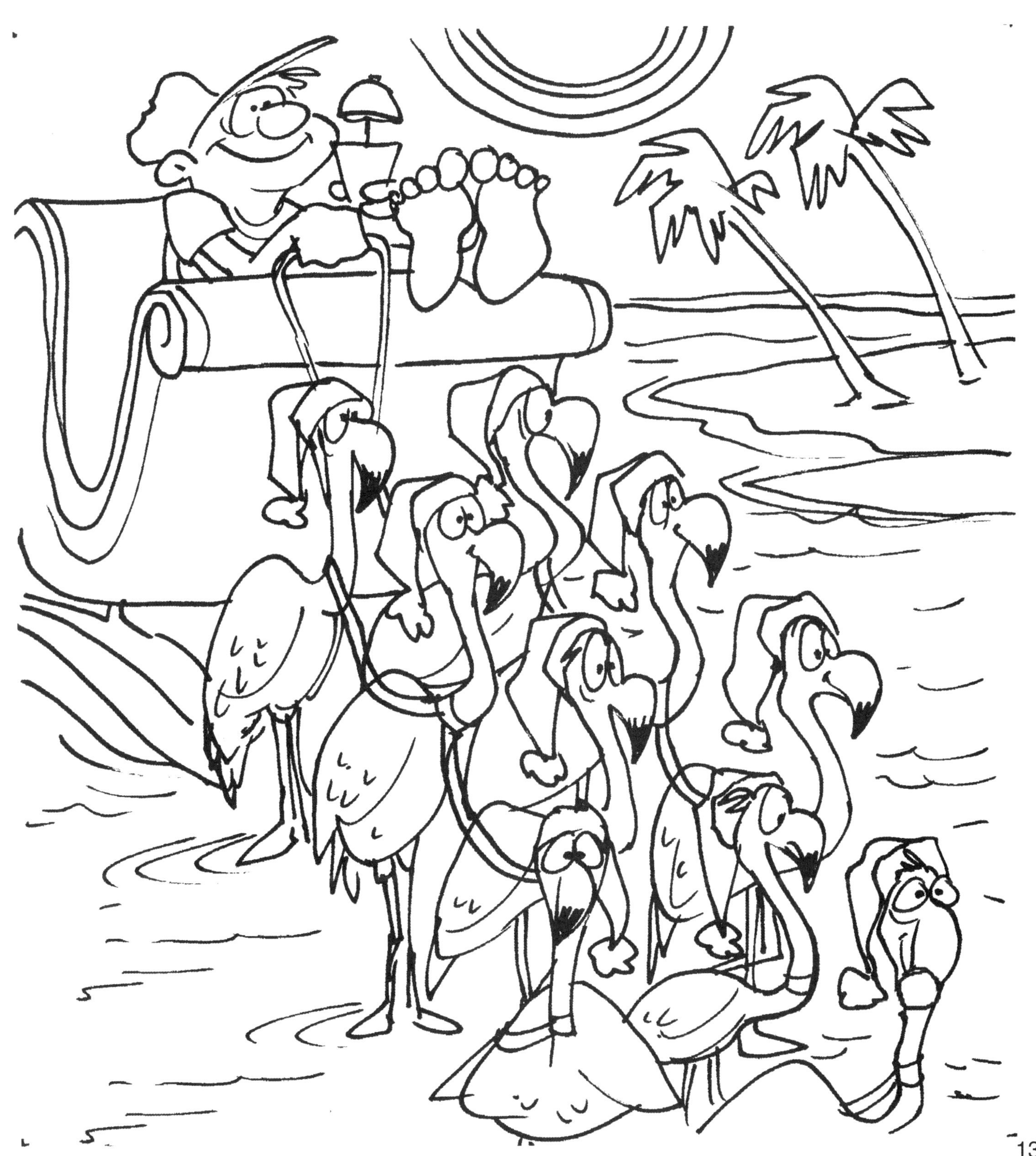

Holiday Shell Ornaments

Coloring Exercise:

Color this cartoon and remember to make every shell ornament a different color.

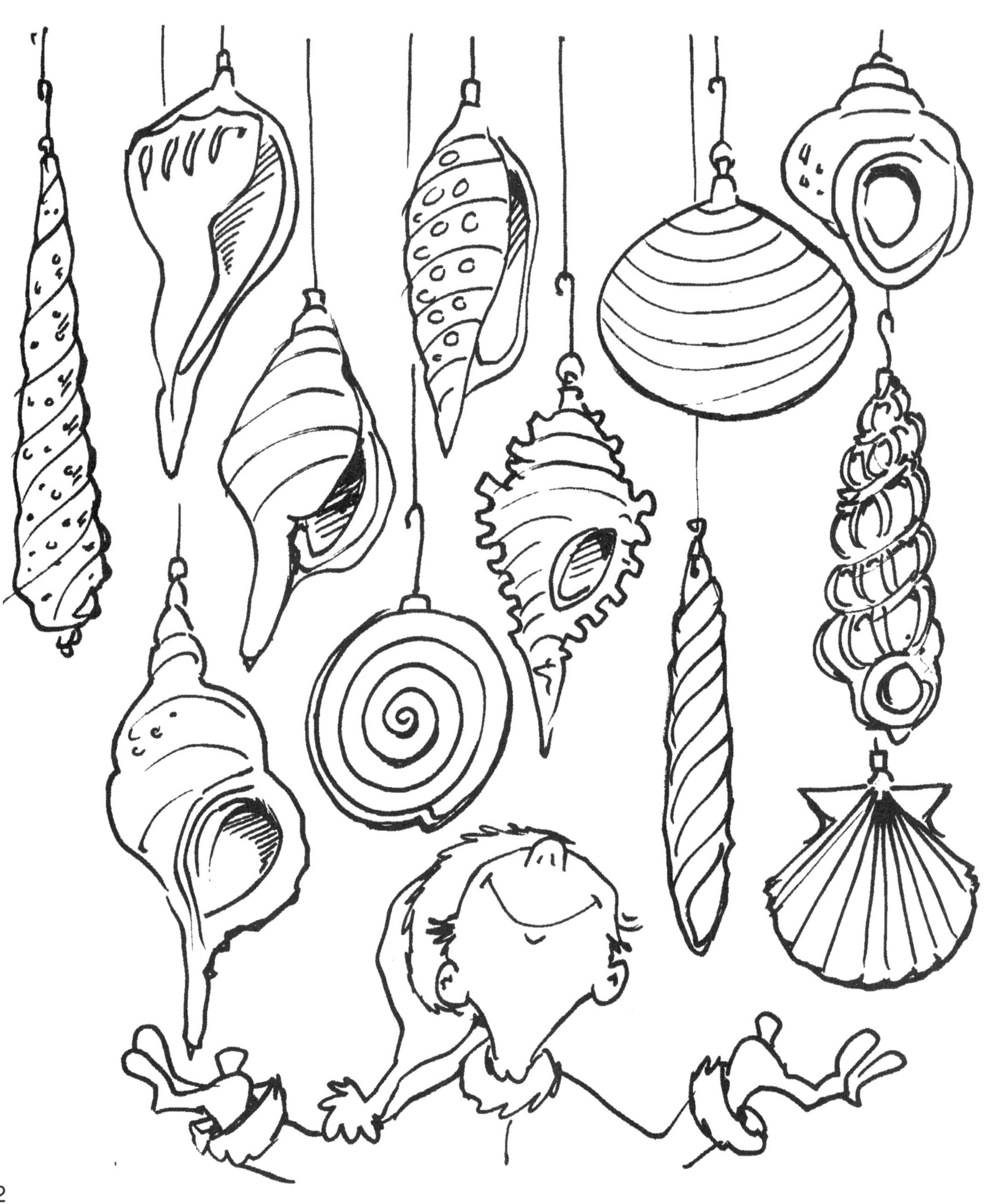

A Thousand Points Of Light

Coloring Exercise:

Color this cartoon. How many bulbs are on the string of lights? Is it more than one hundred? Make each one a different color. If we were to untangle these lights, how many miles would this strand of lights stretch?

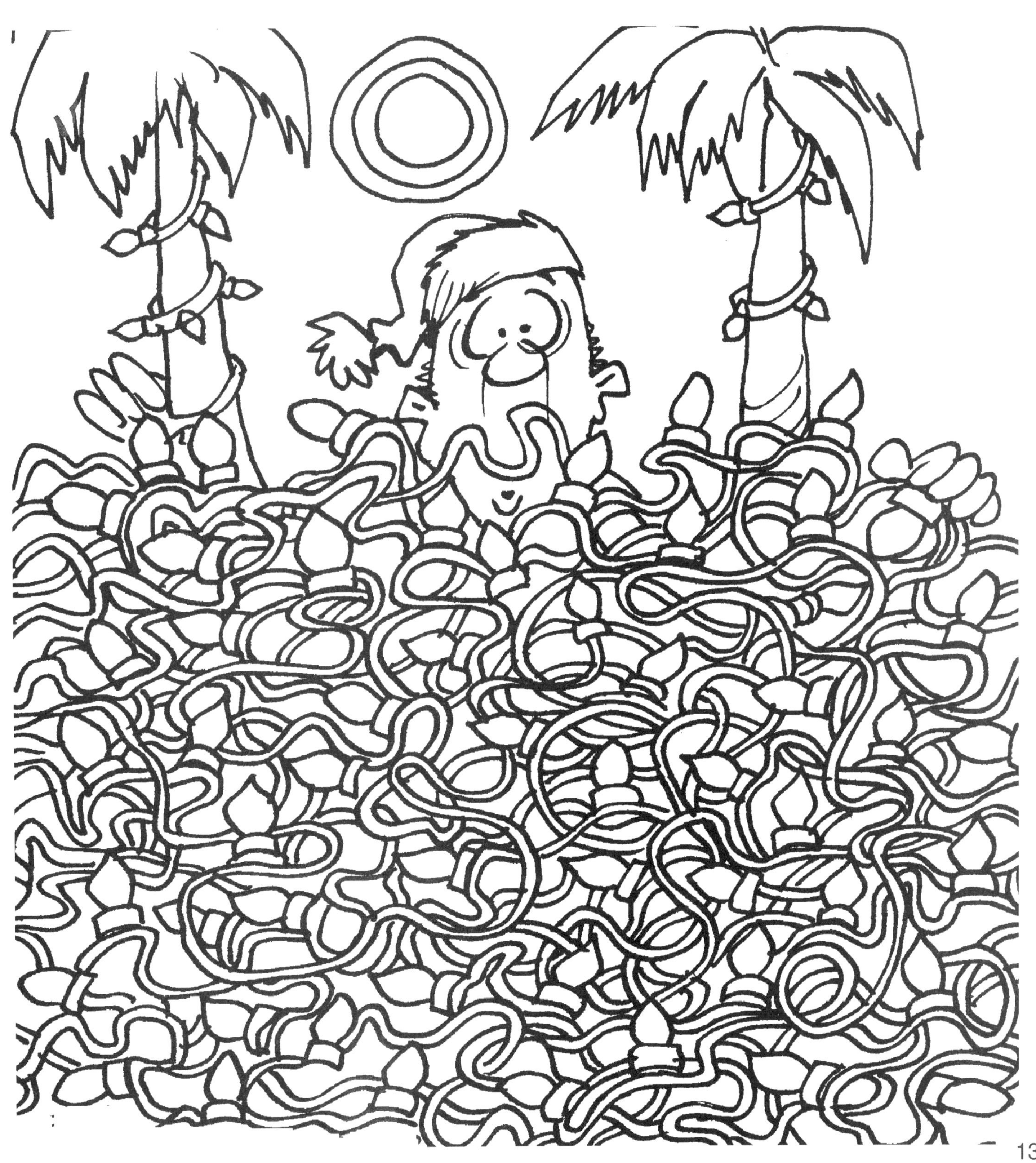

Get Up Offa That Thing!

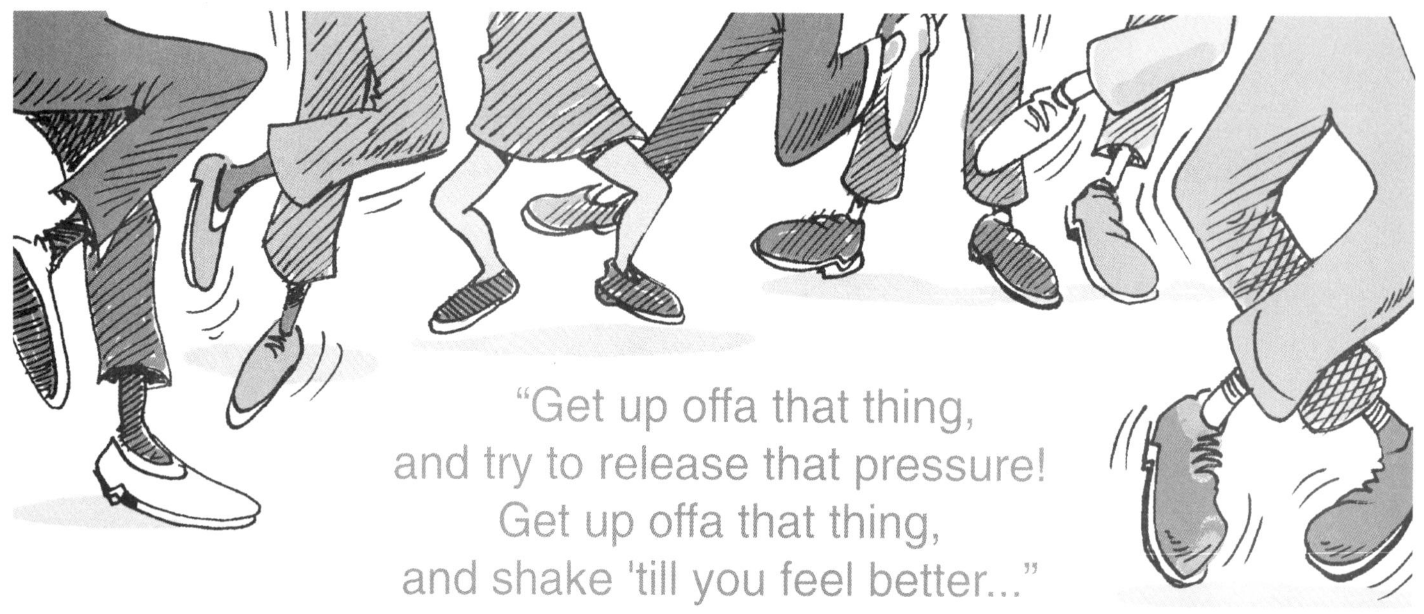

"Get up offa that thing,
and try to release that pressure!
Get up offa that thing,
and shake 'till you feel better..."

- James Brown

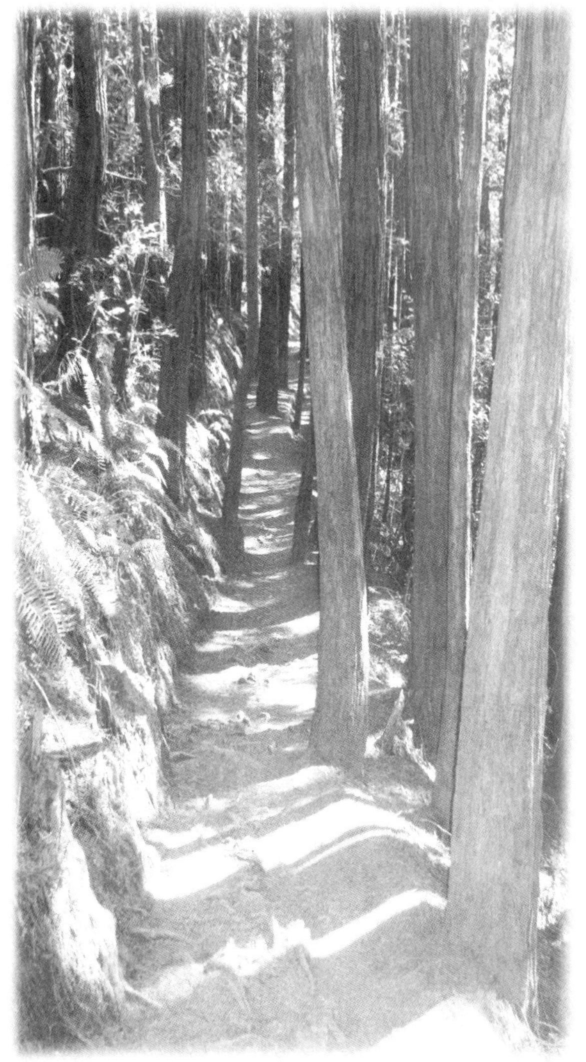

Movement is **kinetic energy**. It is also the energy that helps unlock the creative process. Stuck for an idea when you are writing, drawing, painting or sculpting? Take a break. Take a walk. Removing your **brain block** might be as simple as walking around the block in your neighborhood. Here are some places you can go to help you *unlock your block*.

•the beach •the backyard •the ocean coast
•banks of the nearest brook, stream, or creek
•a forest •a nature trail
•local park, preserve, or refuge

While you are at these places, move and play. Let the inner child out for recess. Dance, sing, skip, sway, roll around, jump, jiggle and flow to the rhythms that you felt as a child.

At home you can close the blinds and turn on some of your favorite music. Dance and sing like a rock star. Belt it out! Any pressure you are feeling from work, home, relationships and family can pass through you. Allow movement and kinetic energy to do the healing. Clear-minded thought will return and you can get back to creating.

*As the late James Brown would say,
"shake 'til you feel better."*

Get Off The Beaten Path!

"Two roads diverged in a wood and I - I took the one less traveled by. And that has made all the difference."

- Robert Frost

Getting into a rut by following the same habitual pathways in our daily lives leads to stagnant thought. It may be time to get off the beaten path. Think about your daily routines. Where do they take you and leave you?

Do you take the same way to work or school each day? Most likely you take the shortest way to your destination. Your brain knows what to expect. Barring a construction detour or an accident up ahead you don't have much diversion in your predictable direction.

Time for ***change***. If you have an extra ten or fifteen minutes take a secondary route to work or back home. Stop at road stands. Pull over and check out that store you always pass and say to yourself, *"I need to check that place out someday."* Today's the day to do it. And if you do stop at the same places everyday, mix it up. If you eat at the same eateries, pick a good mom and pop joint; try their food.

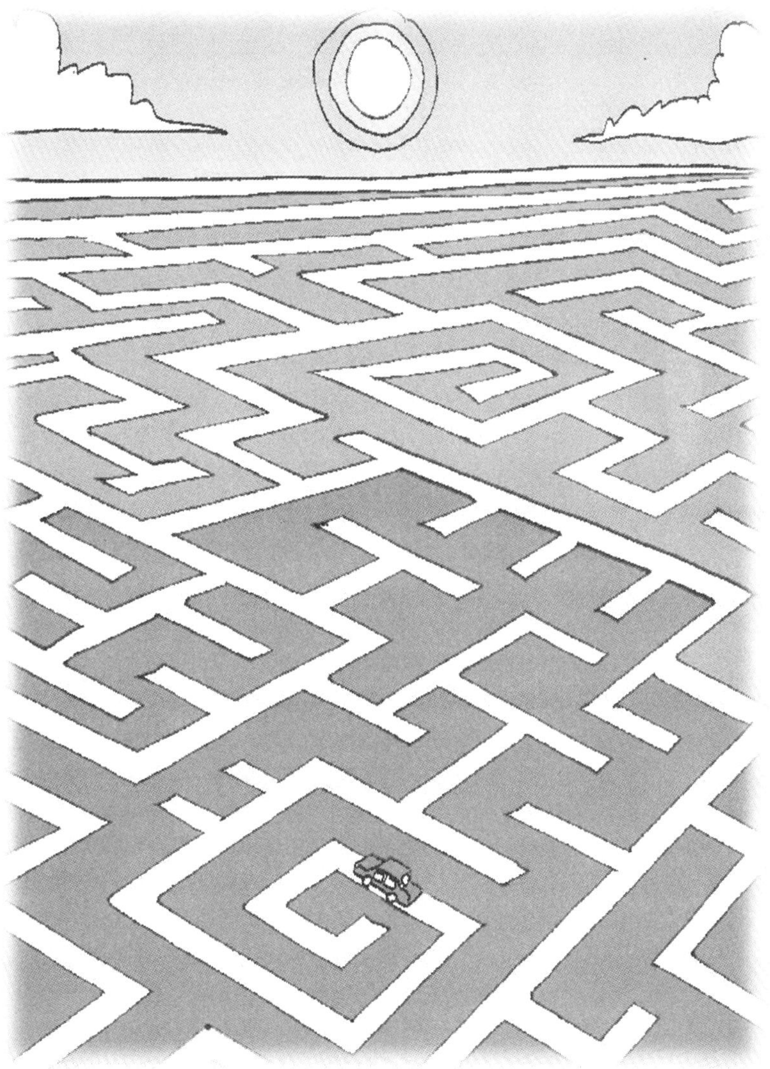

If it is gas you are concerned about take the bus to work if you can. And while you are on the bus you can read, write or draw new discoveries along the way. Distracted driving is dangerous. Having the freedom to collect your thoughts on a bus gives you valuable creative time.

Riding your bike to work is another way off the beaten path. The exercise you'll get doesn't just juice the brain with more oxygen it fills it with more stimuli to process. More stimuli is *more memory bank food for thought* and opens more pathways in the brain. By riding your bike you will hear, smell and feel the trip, instead of sitting inside a car and driving past the outside world.

It may *not* just be the commute to work that needs changing. Consider cutting the lawn in a different pattern. Cut it counterclockwise. If you typically eat your salad first, try eating it last.

Don't starve your brain. Change your pathways! This will bring you more food for thought.

Serendipity

"The creation of something new is not accomplished by the intellect but by the play instinct acting from inner necessity. The creative mind plays with the objects it loves."

- Carl Jung

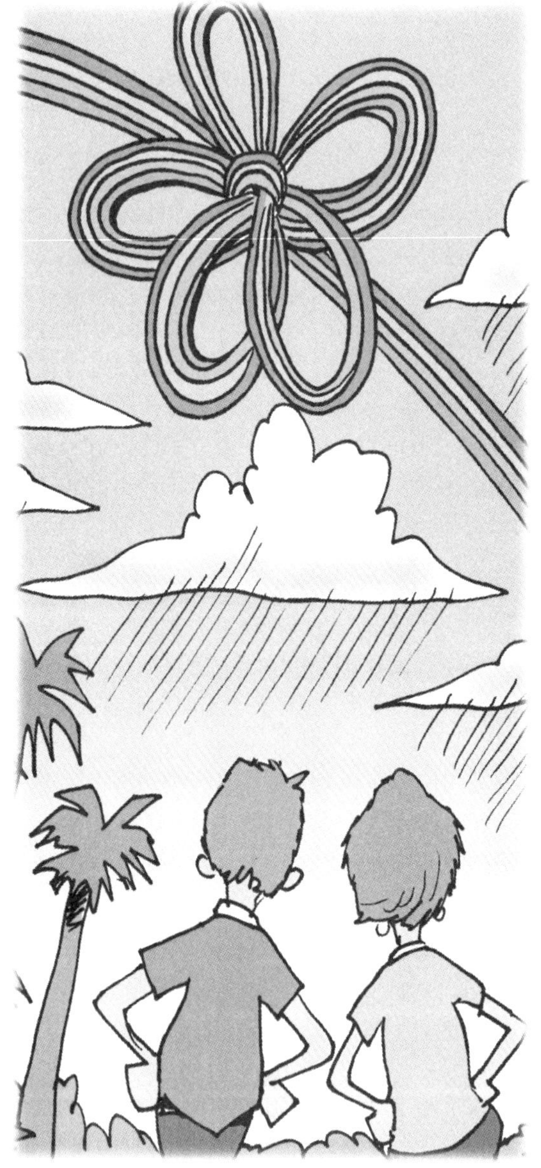

When creative juices are really flowing some incredible things can happen. Not only do you produce a lot more work that is fun, productive, and inspiring, but some interesting coincidences will happen along the way.

Serendipity is defined as "an aptitude for making desirable discoveries by accident...good fortune; luck." Serendipity happens regularly when you are operating at a high level of creativity. If you are creating constantly, thinking of ideas, planning your ideas, or producing them, coincidences will happen more frequently. You'll catch yourself saying, "I was just thinking about that old song this afternoon and now it's playing on the radio while I'm driving home."

Or you may be thinking of an obscure painter you liked years ago and coincidentally you walk into a gallery on vacation and his work is on the wall in front of you. What are the chances of running into a long lost friend at a distant airport while you are observing the public art in the terminal? Having a high level of creative awareness draws those serendipitous moments to you.

As you sense your surroundings while in a highly creative mood, whether its at work, on the road, or at home, frequent discoveries will fall into place. Coincidental good luck, happenstance, surprises and chance findings are all part of the creative flow.

It is this energy, although mysterious, that is certain to follow and lead us further down the artistic path.

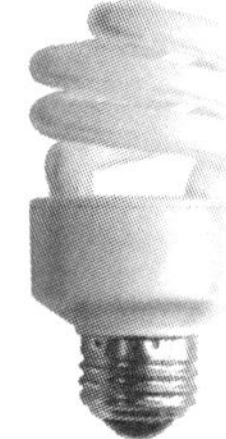

Idea Exercise: Capture the Serendipity

The next time you have an ah-ha moment, record it and write it down. If you experience a coincidence related to your creative day, journal the circumstances. If you make discoveries simply by accident, make a note of it. If you experience a surreal incident, describe it in words. If you see a very unusual Kodak moment, photograph it. If you get a pleasant unexpected surprise remember the time, place and who you were with.

The Mind's Eye

"The intuitive mind is a sacred gift and the rational mind is a faithful servant. We have created a society that honors the servant and has forgotten the gift."

- Albert Einstein

Ever wonder what it would be like if every human inhabitant of our planet could board the space shuttle for just one day. Sure, we would have to squeeze in tight to fit everyone. But, imagine it! We would first soar past the atmosphere, then past the troposphere, past the stratosphere, the mesosphere, even past the thermosphere. As we move further out into space we can see that the earth is curved, and in fact, it is round. Our cities and towns would turn into tiny dots. All we would see is water, land and clouds. No walls and no boundaries.

Finally, we would see what the earth really is - a small ball of stardust whirling through the cosmos; tiny, like most of the other planets. And we would see just how small we humans really are, how small we have always been, even though we like to think we are the most important part of our planet. Yes, it is perspective that we need.

As Jonathon Livingston Seagull once said, "the gull that flies highest, sees farthest." How far can you see? Is it further than your own nose, or is it nearer infinity?

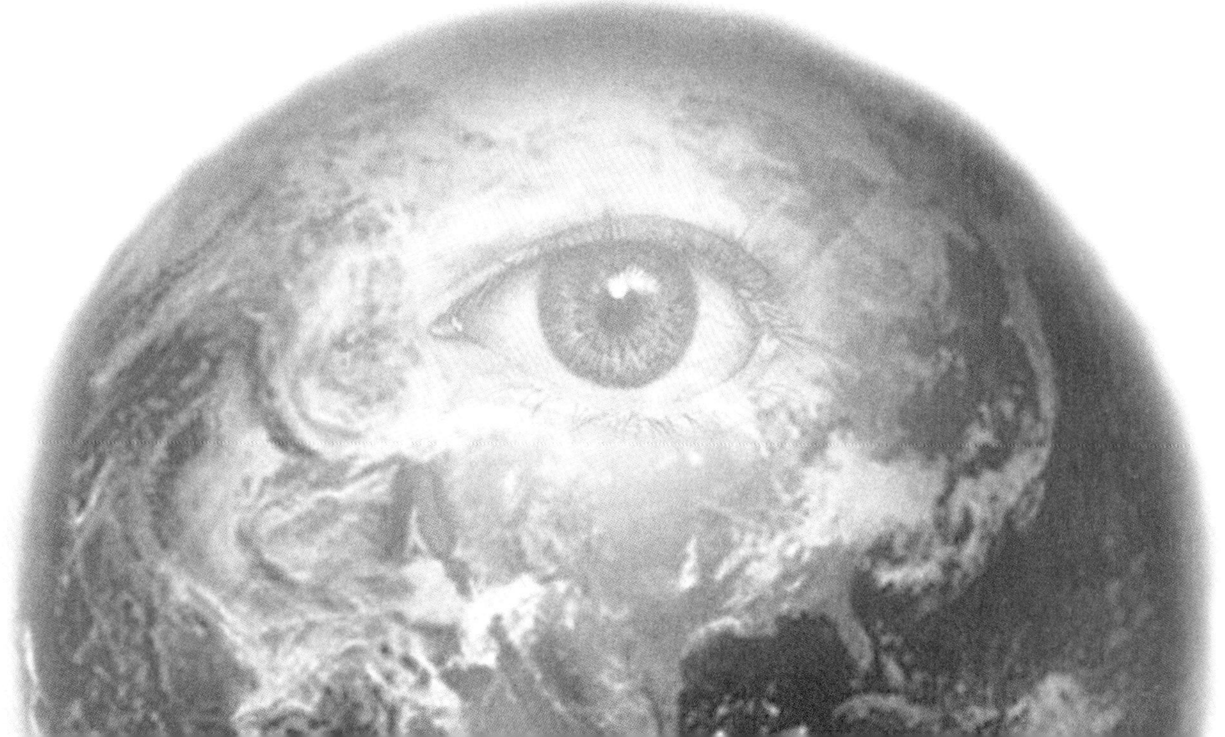

Fill The Senses

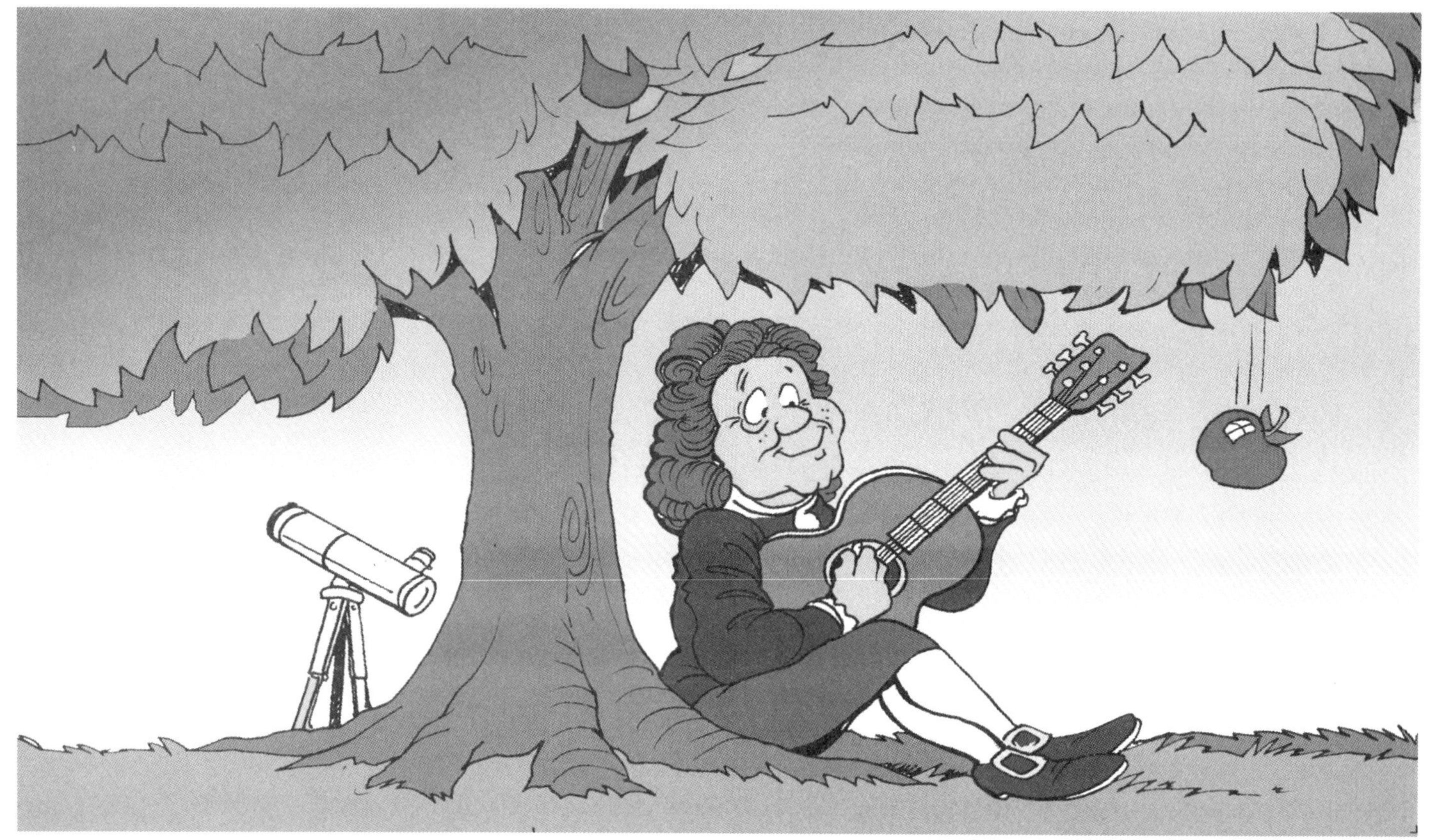

Idea Exercise: Under a Creative Tree with Sir Isaac Newton

Remember Sir Isaac Newton sitting underneath an apple tree? As the story goes an apple falls from the tree, hitting him on the head. It gets him thinking about gravity.

What else would Newton see underneath the tree? What would you see if you sat underneath a tree? Go find out. Bring a pencil and a sketchpad with you. Find your favorite tree in the backyard, park or refuge. Sit underneath it and ponder. Let the wonder and beauty of your surroundings fill your senses.

Hear the birds, the wind and all the sounds nature makes at the moment. Inhale, smell the air, the grass and all the aromas that reach your nose. Take off your shoes and feel the ground. Feel the blades of grass touch your feet. Let your eyes travel up, around and back and forth. Scan and study your surroundings. The tree is there to support you. What do you see from the ground? Imagine what the tree sees. What would it see from the top branch?

In your sketchbook, write down everything you see, everything you smell, everything you hear and everything that touches you. By writing you will enhance your senses and center your thoughts.

When you feel comfortable enough to draw, ask yourself what is the most interesting thing you see, hear, smell and feel. Is it the leaves hanging from the branches above? Is it the sound of the wind passing over the leaves? Is it the distant roar of an airplane, or the streaking cloud contrails passing overhead? Is it the other trees in the distance? Is it the trail leading up where you are now sitting? You decide what will bring your pencil to paper. Now draw it!

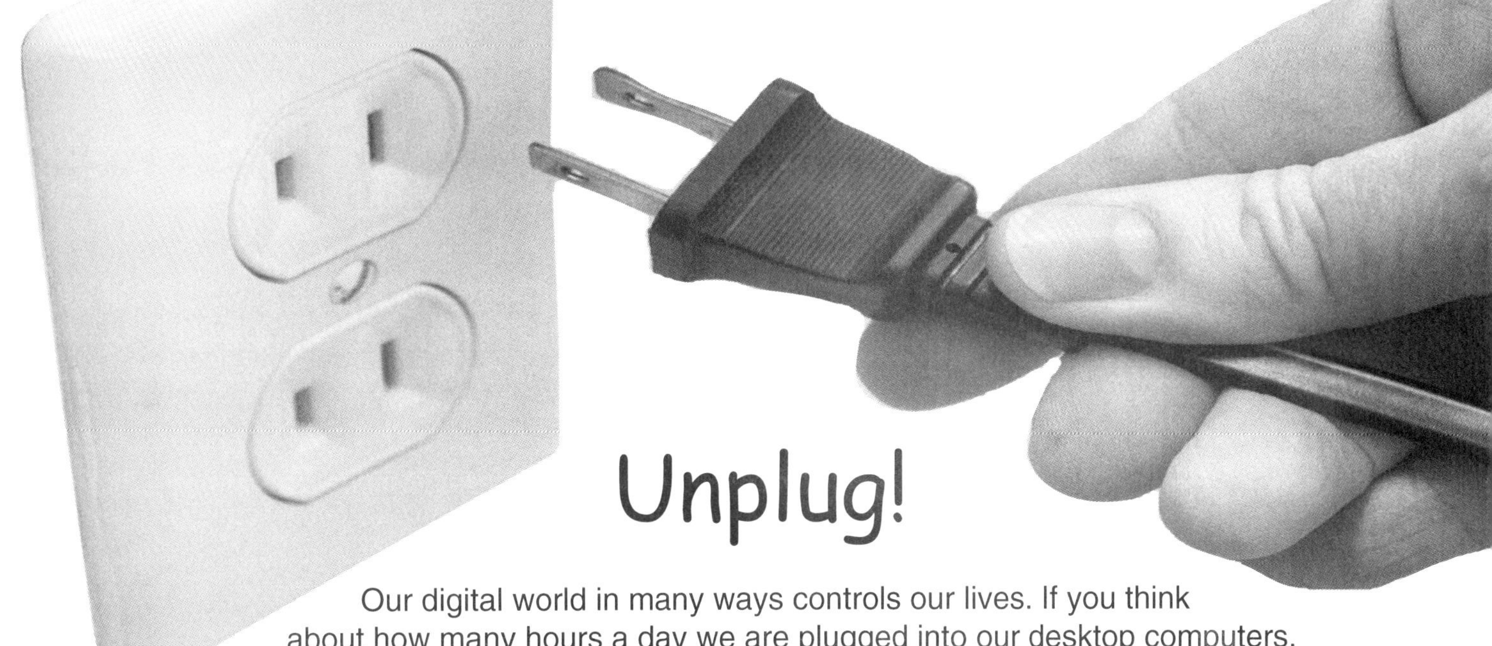

Unplug!

Our digital world in many ways controls our lives. If you think about how many hours a day we are plugged into our desktop computers, TVs, video games, laptops, cell phones, iPods and PDA devices, we are becoming digital robots. Yes, many of these inventions have made us more productive and creative but they have distracted us from some essential qualities of life. It is good from time to time to unplug and concentrate on what is going on around us. The natural world is living, breathing and carrying on around us; but we can be missing it being so plugged in all the time. Below are some ideas to UNPLUG. Or, as they say, "stop and take time to smell the roses."

• Stand looking up at very tall tree • Do a wet walk in a swamp • Look through old scrapbooks • Make funny faces • Dance barefoot in the rain • Lay in a hammock • Listen for bird songs • Hear whispering pines • Go on a sleigh ride or hay ride • Visit a farm • Milk a cow • Make a mud pie • Make a snow angel in winter • Tell a joke • Do cartwheels • Read a book, newspaper or magazine • Open a dictionary and find a new word • Go for a long walk in a nature preserve • Go for a swim in a pond, lake or ocean • Gather and chop forest wood • Build a campfire and stare at the flames • Make smores • Write a handwritten letter or thank you card • Read the comics • Make up your own quotes or favorite sayings • Go fly fishing • Go for a run • Build a sand castle • Go horseback riding • See a sunrise • Play catch with your kids • Shoot baskets • Make soup from scratch • Engage in repetitive rhythm • Draw, paint or doodle • Write a poem to a loved one • Plant a tree • Launch a message in a bottle to the world • Journal your thoughts, hopes and dreams • Drive 50 miles outside of town, draw an "X" on the ground and claim it as yours • Sing in the shower • Swim with dolphins • Collect autumn leaves and press them • Look for northern lights • Look for shooting stars • Look through a telescope • Grow something from seed • Go bike riding • Laugh out really loud • Visit a fragrance garden • Visit the beach • Go body surfing • Watch a sunset

Brace for Creative Turbulence

Ever have those rough days when the light bulb above your head feels like it's just barely lit. Some days are going to feel like 25-watt days and on other days you are going to be as bright as a floodlight.

When those 25-watt days hit you, don't fret. You are probably trying to weather a storm of confusion, boredom, melancholy stress and busyness. Whatever is causing your current power outage, it's time to recharge your brain battery.

There are a few things you can do to up your amperage and restore your creative flow. Try these:

- **Journal:** Get out your pen and journal. Get in your cozy chair and write about anything. Just write. Free flowing thoughts will return. Let your unconscious mind sort itself out. Journaling your thoughts will help piece them together. Finding out what is puzzling you will come into focus. Sunnier skies will emerge and replace storm clouds that are blocking the bright side of your brain.

- **Doodle:** If you don't feel like writing, then doodle. If you are more right-brained this exercise may help you in your storm shelter. Put on some music. Light a scented candle. Sit in a comfortable chair and let your pencil go where it wants to go. Doodle in shapes, words, lines and arrows. Remember, loosen the noodle and doodle your cares away!

- **Power Napping:** Remember nap time in pre-school and kindergarten? You are never too young to nap when you need to. Rest and relaxation are essential to good creative health. Thomas Edison power napped for fifteen minute stretches and woke up with fresh ideas. Get some rest and your unconscious mind will have a chance to recharge. You may wake up and find your bright light bulb is back on.

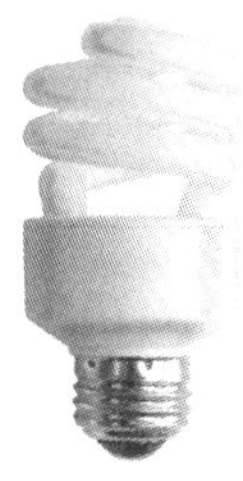

Idea Exercise: Try Humor. Rent a funny movie

If the four ideas to restoring your creative flow didn't work, try renting a funny movie. Laughing, chuckling, and giggling work to release endorphines in the body. Humor is not only a stress releaser, but a bright way to lighten the soul of a heavy heart. Getting your creative juices flowing takes more than a flick of a switch. It takes the right mood to move the muse. When you are under the weather of a dark and cloudy creative day, try some belly laughs to remove the storm clouds. Funny movies will help.

Look on the Bright Side

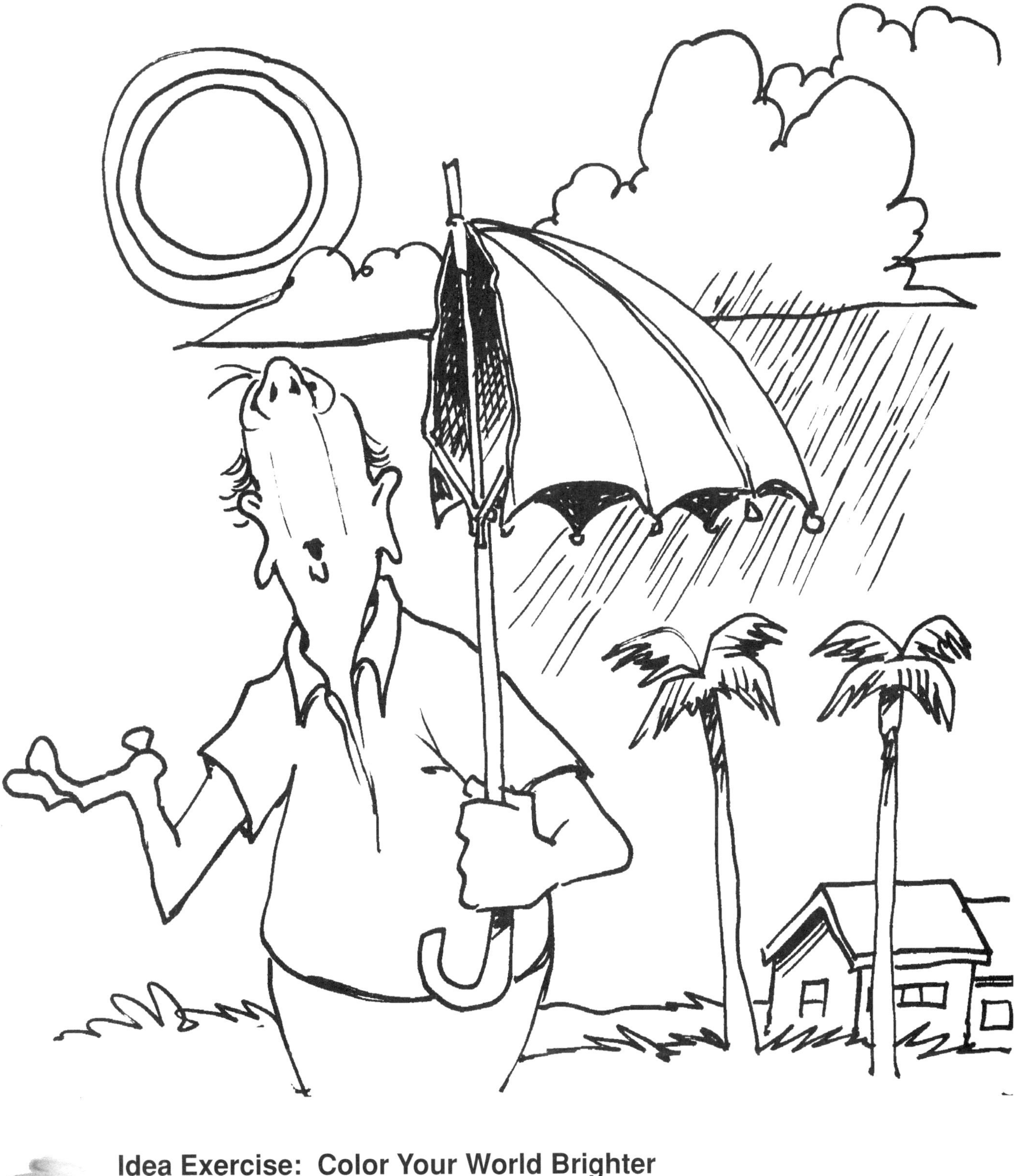

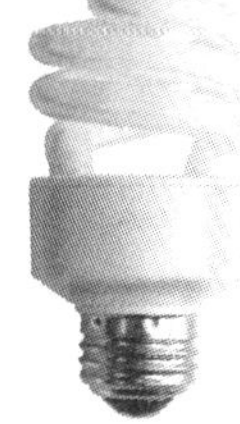

Idea Exercise: Color Your World Brighter

Is the glass half empty or is it half full? Many times being creative is all a matter of attitude. Looking on the bright side of things will also help you weather a bad creative storm. In the cartoon above color both sides differently. On the left side of the umbrella use bright cheerful colors. On the right side use gloomy colors. Then ask yourself how the colors make you feel. What color is your world today?

Dreams

"Go confidently in the direction of your dreams.
Live the life you have imagined!"

- Henry David Thoreau

(author, poet, naturalist, surveyor, historian, philosopher, and leading transcendentalist)

One Last Idea Exercise: Wish upon a dream cloud

Write about your secret and unspoken dreams. In the clouds write in your dream for the present, near future and distant future. No dream is too large. No dream is too small. Remember the Big Picture.

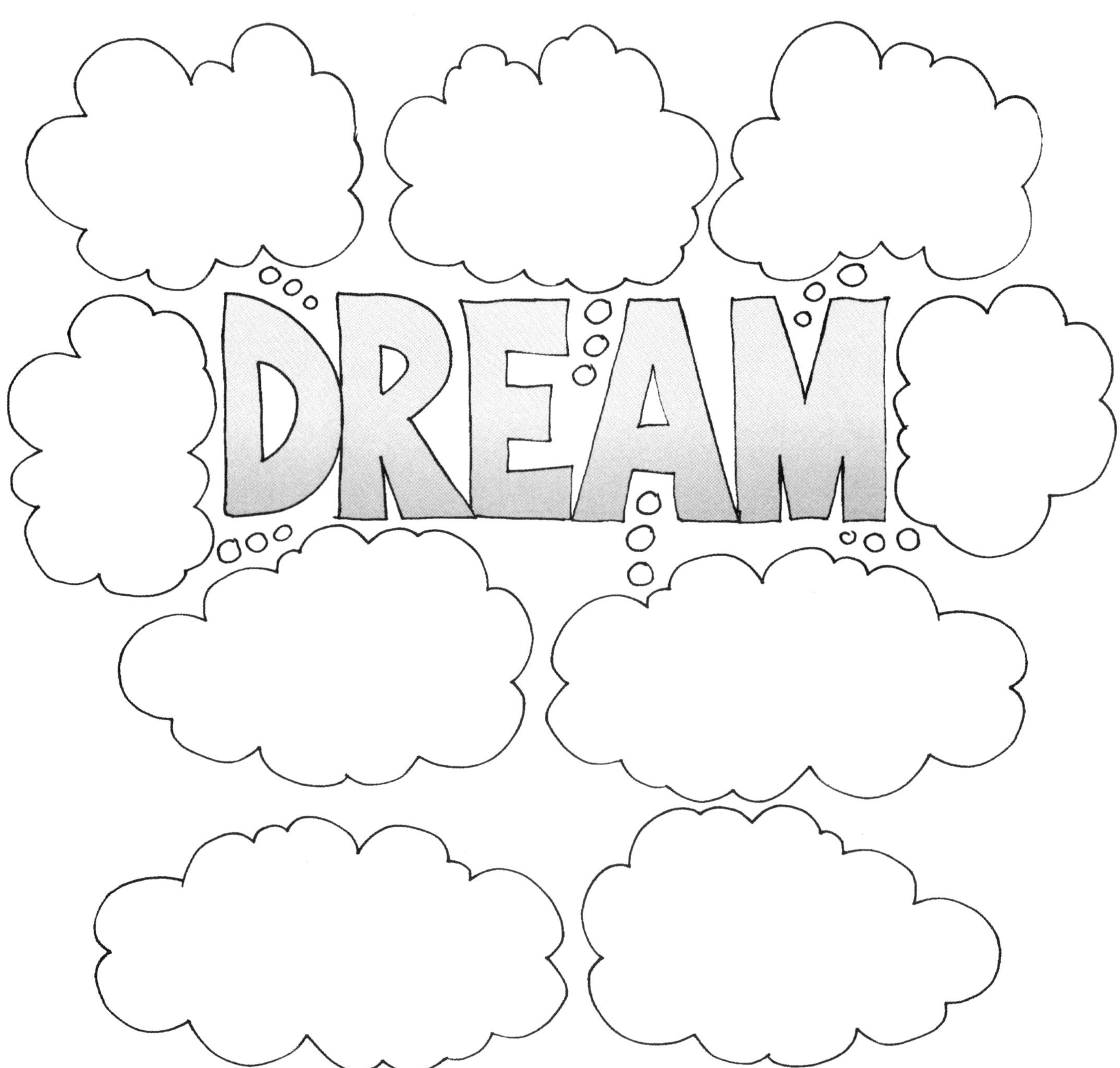

One Last Thought

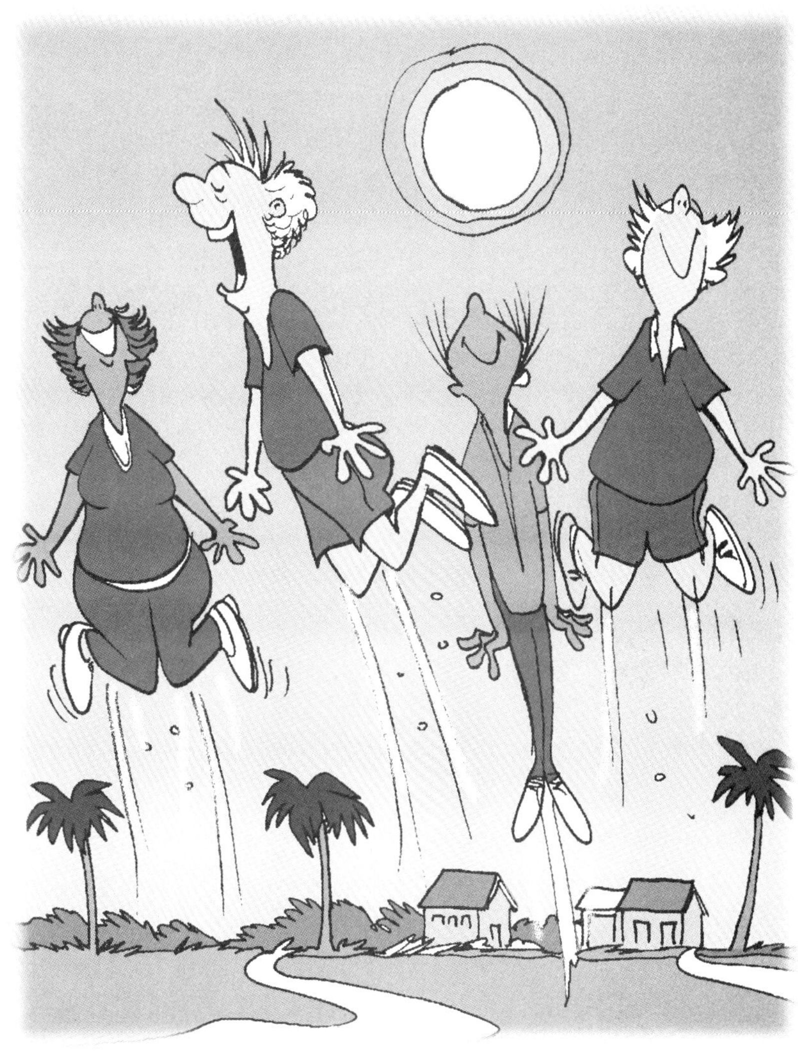

Think about it, you are alive and breathing on planet Earth right here, right now. Why spend it doing the same mundane routines day in and day out? Wouldn't it be more fun to spring into action being more creative every day?

Keeping our inner child alive to sing, wonder, explore, discover, play, act, write, draw, doodle, paint, sculpt, carve, weave, photograph, laugh, giggle, wiggle, dance and create is so important.

Hopefully this book has provided some helpful lessons to keep that inner child healthy.

Staying young is a state of mind. Keeping the body young is hard enough, but keeping the mind young and uncluttered with old habits is a bigger challenge.

And what will you do with all this new found creavity? Maybe you will help solve problems, aid and comfort, spread some magic, share in some laughs, or lighten a load of woes. Try, above all, to bring empathy and creativity together.

Maybe you'll create the next space shuttle to Mars, a solar powered car, a wind turbine, a cure for cancer, or just a beautiful birthday card to give your brother, sister, mom or dad. Your creativity is limitless. Reach for the stars!

Hopefully this book will get you to see more with your mind's eye and less with a myopic (in the box) focus. Maybe you will picture nature in a new perspective. Maybe you will see more of the forest, and less of one tree. Hopefully this work will guide you to be more creative in all your future endeavors.

Remember, it only takes one new thought to change your world.

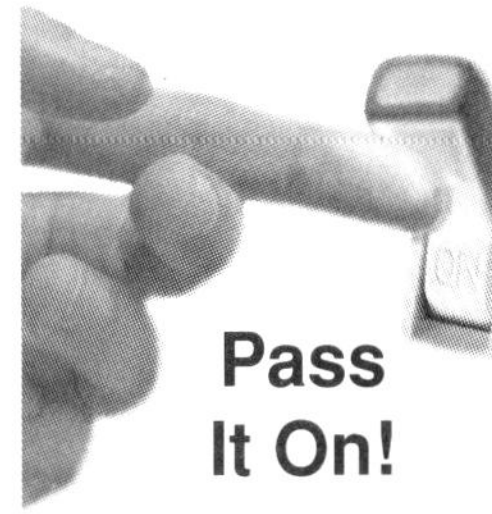

Now Spring Into Action!

Share this book with your mom, dad, grandparents, aunts, uncles, kids, boss, co-workers, teachers, students and anyone who might benefit from being more creative in everyday life. You are never too old to create and let your inner child out on the artistic playground. Draw and write everyday. Get busy. Get creative!

About The Author

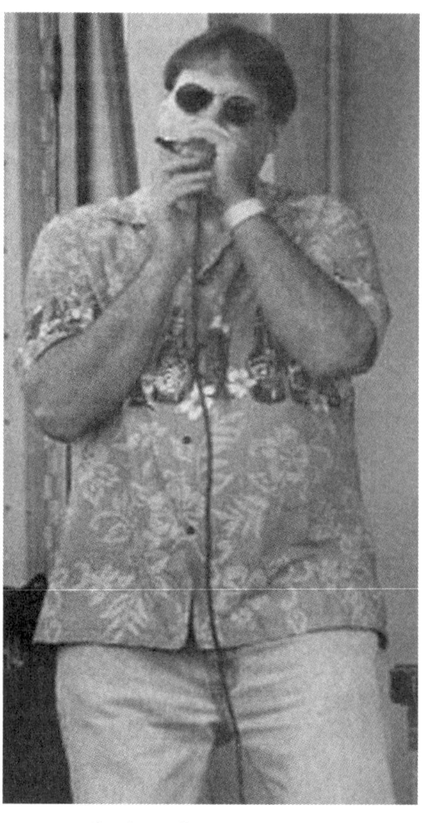

For thirty years **Doug MacGregor** has been creating five editorial cartoons a week. Over seven thousand cartoons later, you can still find him inking away at his drawing table meeting the deadline for the next days newspaper. A graduate of Syracuse University, Doug holds a Bachelor of Fine Arts degree in Illustration. Doug began his cartooning career drawing sports cartoons for the Daily Orange student newspaper. He got his first big break as an editorial cartoonist for the Norwich Bulletin in eastern Connecticut in 1980. While in New England Doug lampooned local and state politics and also had his work published in USA Today.

In 1988 he moved to Fort Myers, FL. and became the editorial cartoonist for The News-Press. He continues drawing daily editorial cartoons as one of only forty full-time editorial cartoonists in the country, a testament to his dedication and passion to his craft. He is also a member of the Association of American Editorial Cartoonists.

Doug is the recipient of several state and national awards, including Best of Gannett eight times. In addition, he teaches and lectures both on an elementary level as well as college level courses. His popular course titled, *"Thinking Creatively"* works to find the inner creative nature in all of us; spilling it over into our daily lives.

Doug has self-published a number of books; compilations of his cartoons dating from his earliest works to the present including, *"The Refrigerator Door Gallery"*, *"The Best of Sunny-Side Up"* and *"Doug MacGregors Cartoons; A Twenty Five Year Retrospective"*. In addition, Doug has written and illustrated several children's books and is an active member of the Society of Children's Book Writers and Illustrators. He is currently working on his next children's book to be published next year.

Also a song writer and musician, Doug can be seen around town playing harmonica in a local blues band. He also produces videos and has made several short movies. Doug contributes much of his time and talents to the community including designing graphic arts for hundreds of local events, and frequently donates paintings to charities. Doug is an active part of the Southwest Florida community.

In 2005, Doug did his most selfless act by donating one of his kidneys to a junior high friend; a man who was a father of two children and was on dialysis. They maintain a close friendship today and golf together whenever they can fit it into their busy lives.

Doug shares this with us. "As a child my father wanted me to play the violin, I found it was not for me. Yet when I picked up a pencil, I knew I had found my lifelong passion...drawing! I've been creating cartoons ever since I learned how to place Snoopy on his doghouse in second grade. Knowing that Charles Schultz already had that gig, I set out to find my own style of drawing. The essence of art for me is seeing life around us, in all of its shapes and forms. The best way for me to express this *wonder* is to never let go of my inner child. Being an artist to me begins with youthful senses; when you add playful humor, compassion and kindness, you will create art from a different perspective. I will never grow old of *wonder*."

"I found in compiling this book, I couldn't fit all of my ideas into it, so I have started my next book with even more exciting ideas. I look forward to sharing that with you soon."

You can see Doug MacGregor's work and hear his music at dougcreates.com.